THE LORD OF THE RINGS

STRATEGY BATTLE GAME

The board is set,
The pieces are moving...

CONTENTS

THE LORD OF THE RINGS
STRATEGY BATTLE GAME

Inspired by the works of
J R R Tolkien

Written by
Alessio Cavatore & Matthew Ward

Additional Material
Adam Troke, Talima Fox

Cover Design
Markus Trenkner

Conceptual Design
Rick Priestley, Alessio Cavatore

Illustration
Alex Boyd & Dave Gallagher

Map
Nuala Kinrade

Production
Michelle Barson, Simon Burton, Marc Elliott,
Kris Jaggers, John Michelbach, Dylan Owen, Mark Owen,
Adam Shaw, Ian Strickland, Nathan Winter

Miniatures Design
Alan Perry, Michael Perry, Gary Morley,
Brian Nelson, Trish Morrison, Tim Adcock,
Dave Andrews, Juan Diaz, Mark Harrison,
Alex Hedström, Steve Saleh & Dave Thomas

Hobby Material
Steve Cumiskey, Mark Jones,
Dominic Murray & Adrian Wood

'Eavy Metal
Kevin Asprey, Pete Foley, David Rodriguez Garcia,
Neil Green, Neil Langdown, Darren Latham,
Keith Robertson & Kirsten Williams

Special Thanks To...
Peter Jackson, Richard Taylor and everybody at Weta;
John Mayo and David Imhoff at New Line Cinema;
Laurie Battle at Tolkien Enterprises; John Blanche,
Rob Wood, Graeme Nicoll, Andy Jones & The Ringwraiths

PRODUCED BY GAMES WORKSHOP

Games Workshop The Lord of The Rings website
http://uk.games-workshop.com/thelordoftherings/

Games Workshop website
www.games-workshop.com

The Lord of The Rings website:
www.lordoftherings.net

UK	US	Australia	Canada
Games Workshop,	Games Workshop,	Games Workshop,	2679 Bristol Circle
Willow Rd,	6721 Baymeadow Drive,	23 Liverpool Street,	Unit 3,
Lenton,	Glen Burnie,	Ingleburn	Oakville,
Nottingham, NG7 2WS	Maryland 21060-6401	NSW 2565	Ontario L6H 6Z8

NEW LINE CINEMA
A Time Warner Company

Tolkien Enterprises

AOL keyword:
Lord of the Rings

THE LORD OF THE RINGS BATTLE GAME

Welcome to Games Workshop's The Lord of The Rings strategy battle game – the game of adventure and battles in the world of Middle-earth.

If you have never played a tabletop battle game before, there is no need to be overwhelmed by the length or apparent complexity of this manual. The core rules are relatively easy to learn, whilst many of the special or detailed rules only apply in rare situations and can be safely ignored to begin with. Similarly, don't be daunted by the prospect of painting all those miniatures – you don't have to paint all your models to enjoy using them on the battlefield. This manual is divided into sections, as you will see if you leaf through the pages to get an overall impression of what it is all about. There is no need to read the whole manual through from start to finish – each section can be consulted as the need arises.

If you're an experienced tabletop gamer but new to The Lord of The Rings strategy battle game, you may be surprised by what is a relatively short set of rules compared to other games. Although the basic game system might seem beguilingly simple, you'll find it requires considerable skill to employ effectively. Players who yearn for more detail (and who doesn't!) will find a growing body of extra material already available, with the promise of yet more to come in the future.

If you're an experienced The Lord of The Rings strategy battle game player and have been with us for some (or all!) of the previous editions of this game, you will find this new rules manual invaluable. This book is a collection of all the rules previously published in the rules manuals and supplement books. Of course we have seized upon the occasion to implement a few rules changes, which make the game even sleeker. It goes without saying that in case of any difference between the rules and profiles presented in this rules manual and those from previous editions of the game and other supplements, the ones in this book supercede and replace the older ones.

For all the latest news about The Lord of The Rings battle game and recent model releases, see Games Workshop's monthly games supplement White Dwarf or check out our website at *www.games-workshop.com*.

INTRODUCTION TO THE GAME RULES

The rules of the game are explained in a conversational style with examples throughout. We have tried to describe rules in a way that enables new players to learn the game as quickly as possible.

WHAT YOU WILL NEED
In order to play you will need a few basic items in addition to this rules manual:

SOMEWHERE TO PLAY
Any reasonably flat surface will do – a kitchen table, table tennis table, or even the floor.

WARRIORS
Any number of model warriors can take part in a battle – from a handful to many hundreds. It is best to start with about five or six models a side and familiarise yourself with the rules before attempting a huge battle.

SCENERY
Strictly speaking you don't need scenery for your playing area at all – but a featureless, flat expanse is a bit dull! A few tumbled ruins, rocks, and trees will help to set the scene. These can be made at home, purchased separately, or improvised from pieces of card or modelling clay.

DICE
You will need a number of ordinary six-sided dice to play this game – at least a couple will do but preferably a half dozen or so.

MEASURE

The movement of models and shooting of weapons requires the use of a measure marked in inches or centimetres. A measuring stick, tape measure or ruler will do just fine.

RECORD SHEET

It is useful to have some means of recording details of the warriors which you can refer to throughout the game. You can do this using a sheet of paper, or photocopy the ready-made record sheet at the back of this book. You will need a pen or pencil to note sundry details.

ADVANCED & SPECIAL RULES

To make the game easier to learn we have divided the Advanced and Special rules from the rest of the text.

Advanced rules introduce extra detail into the game. If you are just starting out, we recommend that you ignore them. Advanced rules are gathered together in the Advanced Rules section which starts on page 30.

Special rules apply only to certain types of creature – they are specific to that individual or race and can be found in their entry.

MEASURING

Throughout these rules you'll often be asked to measure how far a model moves or shoots, etc. Players are allowed to measure at any time they wish – a player might wish to measure before deciding where to move a warrior, for example.

The distance between two models is measured 'base to base' (ie, from the edge of the first model's base to the edge of the other model's base).

All distances have been given in both inches and centimetres. A game can be played using either system – but you can't mix the two systems together. Decide whether you want to play in inches or centimetres and stick to the one method. Note that distances are not exact translations of one system or the other as that would be

extremely inconvenient – for example, centimetres have been rounded to whole even numbers to facilitate easy halving of distances for movement penalties.

ROLLING DICE

When you roll a dice it is sometimes necessary to add or subtract bonuses from the roll – so a roll of 4 with a +1 bonus is a score of 5. Easy enough!

The only thing you need to remember is that the minimum score is always 1 and the maximum score is always 6 – regardless of any bonus or penalty you cannot score better than 6 or worse than 1.

D6 OR D3

Sometimes the abbreviation D6 is used instead of the word 'dice'. These mean exactly the same.

At other times you can find the phrase 'roll a D3'. This means to roll a dice and divide the result by two, rounding up. So, if you roll a 1 or 2 your result will be 1, if you roll a 3 or 4 your result will be 2, and if you roll a 5 or 6 your result will be 3.

RE-ROLLS

Sometimes the rules allow you to 're-roll' the dice. This is exactly as it sounds – pick up the dice you wish to re-roll and roll it again. The second result always counts even if it is worse than the first, and no dice can be re-rolled more than once regardless of the source of the re-roll.

STARTING A GAME – SCENARIOS

Each game represents a conflict between two opposing sides – Good and Evil. This might be anything from a small encounter involving a handful of warriors to a huge clash between two armies. We suggest players begin with smaller encounters as these involve fewer models and are relatively quick to resolve. There are many ways of starting a game, ranging from players just deploying their collection of models on the table and trying to annihilate the opposition, to playing through a very detailed scenario.

The most common kind of scenarios, called narrative scenarios, are games that recreate a specific scene from The Lord of The Rings, or even one that has been created for the occasion by the players. They give a defined set of participants and challenge the players to try to 'change history' (or better it) by achieving a different outcome from the original one. For example, one player can control Lurtz and his Uruk-hai at Amon Hen, seeking to capture the Ringbearer for their master Saruman, while the other player takes the Fellowship of The Ring and tries to ensure that all nine of the Good Heroes – even Boromir – manage to escape the ambush. An enjoyable challenge is for players to swap sides with their opponent and see if they can achieve a better result from the same starting conditions.

Players may also want to play a narrative scenario using different forces from those given in the list of 'historical' participants. For example, they could want to see what would have happened if Saruman had gone in person to command his troops at the siege of Helm's Deep. This is absolutely fine and narrative scenarios normally have a 'points match' section explaining how players can do that and still keep the scenario reasonably balanced.

There are more generic scenarios as well, called battle scenarios, which set some general conditions and objectives, but leave the players with the choice of what forces to use in the game. For example, one of these may represent a small skirmish between a Good patrol trying to stop an Evil warband that is raiding their lands.

CHARACTERISTICS

Because we recognise that all combatants are not the same we must make allowances for their differences. This is achieved by what we call 'characteristics'. There are six different characteristics that define each warrior's abilities. These are Fighting, Strength, Defence, Attacks, Wounds and Courage. Each of these has a value written in the form of a characteristic profile like this:

	F	S	D	A	W	C
Warrior of Minas Tirith	3/4+	3	5	1	1	3

Example: *This is the characteristic profile for a Warrior of Minas Tirith armed with a bow. His characteristic values are typical for a Man. Whilst most ordinary Men have similar characteristic values, Heroes and other individuals have greater values to represent their superior abilities.*

FIGHTING

A warrior's Fighting value (F) consists of two numbers divided by a slash. The first number represents his martial skill in hand-to-hand fighting – the greater this is, the better fighter the warrior is. The second number is the Shooting value and this indicates the minimum dice roll the warrior needs to score a hit with a bow or other long ranged weapon. If a warrior does not carry a long-ranged weapon it is convenient to miss out the Shooting value or replace it with a dash (-). A value of 3 is about average for hand-to-hand fighting and 4+ (ie, a roll of 4, 5 or 6) is average for shooting.

STRENGTH

A warrior's Strength value (S) indicates how strong he is and how powerfully he can strike his enemies. For example, a big creature such as a Mordor Troll is very strong compared to a Man. A value of 3 is about average for a man-sized creature.

DEFENCE

A warrior's Defence value (D) indicates how tough or resilient he is. Many monstrous creatures are especially tough, whilst armour and shields all increase a warrior's resilience to a blow. A value of 3 is about average for a man-sized creature without armour; 6 would be about average for the same warrior fully armoured for battle.

ATTACKS

The Attacks value (A) indicates how many strikes a warrior makes when he wins a fight. Most warriors can strike once per turn and so have a value of 1. Heroic individuals and some big monsters can strike two, three or more times, making them very dangerous in close combat.

WOUNDS

The Wounds value (W) indicates how many wounds a warrior can suffer before he is slain. In the case of most man-sized creatures this value is 1 – a single wound is sufficient to kill. Some Heroes and monstrous creatures can sustain injuries that would incapacitate an ordinary man – they have 2, 3 or more Wounds to represent this.

COURAGE

The Courage value (C) shows how brave and determined the warrior is. A value of about 3 is average, a warrior with Courage of 5 or more is very brave, and a warrior with a value of less than 3 is rather timid.

Mordor Orc with sword & shield	F	S	D	A	W	C
	3/–	3	5	1	1	2

Elf with Elf bow & armour	F	S	D	A	W	C
	5/3+	3	4	1	1	5

Mordor Troll	F	S	D	A	W	C
	7/5+	7	7	3	3	3

Warrior of Minas Tirith with bow	F	S	D	A	W	C
	3/4+	3	5	1	1	3

Mordor Orc with bow	F	S	D	A	W	C
	3/5+	3	4	1	1	2

THE GAME TURN

TURNS

The game is divided into turns. During each turn models can move, shoot with ranged weapons, and fight each other in hand-to-hand combat.

SIDES

There are always two sides in a The Lord of The Rings battle. One side commands the forces of Good and the other the forces of Evil.

Each side is represented by a number of models controlled by one or more players. Refer to the Scenarios section for rules about choosing models (see pages 74-75).

There must be at least one player on each side. If there are more players taking part, each controls a portion of the models. The bigger the game, the more useful it is to have extra players to help with such things as movement and rolling dice.

THE TURN SEQUENCE

During each turn both sides move, shoot and fight in the order given below. This is called the 'Turn Sequence'. Each part of the sequence is called a 'phase'.

PHASE

1   **Priority.** Both sides roll a dice to establish which side has priority that turn.

2   **Move.** Both sides move their models. The side with priority moves its models first. Once the side with priority has made its moves, the other side moves.

3   **Shoot.** Both sides shoot. The side with priority shoots first. Once the side with priority has finished its shots, the other side shoots.

4   **Fight.** Both sides fight hand-to-hand combats. The side with priority decides the order in which combats are fought.

5   **End.** The turn is over. Begin another turn starting with Phase 1 – Priority.

THE PRIORITY PHASE

In the first turn, priority automatically goes to the Good side unless the scenario calls for an exception. This means the Good side will normally move and shoot first in the first turn.

In subsequent turns, both sides roll a dice in the Priority phase at the start of the turn. The side that scores highest has priority for that turn. If the dice rolls are equal, priority automatically changes from one side to the other – the side that had priority in the previous turn will always lose it on a tie.

It is important to remember which side has priority each turn. You can use a token such as a coin or a distinctive model, passing it from one side to the other to indicate which has priority.

There are a few exceptions to the Priority rules. In some scenarios the Good side does not necessarily go first, for example. Also, in the section on Heroes we will be discussing rules that occasionally allow Heroes to override the normal priority and move, shoot or fight before other warriors. These exceptions will be explained in due course.

THE MOVE PHASE

Once priority has been established, the turn proceeds to the Move phase. During the Move phase, each side gets to move its models up to the maximum distance as shown on the chart below. Models do not have to move the full distance – they can move less or not at all if the player prefers.

The distance a model is allowed to move depends upon its race. Some races are faster than others. The following Movement chart summarises the Move distances for each race.

The warrior moves forward 6"/14cm

WHICH SIDE MOVES FIRST?

The side that has priority that turn moves all of its models first. Once all of the first side's moves are complete, the other side gets to move all of its models.

MOVING THE MODELS

Each player can move his models in any order.

Measure the distance each model moves using a measuring tape or ruler. Models don't have to move in a straight line, they can move in curving paths or however you like so long as they move no further than their maximum permitted distance.

Models cannot move through other models whether friends or foes, so players must leave gaps for models to

MOVEMENT CHART

Type	Maximum move over open terrain
MAN/WOMAN/WIZARD	6" / 14cm
ELF	6" / 14cm
EAGLE	12" / 28cm
ENT	6" / 14cm
HOBBIT	4" / 10cm
DWARF	5" / 12cm
GOLLUM	5" / 12cm
ORC	6" / 14cm
MORIA GOBLIN	5" / 12cm
URUK-HAI	6" / 14cm
TROLL	6" / 14cm
SPIRIT	6" / 14cm
GIANT SPIDER	10" / 24cm
FELL BEAST	12" / 28cm
WARG	10" / 24cm
HORSE	10" / 24cm

As you can see, distances are given in both inches and centimetres as they are throughout this rules manual. Either system can be used but stick to one or the other; don't mix them in the same game as the distances have been rounded for convenience.

When friendly models move past each other there must be room for their bases to pass without overlapping.

pass where necessary. The model's base conveniently defines the space it needs to move and fight – so gaps must be at least as wide as a model's base for a friendly warrior to move through.

A model can only move to within 1" or 2cm of an enemy model that it wishes to charge (a charge is a move into contact as described overleaf). In effect, this allows models to block the movement of enemies. This is known as the Control Zone rule.

Once a charger has moved to within 1"/2cm of his target he must complete his move into contact against the target model/models – he will ignore the control zone of other enemies nearby.

There are three exceptions to the Control Zone rule that are worth pointing out right away. Firstly, models already touching an enemy have no control zone – they are already engaged in fighting. An enemy model can therefore move to within 1"/2cm in this case. The second exception is that models are sometimes obliged to move within 1"/2cm because of a rule they have no say over. Where movement

is because of another rule, rather than a deliberate move by the player, a model can move within an enemy's control zone without charging. In this case, models must be clearly separated by a reasonable distance to make it clear that they are not touching once the move is complete. The third exception is that models can sometimes begin their move already within 1"/2cm of an enemy for some reason. In this case, the intruder cannot move closer to the enemy unless he intends to move into touch, but can move around without moving closer if he wants.

Models can be turned to face any direction at any time during the game – not just in the Move phase. Rotating a model on the spot does not count as movement.

Models are not allowed to move off the gaming table unless the scenario being played requires it and includes special rules for this – as discussed in the Scenarios section.

A model cannot move within 1"/2cm of an enemy model unless it is moving into touch. In this situation, the Warrior of Minas Tirith armed with a sword can move into touch with either of the closest Orcs but it cannot move between them to get at the Orc behind.

Once the charger has moved within 1"/2cm of its target, it ignores other models' control zones.

Now that the spear-armed Man has charged, the Orc he touches no longer prevents movement within 1"/2cm, allowing the sword-armed Man to move past to attack the Orc behind.

CHARGES

A model can only fight an enemy it is touching base-to-base. If a player wants a model to attack an enemy, the model must be moved so its base is touching that of its enemy. This is called a 'charge move' or just a 'charge'.

Once a model has moved into base-to-base contact with an enemy, neither can move further in that Move phase. A model that is charged before it gets a chance to move is therefore unable to do so – it is already engaged in a fight.

A model can only fight an enemy it is touching base-to-base.

There is nothing to stop a model moving to charge several enemies at the same time if it can do so. This is entirely up to the controlling player.

WHO CAN CHARGE?

A warrior can charge any enemy model he can see at the start of his own move and which he can reach. It does not matter if he can see his enemy at the start of the Move phase or previously in the phase – only at the start of his own move. A warrior cannot charge an enemy model he can't see when he starts his own move. If a warrior can't see an enemy at the very start of his own move, the model cannot move into touch. A move into touch is a charge by definition.

This is quite an important rule because it prevents warriors charging enemies they couldn't see or react to in a real-life situation. Imagine an enemy is on the other side of a hill, inside a building, or behind a high wall – in these situations a real warrior has no idea where his enemy is.

CAN I SEE?

The easiest way to decide if a model can see another is by bending over the tabletop for a 'model's eye view' of the action. A warrior can turn freely to look in any direction at any time so the model's eye view automatically extends all the way round the model in all directions.

If the enemy is visible from the model's eye view, then the warrior can see it. In many cases you'll be able to see bits of an enemy model but not all of it – in that case the warrior can see so long as part of the enemy's body is clearly visible. For 'body' we mean its torso, limbs and head, but we exclude its tail, which in the case of some creatures is exceedingly long.

If you can't see any part of a model's body, but you can see the tip of a weapon, back pack, its tail or a piece of equipment or decoration we assume the model can't be seen. In principle, the small area of cloth, metal or wood that is visible is not noticed. This is a fair rule because otherwise models with tall or projecting spears would always be seen as it is virtually impossible to position them without their spears poking out somewhere! In reality, the warrior would lay the spear close to the ground or hold it close to his body as he moved – but our models are not that flexible.

Sometimes it can be hard to tell if a warrior can see or not – that's a fact of tabletop gaming life. If you really can't tell then the situation is obviously fairly marginal. In such a case, the best and fairest way to decide is to make a 'random' test. Roll a dice. If a 4, 5 or 6 is rolled the model can see, however a 1, 2 or 3 means it can't.

Tactical note: As models are moved one at a time it is sometimes possible to clear the view for one model by moving another. Similarly, it is easy for models to get in the way of each other if moved carelessly. This can be tricky to begin with – so try to move the models in an order that allows others to see or move.

FIGHTS

At the end of the Move phase, any models that are in base contact with the enemy are paired off into individual combats.

Here there are two separate one-on-one combats to the left, a two-on-one combat in the middle, and a three-on-one combat on the right.

Sometimes you will have situations where a single warrior is faced by two, three or more enemies. This is called a 'multiple combat'. Opponents are always paired off where possible and any other combatants join into a multiple combat against an enemy they are touching.

If a warrior could join one of several combats to create a multiple combat then the player with priority that turn decides which one he joins. Similarly, where matches can be made in one of several different ways, the player with priority decides how the combatants are matched. In both cases, all touching models must be included and any multiple combats must have one model on one side and multiples on the other (never multiples on both sides in the same fight). Always separate the models slightly to make the pairs more obvious and to see what's going on.

TERRAIN

The maximum distances given for movement assume that the going is firm and level and there is nothing to impede progress. Of course that is not always the case – all too often our warriors must struggle through areas of scrub or forest, over bog or mire, or upon rocky scree slopes. We refer to all these and comparable conditions as 'difficult terrain'.

An area of difficult terrain isn't impossible to move through – but it slows progress. To represent this, all distances moved over difficult terrain count as twice the actual distance. For example, a model that moves 6"/14cm normally will move a maximum of 3"/7cm across difficult terrain.

Sometimes a model's move will be split, partly over good ground and partly over difficult terrain. In this case, the model moves normally over the good ground and only the distance over difficult terrain is doubled. For example, a model with a 6" move might move 2" over a marsh (doubled to 4") leaving only 2" for further movement. Always round any remaining fractions of movement up to the next highest half inch or full cm – any distance that is smaller than this is much too insignificant to worry about.

EXAMPLES OF DIFFICULT TERRAIN

Below and overleaf are some examples of difficult terrain features – you may be able to think of more circumstances that would qualify. However, it is important to make sure that players agree which areas are considered difficult terrain/obstacles/barriers, etc, before the game begins.

As difficult terrain counts as double distance, it is important to be able to tell where features begin and end. It is useful to delineate the area in some way – for example, by using a card base to define the area.

TYPES OF DIFFICULT TERRAIN

Very steep, rock strewn or otherwise awkward slopes
Areas of wood or forests
Areas of dense scrub
Bogs, marshes and mires
Areas of shallow water, fords or pools
Areas of ruins, rubble or debris
Areas of deep snow, mud or shifting sand.

BARRIERS

Barriers can take many forms on the tabletop – for example, a stack of barrels, a hedgerow, a rocky outcrop, a low wall or a clump of bushes. A barrier can also be something that cuts into the landscape such as a stream or ditch. The main difference between a barrier and an area of difficult terrain is that a barrier is something you might conceivably leap over, whilst an area of difficult terrain is something you must slog your way through. A good example is a thorny hedge – a barrier you might leap over – as opposed to a whole patch of thorny undergrowth where all you can do is push your way through.

• If a barrier is very low and narrow then a model can cross unhindered – the warrior simply strides over the barrier. A model can automatically cross any barrier if the barrier's height and width are less than half the height of the model. For example, if a model is 28mm tall it can cross a barrier that is less than 14mm high and less than 14mm wide.

• If a barrier is very high or very wide then it cannot be crossed at all or can only be crossed by climbing, as noted later. A model cannot cross or must climb any barrier that is more than twice the height of the model itself. For example, a model that is 28mm tall cannot cross or must climb a wall that is 57mm high. Note that not all barriers are considered climbable – see Climbing (page 20).

• If a barrier is at least half as high or half as wide as the height of a model, but not more than twice as high or wide, then the barrier is described as an '*obstacle*'. For example, a wall 28mm high would form an obstacle to a model that was 28mm tall but not to a model that was 60mm tall.

This steep, rocky slope could slow down progress and, as such, counts as difficult terrain.

This shallow stream could form an obstacle.

OBSTACLES

A model can attempt to cross an obstacle by jumping over it as described below. Sometimes a model will have to jump an obstacle in order to move beyond it as in the case of a stream, for example. On other occasions a model might be able to move around an obstacle, taking a longer route but avoiding the inconvenience of jumping the obstacle itself.

Below are a few examples of barriers that might form obstacles:

TYPES OF OBSTACLE

A length of wall, hedge, barricade, fence or similar barrier
A length of ditch or escarpment
A narrow stream or fissure
A large dense bush or shrub
A substantial rock or rocky outcrop
An open ground floor window
A pile of barrels, sacks, bales or similar
A mound of straw or dung

JUMPING AN OBSTACLE

To get over an obstacle a model must first move up to it and must have at least enough movement remaining to reach the other side were the obstacle not there. A model that does not have enough Move distance to cross the obstacle must wait until the following turn.

A dice is rolled to see if the attempt is successful. If the obstacle is taller or wider than the model's height, deduct 1 from the roll. Consult the chart below:

JUMP CHART

Dice	Result
1	**Stumbles & fails**. The model does not cross and cannot move further this turn.
2-5	**Success**. The model successfully clambers over the obstacle and reaches the other side. The model is placed on the other side of the obstacle with its base touching it and cannot move further this turn.
6	**Effortlessly bounds across**. The model leaps over the obstacle and can complete its move if it has any remaining.

Example. An Elf has a move of 6"/14cm. The Elf moves 2"/4cm forward towards a wall. The wall is 1"/2cm wide and a roll is required to cross. The player rolls a dice. On a score of a 1, the Elf fails to cross and can move no further that turn. On the roll of a 2-5, the Elf crosses and is placed on the other side of the wall. On the roll of a 6, the Elf moves 4"/10cm forward, crossing the wall as he does so.

Steep slopes such as these cannot be traversed normally, but can be climbed.

An area of woodland or copse. The trees block movement or line of sight, and the undergrowth of the base can count as difficult terrain.

Swamps and other kinds of marshy terrain are quite difficult to cross and so can count as difficult terrain.

JUMPING A GAP

A gap, such as a chasm, ditch, or the distance from one part of a ruined building to another, can be jumped in the same way as an obstacle. A model can jump a gap of up to double its own height.

Roll on the Jump chart as you would for jumping an obstacle. On a 1, the model does not simply fail to cross but falls down to the ground. A model falling further than twice its own height may be injured as a result – see Climbing for details about damage from falls.

CLIMBING

In areas of ancient ruins, models often have the opportunity to climb onto old tombs, or up to the ruined upper floors of buildings. If the total ascent is not more than twice the height of the model, this is accomplished in the same way as for crossing an obstacle and a Jump roll is made as described previously.

Very occasionally a tall vertical or near vertical surface will offer enough handholds so that it can be climbed steadily. In this case, treat the vertical surface as difficult terrain and move the model upwards or downwards counting the distance as double the measured distance. In addition, roll a dice when the model starts to climb and at the start of each move whilst climbing and refer to the Climb chart below:

CLIMB CHART

Dice	Result
1	**Fall**. The model slips & falls to the ground. See rules opposite.
2-5	**Continue to climb**. If the top/bottom is reached place the model at the edge. The model cannot move further that turn.
6	**Continue to climb**. If the top/bottom is reached the model can complete its remaining move.

A model can jump, climb or fall down a vertical drop of up to double its own height without a dice test, move penalty, hindrance, or risk of injury. Eg, a model with a move of 12cm could move 6cm to the edge of a ruined platform, jump down to the ground, and move 6cm further. No Jump roll is required to jump down in this way.

Jumping or falling down a drop more than twice the model's height is dangerous. If a model jumps/falls in this way it is automatically placed lying on the ground at the foot of the drop and suffers one Strength 3 hit for each full 1" or full 2cm of fall. So, a model that falls 4"/10cm suffers four Strength 3 hits, a model that falls 12cm suffers six Strength 3 hits, etc. See the Shooting section for how to calculate the effect of hits. Note that when jumping a drop of more than double the model's height, no Jump roll is required to make the descent no matter how far. The warrior plummets to the ground quite effortlessly! Assuming the experience does not prove fatal, the model is considered to have expended all of its movement for that Move phase.

MODELS ON THE GROUND

Real warriors on foot can conceal themselves from view by crouching or lying behind cover. Models can also be knocked to the ground by charging cavalry. To represent this, players must lie the model down.

If no part of the model's body is visible to an enemy warrior's model's eye view, it cannot be seen. Note that it is only the model's body that is taken into account – not its base, weapons, etc.

If a model is on the ground but its body is still visible in its entirety to the enemy warrior's model's eye view (with no interposing cover, terrain, or other models) the model can be seen.

If a model is on the ground and the model's eye view of its body is partially obscured by scenery, cover or other models then it can only be seen by an enemy if a dice is rolled and scores a 4, 5 or 6. On the roll of a 1, 2 or 3, the model can't be seen because it is too cleverly concealed. It is necessary to roll a 'spotting' dice for each enemy trying to spot the model – only enemy models that successfully spot the model on the ground will see it.

When a player gets to move a warrior, he can lie the model down. This costs the model half its entire move distance.

A model that is on the ground can get up. This costs the model half of its entire movement distance. The model can then complete the rest of its move normally, including charging an enemy.

Whilst on the ground, a model does not have a control zone and is unable to charge an enemy, employ magical powers, shoot or do anything else except for moving as described below. He also cannot use any weapon except shields, hand weapons, knives and daggers.

A lying down model's Move rate is reduced to 1" or 2cm regardless of its race. This represents the warrior crawling along on its hands and knees.

A lying down model can be jumped over by friends and foes alike, in the same way as an obstacle (though, of course, it cannot be defended like an obstacle – don't even think about it!).

If a model is lying directly behind cover, we assume that the warrior is capable of peeking through or over its cover without exposing itself to view. A model lying behind cover is therefore assumed to be able to see as if the model were standing, even though the cover might be in the way of the model's eye view.

If a model is charged whilst on the ground, it cannot stand up in the Move phase but will attempt to stand in the Fight phase. Determine who wins the fight as normal. If the model on the ground wins the fight then it cannot strike but automatically stands instead. If the model on the ground loses, it remains down, is pushed back 1"/2cm and counts as trapped as described in the Fight Phase section (see page 29).

A model lying down behind a barrier cannot count as defending it – to defend a barrier a warrior must be on its feet ready to repel the enemy.

THE SHOOT PHASE

Once both sides have moved it is time for the Shoot phase. In this phase, models from both sides can shoot their bows, crossbows, or other ranged weapons.

The side that has priority works out all shooting first, followed by the other side. Warriors that are slain before they have a chance to shoot cannot do so. A player can shoot with his models in any order.

MISSILE CHART

Different kinds of weapons have different ranges, some shoot further than others whilst some are harder hitting and more dangerous. The chart below indicates the range of each type, its Strength value, and the proportion of the model's move it must give up in order to shoot that turn.

Weapon	Range (Inches/cm)	Strength	Move Penalty
Short bow	18"/42cm	2	Half
Bow	24"/56cm	2	Half
Orc bow	18"/42cm	2	Half
Elf bow	24"/56cm	3	Half
Dwarf bow	18"/42cm	3	Half
Uruk-hai crossbow	24"/56cm	4	All
Throwing weapon	6"/14cm	3	None

A model can shoot once in the Shoot phase at a target within range that it can see. We have already discussed what is meant by what a model 'sees' in the Movement rules. The rule is exactly the same whether a model is moving or shooting. If you wish to remind yourself of the rule refer back to page 16.

The player starts by selecting the model that is to shoot and indicates the target. It is a good idea to turn the shooter to face his target – this is not strictly necessary but it looks better that way.

Not all warriors are equally good marksmen, as reflected by the Shooting value in their profile. This is the second number shown on the Fight characteristic. If a warrior does not have a weapon to shoot with it is convenient to miss out the Shooting value – this is shown by a dash (–).

The Shooting value indicates the minimum dice roll which is needed by the shooter to score a hit on its target. So, a shooter with a Shooting value of 4+ needs a dice roll of 4, 5 or 6 to score a hit, a shooter with a value of 5+ needs to roll a 5 or 6, and so on. Roll a dice and if you score a hit refer to the Wound chart below and roll the dice again to work out if the hit inflicts a wound.

WOUND CHART

		DEFENCE									
		1	2	3	4	5	6	7	8	9	10
STRENGTH	**1**	4	5	5	6	6	6/4	6/5	6/6	–	–
	2	4	4	5	5	6	6	6/4	6/5	6/6	–
	3	3	4	4	5	5	6	6	6/4	6/5	6/6
	4	3	3	4	4	5	5	6	6	6/4	6/5
	5	3	3	3	4	4	5	5	6	6	6/4
	6	3	3	3	3	4	4	5	5	6	6
	7	3	3	3	3	3	4	4	5	5	6
	8	3	3	3	3	3	3	4	4	5	5
	9	3	3	3	3	3	3	3	4	4	5
	10+	3	3	3	3	3	3	3	3	4	4

Compare the Strength value of the shot down the left-hand side of the chart with the target's Defence value across the top. The result indicates the minimum dice roll required to inflict one wound on your enemy. For example, a Moria Goblin shoots an Elf and hits. The Goblin's bow has a Strength of 2, the Elf has a Defence of 5.

The Goblin therefore requires a dice roll of 6 to inflict a wound on the Elf. A score of 6/4 or 6/5 or 6/6 means you must roll a single dice and score a 6, followed by a further dice that must score either a 4+, 5+ or another 6. A '–' indicates the target is impossible to hurt – it is just too tough!

CASUALTIES

If a model has 1 Wound on its characteristic profile it is slain if it suffers a wound (most warriors can only take one wound). The model is then removed from the game as a casualty.

If the shot fails to inflict a wound, the target is unharmed – the shot has bounced off the warrior's armour or caused only superficial hurt that is easily ignored.

MULTIPLE SHOTS

Some Heroes can shoot more than once in the Shooting phase. If a Hero has multiple shots you must work out all of his shots before going on to shoot with another model. Work out each shot separately.

The player can shoot at the same target or change targets with each shot – it's up to the player.

MULTIPLE WOUNDS

Some Heroes and larger creatures have more than 1 Wound on their characteristic profile. If a model has 2 Wounds it simply means it takes 2 wounds to kill it, 3 Wounds means it takes 3 wounds to kill, and so on. If such a warrior suffers a single wound make a note on your record sheet that its Wounds value has fallen by -1. The warrior carries on fighting as normal, with no other effect.

When the model loses its last wound, the warrior is slain and the model is removed from the tabletop.

MOVING & SHOOTING

A bow-armed model must give up half its permitted move distance in the Move phase in order to shoot in the Shoot phase. If the model moves further than half of its move it may not shoot that turn. Eg, a model with a potential move of 5"/12cm cannot shoot if it moves further than 2.5"/6cm.

A crossbow-armed model must give up its entire move to shoot. Such a model cannot therefore move in the Move phase and then shoot in the following Shoot phase. Crossbows are much more time consuming weapons to load and fire than bows.

A warrior armed with a throwing weapon suffers no reduction in its move on account of throwing the weapon. The model can move its entire permitted Move distance and throw its weapon.

Note that if the distance a bow-armed model moves is reduced by difficult terrain then it must still give up half of its remaining move to shoot. So, a model with a 12cm move travelling over a bog would find its permitted movement reduced to 6cm. If the model also wishes to shoot a bow, its move must be further reduced to 3cm.

A model attempting to cross an obstacle, jump, climb or mount a steed during the Move phase cannot shoot that turn. A model that fails to cross an obstacle or jump a gap (on the roll of a 1) cannot shoot as the warrior was attempting to cross even though he failed to do so. A model cannot shoot whilst it is on the ground. A thrown rider cannot shoot that turn unless it shoots before it is thrown.

SHOOTERS IN COMBAT

Models that are touching an enemy in the Shooting phase cannot shoot that turn. They are already busily engaged in hand-to-hand fighting using swords, daggers or whatever they have about them. Hand-to-hand combat is worked out in the Fight phase (see page 26).

The Orc fires into combat even though he risks hitting the other Orc.

TARGETS IN COMBAT

Good models are not allowed to shoot at enemies that are already fighting other Good models – not even if they have a clear shot. There is a great risk of hitting an ally in the hurly-burly of close combat. Evil players are free to attempt such a shot if they wish even though their target might be partially blocked by friendly combatants (we find they usually do!).

Roll to hit the target in the usual way. If the shot misses then it misses altogether, the shot flies off hitting no one and causing no harm.

If the shot scores a hit, roll another dice to determine which side has been hit. On a 1, 2 or 3, you have hit a warrior from your own side, on a 4, 5 or 6, you have hit your intended target.

If you hit your own side and there are two or more of your own models fighting, you will hit the nearest. Roll to wound as normal, but don't worry there's plenty more where he came from!

IN THE WAY!

Often a shooter's view of the target's body will be partly obscured by another model or some other object that lies between the shooter and target. The model or object is in the way of the shot. Remember that for 'body' we mean a model's torso, limbs and head, but we exclude its tail and all its equipment (see the Charges section).

A Good warrior is not allowed to shoot at a target if another Good warrior is in the way. He wouldn't want to risk hitting a friend, after all. However, an Evil warrior can shoot if other Evil warriors are in the way (life is cheap – especially when it's not your own!).

Where a shooter's view to his intended target is partly obscured by someone or something in the way then there is a chance a shot will hit whatever is in the way instead of the target. This is worked out as follows:

First roll to see if a hit is scored as normal. If you miss, the shot flies wide and hits nothing. If a hit is scored, roll a dice on behalf of the first thing in the way of the shot.

If you roll a 1, 2 or 3, the shot has hit whatever is in the way. If this is another model, work out the effect of the hit. If it is a physical object, the arrow strikes it and is stopped or deflected, causing no harm.

The Man cannot shoot at the Orc – his friend is in the way.

If you roll a 4, 5 or 6, the shot has missed whatever is in the way and flies on towards its intended target. Roll for the next thing in the way, and continue rolling for each thing in the way of the shot until it hits something or reaches the intended target.

For example, a Man shoots his bow at an Orc and scores a hit. However, the Orc is behind a wall and there is a tree in front that partly obscures the Orc from view. The Man rolls to see if the tree is hit and, scoring a 5, avoids the tree. The Man next rolls for the wall and scores a 4, avoiding that also. The arrow reaches the Orc and hits him.

The tree and wall are both in the way of this shot.

Note that an Evil warrior who is fighting an enemy won't be both 'in the way' and a 'target in combat'. The warrior will just be a target in combat and only one roll is required to see if he's hit. Life is difficult enough when you're a minion of Evil so we won't penalise him further!

On the other hand, a model might wish to shoot at a target that is partially obscured by two or more models engaged in combat. Good models, as usual, cannot take this kind of shot, but Evil ones can. If the shot hits the intended target,

then the fight will be treated as an obstacle 'in the way' of the shot. If a 1-3 is rolled, the arrow is stopped by the fight and the hit must be resolved in the same way as a shot directed against targets in combat (see opposite).

SHOOTING FROM COVER

If a model is shooting from behind cover; a low wall or other barrier; or from behind a rock, bush, or similar object; its own cover isn't considered to be in the way of its shooting so long as the model is touching the cover and is tall enough to see over or around it.

This is one of those cases where in real life a warrior could quickly lean out of or over his cover to shoot – so the model is allowed to shoot so long as its head is clear to see the target.

SHOOTING FROM BEHIND FRIENDS

If a model is shooting from behind a friendly model, this model isn't considered to be in the way of its shooting so long as the base of the shooter is touching the base of the friendly model, and the friendly model's base is of the same size as the shooter's or smaller.

As the two Men are in base contact, the Man with the bow can shoot the Orc as if the other Man was not in the way.

This rule represents a warrior taking a shot from above the shoulder of a comrade who is standing in front of him.

THE FIGHT PHASE

During the Fight phase, both sides work out combat between opposing models in base-to-base contact. Enemies are only allowed to touch where one has charged the other as we have already described in the Move phase section of the rules (see page 16).

WHEN TO FIGHT

The side that has priority that turn decides the order that fights are resolved. The deciding player chooses which combat he wants to work out first, the players work out the result, then the player with priority nominates the second combat, and so on until all fights have been resolved.

WORKING OUT A FIGHT

The easiest way to explain how combat works is to consider a fight between a Warrior of Minas Tirith and an Orc. Both have 1 Attack and 1 Wound on their characteristic profile and a Fight value of 3.

Where the combatants have 1 Attack, both players roll one dice on behalf of their warrior. The highest scoring warrior wins the fight. If both warriors roll the same result, the warrior with the highest Fight value wins – if both have the same Fight value roll a dice – 1, 2 or 3 the Evil side wins; 4, 5 or 6 the Good side wins.

The Orc rolls 3 and the Warrior of Minas Tirith rolls 4. The Warrior of Minas Tirith wins the fight.

The Orc is moved 1"/2cm back to show that he has lost the fight. Note that this means combatants will always separate once their fight is over.

The loser must 'back away' 1"/2cm from his opponent to represent he has lost the fight. The loser cannot move into touch with another enemy as it backs away but it can move within the 1"/2cm control zone of other enemies because models are assumed to back away as the combatants struggle. Also, a model cannot back away over an obstacle, climb or attempt to mount up on a steed. If unable to comply, the warrior is trapped – see the rules for trapped fighters (page 29).

The winner strikes at the loser and might hurt him by inflicting a wound. Where the winner has 1 Attack, roll one dice and refer to the Wound chart below. The Wound chart is the same as that used for shooting except that it is the warrior's own Strength that is compared to the enemy's Defence value rather than that of his weapon.

Most warriors have only 1 Wound on their characteristic profile. Where this is the case, the loser suffers a wound and is slain. The model is removed as a casualty. If the dice roll is insufficient to inflict a wound the loser is unharmed.

Once wounds have been worked out, the combat is complete and the side that has priority selects which combat to work out next. Once all combats have been worked out, the Fight phase is over.

Combats involving models lying on the ground are resolved with slightly different rules (see page 21).

MULTIPLE ATTACKS

Some Heroes and large creatures have more than 1 Attack on their characteristic profile. If a model has 2 Attacks then roll two dice when working out fights instead of one and choose the best score. If a model has 3 Attacks, roll three dice and choose the best score, and so on. A model with multiple Attacks is therefore more likely to win a combat.

If a model with multiple Attacks wins a fight then it strikes the enemy once per Attack. So, a Hero with 2 Attacks rolls two dice to see if he inflicts a wound – both dice count so he either inflicts no wounds, 1 wound, or 2 wounds.

When working out who wins a fight, a Hero with 2 Attacks rolls two dice – an ordinary warrior with 1 Attack rolls one dice.

WOUND CHART

DEFENCE

	1	2	3	4	5	6	7	8	9	10
1	4	5	5	6	6	6/4	6/5	6/6	–	–
2	4	4	5	5	6	6	6/4	6/5	6/6	–
3	3	4	4	5	5	6	6	6/4	6/5	6/6
4	3	3	4	4	5	5	6	6	6/4	6/5
5	3	3	3	4	4	5	5	6	6	6/4
6	3	3	3	3	4	4	5	5	6	6
7	3	3	3	3	3	4	4	5	5	6
8	3	3	3	3	3	3	4	4	5	5
9	3	3	3	3	3	3	3	4	4	5
10+	3	3	3	3	3	3	3	3	4	4

*(left side of chart, vertical label: **STRENGTH**)*

Compare the Strength value of the attacker down the left-hand side of the chart with the target's Defence value across the top of the chart.

The result indicates the minimum dice roll required to inflict one wound on your enemy. A score of 6/4 or 6/5 or 6/6 means you must roll a single dice and score a 6, followed by a further dice that must score

either 4+, 5+ or another 6. A '–' indicates the target is impossible to hurt – it is just too tough!

For example, a Man defeats an Orc in a fight. The Man has a Strength of 3, the Orc a Defence of 5, and both have 1 Attack. The Man therefore requires a dice roll of 5 or more to inflict one wound on the Orc.

or more enemies the retreating player can retreat through any gap that is wide enough for the model's base to pass – if there is no gap the model is trapped as described opposite. Where multiple models are backing away from a single model, each retreats exactly as in a one-on-one combat, which means none, some or all might be trapped. Once models have backed away work out strikes.

If the multiple side wins the fight, each model strikes against the loser. It doesn't matter whether individual models score higher or lower than their opponent – all models strike if their side wins.

If the single model wins the fight it can strike against one of the enemy if it has 1 Attack. If the model has more than 1 Attack, it strikes once per attack and can divide its strikes amongst its opponents as the player wishes. This is important as some enemies might have different Defence values or might be trapped. The player can roll for each strike before allocating the next if he prefers.

MULTIPLE WOUNDS

Some Heroes and larger creatures have more than 1 Wound on their characteristic profile. If a model has 2 Wounds it simply means it takes two wounds to kill it, 3 Wounds means it needs three wounds to kill, and so on. If such a warrior suffers a single wound make a note on your record sheet and carry on fighting. When the model loses its last wound it is slain.

MULTIPLE COMBATS

If two, three or more warriors are fighting a single enemy roll one dice for each warrior as before. For example, where three Orcs fight one Warrior of Minas Tirith, the Orcs roll three dice and the Man rolls one. The player rolling multiple dice takes the highest scoring dice and ignores the rest. In this example, the highest scoring dice for the Orcs is compared to the Man's dice score and the highest score wins.

If any models involved in a multiple combat have 2 or more Attacks then just total up the number of attacks on both sides and roll the appropriate number of dice. Pick out the best scoring dice for each side. In the case of a draw, compare the single model's Fight value to the best Fight value from the multiple side. If they are equal, roll one dice – 1, 2, 3 the Evil side wins; 4, 5, 6 the Good side wins.

All the models on the losing side are beaten back from their enemy 1"/2cm. Where a single model is beaten back by two

Three Orcs each have 1 Attack so roll one dice for each – 3 Attacks against the Warrior of Minas Tirith's 1 Attack.

Both sides compare their highest score – in this case the Orc's 6 wins the day.

A model surrounded by three equidistant enemies – he has nowhere to back away to, so he is trapped.

TRAPPED FIGHTERS

Warriors who have been defeated must back away from their opponent as described earlier. Sometimes a model will be unable to back away because its path is blocked by an impassable feature, obstacle, the edge of the table, or by other models. This is always the case where a defeated warrior is surrounded by three roughly equidistant enemies.

Note that a model is not allowed to back away by jumping an obstacle, climbing or mounting up – but it can back away by leaping over a sheer drop. This is up to the player. If the warrior leaps a drop of more than double the model's height, the player must roll to see if it is hurt as described in the Move Phase section (see page 21).

A model is surrounded by two equidistant enemies and a terrain feature – he is trapped.

If a defeated warrior can't back away the full 1"/2cm, the model is trapped. Any strikes made against a trapped model are doubled. So, a model with 1 Attack will make two strikes, a model with 2 Attacks makes four strikes against a trapped model or two strikes against two different

trapped models, and so on. The defeated model must be moved back as far as possible so that enemies are no longer touching – if necessary other models, even the very enemies that are trapping it, must be moved slightly to make sure there is a gap.

In a multiple combat where several models must move, the player whose models are backing away can move them in any order he wishes.

MAKING WAY FOR TRAPPED FIGHTERS

If a defeated warrior can't back away from his opponent because of friends blocking his path, then these friends can move up to 1"/2cm in order to make room. This is called 'making way for friends'. Models lying on the ground can make way for friends. Models don't have to make way – it is up to the player.

The spear-armed warrior makes way for his friend backing away.

Models cannot make way if they are still engaged in combat with an opponent. Otherwise, the same rules apply as for backing away, so models can move into enemy control zones, but cannot move into a fight, for example.

The idea behind this rule is that it enables friends to move 1"/2cm to allow their comrades to avoid taking double strikes because they are trapped.

Note that the rule for making way only allows a model to make way for a friendly model that has been defeated in a fight. A model cannot usually make way for another model that is making way. This means that in a dense mob, the models at the front will be pushed onto the enemy as those at the rear will be unable to make way (a common Orc tactic!).

Tactical note: *As models don't have to charge enemies in a straight line, it's a good idea to try to surround the enemy models as your warriors charge in, making sure the enemy will be trapped in the ensuing combat.*

ADVANCED RULES

*T*he pages that precede this section constitute the core rules of the game. The pages here deal with additional rules. You don't need to use any of these extra rules to play a game, though they add further depth to the tactical options. It is a good idea to make sure you are reasonably familiar with the core rules before using the advanced rules.

DEFENDING BARRIERS

If a warrior is placed directly behind a barrier then he is especially well placed to counter any foe that tries to cross. The model is said to be 'defending' the barrier and is placed with its base touching it.

To count as defendable, a barrier must be at least half as tall or wide as an attacking enemy (otherwise the enemy can step over it without penalty) and the defender has to be able to see over it.

When a model is defending a barrier, its zone of control applies to the whole area immediately in front of the defender's base plus 1"/2cm either side. This is the part of the barrier he is defending. No enemy can move into the defender's zone of control except to fight him.

The defender's control zone extends 1"/2cm either side of his base.

Where a model is placed behind a barrier it will be impossible to place an enemy into base contact because the barrier will be in the way. To allow for this we introduce the following rule: a model can charge an enemy that is defending a barrier by moving into the enemy's zone of control and contacting the barrier. The two models are assumed to be touching even though they are not actually in base contact.

These two models are considered to be touching.

Note that, differently from normal, the defender's control zone is not cancelled by enemies engaging him in combat across the barrier, so the defender can stop up to three man-sized opponents attempting to cross the barrier within its control zone, as shown in the diagram below.

Three warriors fighting against a single defender.

It is also possible for up to three defenders to fight against a single charger because their control zones overlap. This is shown in the diagram below.

A single warrior is fighting against three defenders.

Enemies are of course free to try and cross the barrier further away, outside the defender's control zone. If they roll a 6 on the Jump chart and have enough movement left to reach the defender, they can even finish their move and charge the defender from his own side of the barrier, denying the advantage of defending the barrier. The only way to cross a barrier within the defender's control zone is to fight and kill the model behind it as described below.

The Orc rolls a 6 to jump the barrier, and has enough movement to reach the defender, attacking him from his own side of the barrier.

DEFENDING ONE-ON-ONE

The procedure for defending is slightly different to the basic combat rules that we have already learned. In the case of ordinary combats, warriors who lose a fight are immediately moved back 1"/2cm before working out the effect of blows. In the case of defending combats, the defender does not move at all even if he is beaten. If the defender survives he repels the attack and the charger is automatically moved back 1"/2cm as if he had been beaten. Only if the defender is slain is the model removed and the charger is automatically moved over the barrier to occupy his space.

To work out a one-on-one fight, roll to determine which side wins the fight as normal. If the charger wins, roll a dice to see if he strikes the barrier or his foe. On a roll of 1, 2 or 3, his blow strikes the barrier and has no effect, on a roll of a 4, 5 or 6, the blow strikes the defender and is worked out as normal. Roll for each strike separately when striking more than once.

If the defender wins the fight, his blows are struck as normal. It is not necessary to roll to see if he strikes the barrier. Because he is defending he has already thrust his weapon through or over the barrier in order to fight his opponent.

If neither model is slain at the end of the fight, the charger is moved back 1"/2cm, whilst the defender remains in place. If the defender has been slain, the charger is moved over the barrier to occupy the defender's space.

If a single charger moves into the zones of control of two or three defenders (or more defenders move so that the attacker is now inside their control zone, joining in the defence to help the friendly model who has been attacked) then he must fight them all.

All the defenders fight at once, rolling all their dice at the same time as they would for a normal multiple combat. This is because the defenders are all prepared to strike and don't have to struggle over the barrier to press their attack. If the charger wins the fight he must still roll to see whether his blows hit the barricade. If he should succeed in killing any of his opponents then he crosses the barrier automatically, immediately taking the place of a model he has slain. If necessary, move the other defenders aside to leave some space between the attacker's base and the defenders'.

DEFENDING IN MULTIPLE FIGHTS

If two or three chargers attack a single defender then the chargers must fight the defender one at a time. The charging player can decide which of his models will fight first. This means that a defending model can potentially fight two or three times in the same combat round.

Once each charger has fought he is moved back 1"/2cm unless he has slain the defender or been slain himself. If the defender is slain then his opponent and any other chargers who have yet to fight will automatically cross the barrier. The charger who slew his foe moves into the space vacated by his enemy and remaining models are moved directly forward and over the barrier. If remaining models cannot be moved directly over the barrier for whatever reason, they can be moved next to the model that has already crossed or otherwise not at all.

The attacking Orc wins the fight against two defenders and kills one.

He can now immediately cross the barrier, replacing the model killed.

As the defender has been killed by the first attacker, all three Orcs move across the barrier.

MULTIPLE FIGHTS ON BOTH SIDES

Where there are several models on both sides of a barrier the combats are divided into as many separate one-on-one fights as possible by the player with priority. Remaining multiple fights are resolved as multiple combats with one model on one side as already described.

ATTACKED FROM TWO SIDES

If a defending model is also attacked from his side of a barrier, then the fight becomes a regular combat and the defender loses all his advantages. All attackers engaged against the defender, from both sides of the barrier, fight together as normal, ignoring the barrier. The only exception to normal fights is that if the attackers kill the defender, they can still cross the barrier.

If attacked from both sides of the barrier, work out the fight as a normal three-on-one multiple fight. If the defender is killed, all attackers can cross the barrier.

It's also possible, though unlikely, that a model attacking across a barrier is then charged by other defenders from his own side of the barrier. In this case, treat the fight as a normal multiple combat, ignoring the barrier. Note that in this case the attacker cannot cross the barrier even if he wins and kills the defender behind the barrier.

The Orc has charged the defender and has subsequently been charged by another Man from his own side of the barrier.

DEFENDING ELEVATED POSITIONS

A warrior who climbs to the top of a cliff, wall or other vertical surface automatically charges the nearest enemy whose zone of control overlaps the top edge of the surface. He holds on just below the top of the vertical surface and fights the warrior on the top. If no enemy zone of control overlaps the edge of the vertical surface, the warrior can position himself on the top – but he cannot charge any other enemy on the top if they were not visible at the start of his move.

Models stood on the top of a vertical surface fight by defending its edge against attackers climbing up from below.

A warrior on the top of a wall/cliff can be placed immediately behind its edge and can then defend the edge immediately in front of him and 1"/2cm either side. This is exactly the same as for defending barriers and is shown on the diagram below.

The defender's zone of control extends 1"/2cm either side of his base. The elevated position counts as a defended barrier.

No enemy can attempt to ascend over the edge of a vertical surface if he has to enter the control zone of a model that is defending the edge. The attacker must fight the defender and kill him in order to climb over the edge and occupy his enemy's place on the top.

The rules for defending fights are used to work out the combat. This is exactly the same as for a combat over a wall, hedge, barricade or similar defence work. The only difference is that the chargers are climbing a vertical surface and so risk falling off if they fail to get over the edge as noted below.

FALLING OFF

The following rules apply to warriors attacking whilst climbing vertical surfaces:

If a model is fighting in this way and is forced to back away 1"/2cm, he can only move down the vertical surface. As he backs away he risks falling. If physically unable to back away for whatever reason, the warrior still risks falling. A model making way for a friend who is backing away from a fight does not have to roll – he is not retreating in the face of the enemy.

Make a random roll to see if the warrior falls as he is beaten back. On a 4, 5, or 6, the warrior keeps his footing and backs away as required. On a 1, 2 or 3, the warrior loses his footing and falls to the ground before he can back away. He falls the full distance to the ground and suffers falling damage in the usual way. (See page 21).

If the warrior at the top of the vertical surface falls, then roll a dice for every other model that is climbing right below him. Any model that rolls a 1, 2 or 3 is also knocked from the vertical surface by their own friend. Models fall from wherever they are on the surface – so warriors that are nearer the ground suffer fewer hits. See page 21 for the rules on falling damage.

COURAGE

Of course all of our warriors are courageous – it's just that some are more courageous than others! The rules that follow represent the fact that warriors will not always act as you, the player, might wish them to. There are times when even the bravest warrior would sooner retreat than fight. To take this into account we have the 'Courage test'.

If you're learning the game we recommend you ignore Courage until you're confident with the rules for moving, shooting and fighting. You can always introduce the Courage rules later. To begin with, it is reasonable to assume that any Courage test required by the following rules is passed.

COURAGE TESTS

A Courage test is always taken in the same way. Two dice are rolled and added together, and the warrior's Courage value is added to the total.

If the total score is 10 or more, the test is passed.

If the score is less than 10, it is failed.

In the case of mounted warriors only the rider needs to test – mounts do not need to make a Courage test so long as they have a rider.

WHEN TO TEST

A model must take a Courage test for the following:

1. When attempting to charge a terrifying enemy.

2. At the start of a move once its force is Broken.

3. Mounts must test if they are separated from their rider.

ATTEMPTING TO CHARGE A TERRIFYING ENEMY

If a warrior wishes to charge one or more terrifying enemies, he needs to take a Courage test before he moves. If the test is passed, the model can make its charge by moving into base contact with the enemy. If it is failed, the model will not charge, losing heart and immediately freezing on the spot, not moving at all.

Models that fail this test cannot use any missile weapon or magical powers during that same turn, but are otherwise unaffected.

The ability to inspire terror is a special quality of some monstrous creatures, as noted in the Forces section.

Note that a model armed with a spear/pike supporting a friend who is fighting a terrifying enemy does not need to take this test, since he is not going to charge the terrifying enemy.

AT THE START OF EACH MOVE
ONCE THE FORCE IS BROKEN
At the beginning of the game, count the number of models in your force (cavalry models count as a single model) and note it down. If, at the beginning of a turn, half or more of the warriors on your side have been lost then your force is said to be Broken. From then on, every remaining warrior must test every turn before moving in the Move phase. Make the test for each model before it moves. Models that do not intend to move must still test as if they were about to do so unless already engaged in a fight. Models already fighting when it is their turn to move do not test for courage; they are too busy fighting for their lives.

If the test is passed, the warrior can be moved normally or not at all as the player wishes.

If the test is failed, the warrior will lose his nerve, turn tail and flee the battlefield. The model is immediately removed from the game just as if it had been slain.

Note that such models count as casualties, in exactly the same way as models that have actually been slain.

Stand Fast!
The following rule applies only to Courage tests which are taken on account of the army being Broken. This is often the point where battles will be won or lost and where only the Heroes can force ordinary warriors to stand fast. Rules for Heroes are given later.

Ordinary Warriors do not have to test their courage for their force being Broken if there is a visible Hero within 6"/14cm who has already tested his courage and passed (including those Heroes that pass this test automatically because of a spell or special rule). To benefit from this rule, players must test and move their Heroes before testing for ordinary Warriors. Remember that other Heroes are not affected by this rule and must therefore test even if a Hero within range has already passed his test.

Heroes that are engaged in combat do not test on their Courage, so they cannot use the Stand Fast! rule (they are too busy defending themselves to think about leading the troops around them).

MOUNTS MUST TEST IF THEY
ARE SEPARATED FROM THEIR RIDER
If a mount finds itself separated from its rider, whether because the rider is killed, thrown or simply dismounts, the animal may decide that it's time to leave the battlefield.

Whenever a mount loses its rider, the mount must immediately take a Courage test. If the test is failed, the mount is scared by the death of the rider and the cavalry model is removed. If the test is passed, the mount continues to fight and the cavalry model must be replaced with a suitable unridden mount. If the player does not have such a model available, then the mount is assumed to have failed the test as described above and the cavalry model is simply removed.

Mounts that have a value of 0 in their Attack and Fight characteristic (like in the case of horses), are rather timid and will always fail this test and run away as soon as they don't have a rider.

HEROES

Heroes are extraordinary individuals – stern, mighty, and dangerous. A hero can fight and defeat several ordinary warriors with ease. In terms of our game, Heroes are not necessarily good or evil. The Forces of Darkness also have their own evil Heroes who are just as powerful as those of the Free Peoples. Aragorn, Gandalf and Boromir are obvious examples of Heroes, and opposing them are the Witch-king, Saruman, and the monstrous Balrog.

MIGHT, WILL & FATE

Heroes have characteristic profiles just like ordinary warriors. In addition, they have three heroic characteristics, namely Might, Will, and Fate (abbreviated as M/W/F). An example of a Hero's characteristic profile is shown below.

Unlike other characteristics these are represented by a store of points that are used up during the game. Players must decide for themselves the best time to use their rare and precious Might, Will and Fate points.

	F	S	D	A	W	C	M/W/F		
Éomer	5/4+	4	6	2	2	5	3	2	2

MIGHT

This represents a Hero's ability to perform heroic feats. When a dice is rolled on behalf of a Hero to resolve the effect of something it has done, its score can be adjusted by expending Might. Might can also be used to perform heroic actions as described later.

Each point of Might that is expended can be used to adjust the dice score up or down by one to a maximum of 6 or minimum of 1. No dice can be adjusted to more than 6 or reduced to less than 1. If a player rolls a 3, for example, he can expend two points of Might to turn the score into 5.

A player does not have to decide to use his Might until the dice has been rolled, or until both sides have rolled in the case of a roll to see who wins a fight. This means a player can always ensure the result he wants so long as he has enough Might points left. Note that if the players may employ re-rolls, these must be used first and only once the final scores of the dice have been determined, the players may decide to modify this final score with Might.

If two opposing Heroes are fighting and both wish to use Might to win, both players must secretly indicate with hidden dice or written notes how much Might they are going to expend (minimum 1) and reveal simultaneously.

When rolling to determine the effect of a successful strike or missile hit, two rolls are sometimes required to inflict a wound (eg, 6/4+). In this case, the Might bonus is added to both rolls – so 1 Might point expended on the first roll automatically adds to the second roll.

When a modifier applies to the dice, the modifier is applied to the roll first and then the Hero is allowed to use his Might to modify the result. For example, a Hero fighting with a two-handed sword rolls a 6 to win the fight. His score is modified to a 5 because of the penalty from the weapon, but then the Hero can choose to use a point of Might to bring the final result back up to a 6.

At the start of the game you must record the Might points available for each of your Heroes. As Might is used up you must keep track of the remaining points. Once all a Hero's Might is gone he can no longer adjust dice rolls.

It is important to remember that a Hero can only use Might to affect his own dice rolls – not those of other characters whether friend of foe. In a multiple combat, it is therefore necessary to roll separately for a Hero's Attacks or use distinctly coloured dice to differentiate his rolls from those of other warriors. Might is never used to affect random rolls, for example, deciding if a model can be seen if you are unsure, the roll-off to solve a tie in a fight between models with same Fighting value, rolling for objects in the way of a shot, rolling for hitting a barrier when fighting a defending enemy, rolling to see if the rider or the mount is hit by a shot, shooting into combat, etc. Also, Might cannot be used to affect the Priority roll made at the start of each turn.

CAN I USE MIGHT?

Might points can be used to add to or subtract from any dice roll made to resolve something the Hero has done. The most usual occasions are:

When fighting
To boost a dice roll to win a combat.

When shooting
To hit a target.

Shooting and Combat
To inflict a wound on an enemy the model has hit or struck.

Courage
To pass a Courage test.

Making tests
To affect Jumping, Climbing or Thrown Rider results.

When using Will
To cast a spell or pass a Magical Resistance test.

When using Fate
To pass a Fate roll.

WILL

This represents the Hero's willpower and determination, and is also a measure of his ability to employ or resist magical powers.

Will points can be expended by the Hero in the same way as Might points, but only to modify the result of dice rolls to pass a Courage test.

Will points can also be used to employ or resist magical powers, as described below. Each time a power is employed, the Hero's stock of Will is reduced. Each time a Hero attempts to resist a magical power, his stock of Will is reduced. Once a Hero's Will has been used up he may neither employ nor resist magical powers.

MAGICAL POWERS

If a Hero has magical powers he can attempt to use one power once in any turn. A Hero can resist any number of magical powers during a turn so long as he has Will points remaining.

A Hero can employ a magical power in the Move phase when it is the model's turn to move. The Hero must be able to see the target as we have already discussed. The Hero can target a visible model even if it is engaged in combat, unless specified differently in the magical power's description. In addition, a Hero must be free to move in order to use a magical power. A Hero already fighting an enemy when it is his turn to move cannot use a magical power.

A magical power can be used at any point during the model's movement – before moving, afterwards, or at any point between. A Hero can use a magical power against an enemy and then move into combat against the same (or a different) enemy, for example.

When a Hero employs a magical power, the player states which power the Hero is using and nominates how many dice he will roll. The Hero's Will value is immediately reduced by 1 for each dice rolled. The player rolls all the dice together. If the highest scoring dice equals or beats the value required to use the power then the Hero has succeeded. If none of the dice score the minimum value needed, the Hero has failed to use the power – there is no effect and the Will points have been wasted. You will notice that the more dice a player uses, the greater is his chance of scoring the value required and the greater his Hero's expenditure of Will.

If a Hero is the victim of a magical power he can resist it by rolling one or more dice. This is called 'magical resistance'. The player declares how many dice he will roll and the Hero's Will value is immediately reduced by 1 for each dice rolled. The player rolls all the dice together and picks out the highest score. If the highest scoring dice equals or beats the highest scoring dice of the attacker then the power is resisted and has no effect. If none of the dice equals or beats the highest scoring dice of the attacker then the Hero has failed to resist the spell's effects.

Of course, when a Hero is rolling to employ a magical power, he can modify his highest roll by using Might, either to get to cast a spell he would have otherwise failed to cast or to increase the number rolled in order to make it more difficult for the target to resist the spell. He must do this, generating a final casting score, before the enemy decides to resist the spell or not. The victim then gets to use his own Might to modify his resist roll, if he wishes.

FATE

Fate represents a Hero's destiny and as such preserves him from harm, where ordinary warriors would otherwise die. If a Hero loses a wound then he would normally reduce his remaining Wounds value by 1. However, if the Hero has Fate points left he might be able to avoid harm by some heroic ruse.

If a Hero loses a wound then he can immediately expend one or more of any Fate points he has to 'avoid' it. The player rolls a dice and simultaneously reduces the Hero's Fate store by 1. If the dice scores a 4, 5 or 6 then the roll is successful and the Hero avoids the wound. Any number of wounds can be avoided in this way.

A player can use as many Fate points as he has available to try to avoid a wound. The player can roll one dice at a time until he makes the score required, runs out of Fate, or decides to suffer the wound. Note that Might must be used only to modify the last dice rolled (if, for example, you roll a 3 for your Fate, decide to use another Fate point, and then roll a 2. You cannot at this stage decide you want to modify the original score of 3. You are stuck with the 2 and now need to use two points of Might if you want to avoid the wound...).

Fate points are most commonly expended in combat but a player can also use them if a Hero dies as a result of a fall or similar mischance. In this case, a successful result might mean that the Hero has not fallen to his death but landed on something soft placed in his path by fortune.

Note that Fate points cannot be used to save a Hero that has failed a Courage test for his force being Broken. Such a cowardly Hero is removed as a casualty exactly like the lowliest warrior and cannot benefit from his Fate.

USING MIGHT, WILL & FATE TOGETHER

Might can be used to adjust Will or Fate dice rolls if the player wishes, so long as the Hero has sufficient Might points remaining. In the same way, a Hero may use a mix of Might and Will points to pass a Courage test he would otherwise fail. A very powerful Hero will be able to cheat death and resist the most potent of sorceries – for a while – but sooner or later even the greatest Hero will run out of Might, Will and Fate.

Most Heroes will have only a few points of Might, Will or Fate for an entire game, and will have to consider how to use them very carefully indeed. The more junior Heroes may have little more than a single Fate point or a couple of Might points to back their claim to fame. Others not only have a large store of points, but depend upon them utterly, such as the Ringwraiths.

HEROIC ACTIONS

As we have already described, priority is usually established at the start of each turn by rolling a dice. Whichever side has priority that turn takes all its moves and shots first, and decides the order in which combats are fought. This is the normal priority rule as described in the Turn Sequence (see page 13).

During the Move, Shoot, or Fight phase, any individual Hero can override the normal sequence by giving up one point of Might to make a 'heroic action'. The players must declare that they wish to make heroic actions at the start of the phase, beginning with the player that has priority for that turn. If the player with priority does not want to make heroic actions, then the opponent may decide to do so, but the player with priority is then allowed to change his mind and declare he wants to make heroic actions as well.

If both players wish to make heroic actions in the same phase, then the sides alternate picking a Hero to make a heroic action. Roll a dice to randomly determine which side has the first pick – 1, 2 or 3 the Evil side goes first; 4, 5 or 6 the Good side goes first.

Once all the Heroes who are making heroic actions have been indicated, work out their actions in the order they were picked. It is easier to remember the order if you place a dice beside each model as it is nominated – 1 is first, 2 is second, 3, 4, and so on. This sometimes allows Heroes to anticipate the enemy and cancel their heroic action, for example, by moving into base contact with a Hero who has declared a heroic move or by shooting before the Hero and his friends can do so and killing the Hero. If this happens, the points of Might used to declare the heroic action are spent and cannot be restored because the heroic action has not happened – the enemy has been quicker!

HEROIC MOVE

A Hero who makes a heroic action at the start of the Move phase will move before other models that are not making heroic actions. In addition, the Hero can shout "With me!" as he moves, and all friends within 6"/14cm will move at the same time. Friends moving in this way must begin and end their move within 6"/14cm of the Hero who is making the heroic action, otherwise they cannot move with him. A Hero that is engaged in combat cannot execute heroic Moves nor can he shout "With me!".

HEROIC SHOOTING

A Hero can call a heroic action at the start of the Shoot phase by shouting "Fire!". This enables the Hero himself and all friends within 6"/14cm to shoot before other models that turn at whatever targets they wish, assuming they are able to. Note that a Hero does not need to be shooting himself to call a heroic shooting action, but he cannot do so if he is engaged in combat.

HEROIC COMBAT

If a Hero gives up one point of Might at the start of the Fight phase, the combat he is involved in is worked out before other combats that turn. In addition, if all enemy models in base contact with the Hero are slain, the Hero and any friends in the same multiple combat can move again before proceeding with the Fight phase. For example, the Hero and accompanying friends can charge other enemies or move to join other fights, although they don't have to, and can simply move away if they so wish.

When warriors fight heroic combats they will often move to join existing fights and in some cases this can change the way the fights are divided. Once the heroic combats have been worked out it may be necessary to rematch other fights as a result. The player with priority decides how combatants are matched as normal.

A warrior who fights a heroic combat and then moves to join a further heroic combat cannot then move and fight again. A warrior can only benefit from one heroic combat during a single Fight phase.

Designer's Note. *It's possible for a Hero's heroic action to affect another Hero – so two Heroes within 6"/14cm could benefit from either of them making a heroic move or shot. Similarly, two Heroes fighting together in a multiple combat would benefit if either used the heroic combat ability.*

Once a model has moved or shot it has completed its movement and shooting for that phase. The heroic action enables the model to move or shoot first but does not enable it to move or shoot twice. A model that happens to be within 6"/14cm of a series of Heroes making a heroic move cannot move along with each – it only moves once!

Heroic combat is slightly different because a model gets the chance to move and fight a second time. However, a model can only benefit from a heroic combat action once per turn.

MAGICAL POWERS

Wizards and other supernatural creatures of Middle-earth wield terrible and mysterious powers of sorcery. In the game, this is represented by Magical Powers, as described in the Heroes section. The most common magical powers are listed here, together with their effects. The range at which these powers can be cast and the number that the caster needs to roll to cast them often vary, so they will be given in each model's entry.

Aura of Command. While this spell is in effect, all friendly models within 6"/14cm of the caster will automatically pass any Courage tests they are compelled to take. Once cast, this power lasts for the remainder of the game so long as the caster has at least 1 point of Will remaining. If the caster's Will drops to zero, the aura fades away.

Aura of Dismay. This power can only be cast at the end of the caster's move. If successfully cast, any friendly models that end their move within 6"/14cm of the caster (including the caster himself) count as causing terror for the remainder of that Move phase.

Black Dart. The victim suffers a hit with a Strength of 9. If a cavalry model fails to resist this power, the caster can choose whether the Dart hits the rider, any passenger or the mount, even if the target is engaged in combat (no need to roll).

Cast Blinding Light. This power enables the caster to cause his hand or weapon to glow brilliantly. In darkness this illuminates an area 12"/28cm around him and anyone within this area can be seen as if it were daylight. Once cast this power lasts for the rest of the game so long as the caster has at least 1 point of Will remaining. If the caster's Will drops to zero the light is extinguished. Because of the light's brightness any enemy shooting at the caster, at a target that is partially obscured by the caster or at a target within 6"/14cm of the caster will require a roll of 6 to score a hit.

Chill Soul. The victim suffers a wound exactly as if wounded in close combat. If a cavalry model fails to resist this power, the caster can choose whether the rider, the mount or a passenger will suffer the wound, even if the target is engaged in combat (no need to roll).

Command/Compel. The victim can do nothing further that turn as described for Immobilise/Transfix (below), except that the caster can move the victim up to half a move as soon as the power takes effect, even into base contact with an enemy (there is no need for a Courage test in order to charge a terrifying enemy). The player can do this even if the model has already moved that turn or even if the model has already been compelled that turn. The model cannot be moved out of a combat if it is already engaged. The model cannot be forced to lie down, climb, jump, mount, dismount or other complex movements, it can only be moved up to half his normal movement value. The model cannot be forced to perform any actions that would cause direct harm to it (such as moving over the edge of a cliff…). If the victim has the Ring, he must put it on if the caster wishes.

Drain Courage. The victim loses 1 point of Courage from his characteristic profile. This penalty applies for the rest of the battle. This ability can take effect several times on the same target – reducing a model's Courage value each time.

Fury. This power is targeted on the caster himself and, once in action, its 6"/14cm area of effect follows the caster as he moves around. The caster and all models of its race (Orcs, Goblins or Uruk-hai, including Heroes) within range of the power are possessed by an insane fighting frenzy, which allows them to ignore the most serious of wounds. They always automatically pass any Courage test they are required to take. In addition, every time they suffer a wound, they can roll a dice: if a 6 is rolled, the wound is recovered. This is effectively like using a point of Fate, with the only exception that the Wound is recovered only on the roll of a 6 rather than on a 4+. If the wound is not recovered, Heroes can then make use of their Fate as normal. Once the magical power is in action, both of its effects will last until the caster is engaged in a Fight and his side loses the fight. The caster can, of course, employ the power again later as long as he has Will left.

Nature's Wrath. The spell affects all enemies within 6"/14cm of the caster – but only one affected foe can attempt to resist it. If resisted, all foes are unaffected; if the foe fails to resist, then all are affected. All enemies within 6"/14cm of the caster are knocked to the ground. Cavalry models are automatically thrown and both the steed and the rider are kocked to the ground.

Immobilise/Transfix. The victim can do nothing further that turn. In combat, his Fight value counts as 1 and he rolls one dice regardless of how many attacks he normally has. If he wins a combat he will not strike. The victim can still use Might, Will and Fate but cannot make heroic actions. The effect lasts for the remainder of that turn.

Panic Steed. This power may only be directed against a mounted model. The rider is immediately thrown as the steed rears and throws him from the saddle. Remove the steed from play and roll on the Thrown Rider chart to determine the effect of the fall.

Renew. The caster can use this spell to restore one lost Wound to one friendly model.

Sap Will. The victim's Will value is reduced to 0. The effect lasts for the remainder of the battle – although it can be increased by the Strengthen Will magical power.

Sorcerous Blast. This power can be used against a single enemy model. If the power is employed successfully the target is blasted directly away from the caster and knocked to the ground – roll a dice and move the target that number of inches or double that number of centimetres (1"-6" or 2cm-12cm). Except as noted below, any other models that lie within the path of the blasted model are automatically moved aside and knocked to the ground. If the target or one of the models lying within the path of the target is fighting, then all other models in the same fight are knocked to the ground whether friends or foe. The target model counts as having been struck one blow at a Strength value of 5 and every model knocked to the ground is struck one blow at a Strength value of 3. If a model with a Strength of 5 or less is blasted into a model which has a Strength of 6 or more, it stops immediately. The model with Strength 6 or more is not moved or knocked to the ground, but it is struck one blow from the impact as normal. If the model blasted away has a Strength of 6 or more, then it will affect any other model along its path. Eg, if the Balrog is blasted into a Goblin it will knock it to the ground but if a Goblin is blasted into the Balrog, the demon won't budge.

Strengthen Will. The caster can use this spell to give one point of Will to a friendly Hero within range. The target's Will can be increased up to the starting amount shown on the target's profile, except that the caster can give a point of Will to Heroes whose original Will value is 0. The caster cannot use this magical power to restore his own Will.

Terrifying Aura. Once this power has been successfully cast, the model counts as terrifying to all enemies as long as he has at least 1 point of Will remaining. If his Will drops to 0 the terrifying aura is extinguished. See pages 34-35 for the rules concerning terror.

Your Staff is Broken! This power enables the caster to destroy the Staff of Power of an enemy wizard. Once this power has been successfully cast, the enemy loses all the advantages related with his magical staff (both the free point of Will and the possibility of using the staff as a two-handed weapon).

WARGEAR

So far in the game it makes no difference whether a warrior is armed with a sword, spear, or any other weapon – all warriors fight in the same way. Whilst this is perfectly good when it comes to learning the rules and making a start, there is clearly a good case for introducing unique rules to reflect the differences between one type of weapon and another.

SWORDS AND OTHER HAND WEAPONS

All warriors carry a sword, axe, club or similar weapon in one hand – these are collectively called 'hand weapons' for that reason. All hand weapons are used more or less in the same way and how effective they are is more dependent upon a warrior's familiarity with his armament than any inherent difference between swords, axes, etc.

The rules already given assume a warrior is armed in this way so we need not burden ourselves with additional rules for hand weapons.

MORE THAN ONE WEAPON

Warriors often carry several weapons; for example a bow, sword and a spear. If a warrior is armed with several different shooting weapons, eg, a throwing spear and a bow, he can use either one of them in the Shoot phase but he cannot use both in the same turn. If a warrior has several close combat weapons, eg, a sword and a two-handed axe, he can use either one of them in the Fight phase but he cannot use both in the same turn.

UNARMED MODELS

Occasionally a model may carry no weapon at all, and when this is the case it will be clearly specified in its entry.

An unarmed model is not well equipped for combat and therefore suffers a -1 dice penalty when working out who wins a fight – a roll of 4 counts as 3, a roll of 6 as 5, and so on. Rolls of 1 still count as 1 because it is the lowest score possible. Note that separate dice rolls will be required in multiple combats for unarmed models.

Savage animals and monsters which would not normally need weapons to fight are not penalised just because they have no visible weaponry. They have claws, teeth, and whatever else nature has endowed them with.

SPEARS

Due to a spear's length, a spear-armed warrior on foot can contribute one attack to a fight if he is in base contact with a friend who is touching an enemy. The extra length of the spear allows him to 'support' his own comrade against the foe. The spear-armed warrior does not need to be touching the foe to lend support in this way – he only has to be touching a friend who is himself touching the enemy. The friend must have a base of the same size as the spear-armed warrior, or smaller, for the spear-armed warrior to be able to support him. If the friend's base is bigger than the spearman's, the spearman cannot support his friend.

The spear rule allows a warrior to support a friend.

A spearman cannot offer support if he is himself engaged in combat or if he has shot in the Shoot phase.

A spear-armed warrior who is supporting a friend as described is not part of the combat for all intents and purposes (ie, the Fight value, Strength and Might of the spearman do not come into the fight at all). The friend supported in this way by a spearman gets one extra attack for that combat. A model with 1 attack will have 2, a model with 2 will have 3, and so on. This extra attack represents the advantage offered to the friend by the support of the spearman, which allows the friend to be more effective in combat.

This fight is a multiple combat between two Men and one Orc, with a second Orc supporting with a spear.

Only one spear-armed warrior can support one friendly model at a time. If several spear-armed warriors are touching a single friend, only one of them can give an extra attack to the friend.

As noted overleaf, spear-armed models cannot support warriors using two-handed weapons or defending themselves by shielding. See the rules for these weapons.

The spear rules allow warriors with spears to support their friends, and enables a huddle of spear-armed troops to bring their numbers to bear against the foe. This offers spear-armed warriors a different way of fighting that is especially valuable in larger battles where bringing as many men into a fight as possible can often carry the day.

PIKES

A pike is a very long spear. Only a warrior on foot can carry a pike – the weapon is so long that it is impossible to use whilst mounted. Models armed with pikes cannot carry bows, crossbows or shields as they need both hands to carry their weapons.

The rules for pikes are the same as those for spears except:

A pike-armed warrior can support a friend engaged in combat by being in base contact with a spear- or pike-armed warrior who is already supporting the same friend, as shown below. This will give another attack to the friend engaged in combat, for a total of +2 attacks.

Otherwise – all the rules for spears apply.

In this situation, the Uruk-hai fighting against the Warrior of Minas Tirith is being supported by two friends and therefore has three attacks.

A pikeman and a spearman supporting a friend.

TWO-HANDED WEAPONS

A two-handed sword or axe is a large, heavy weapon that needs two hands to wield it effectively (heavy glaives, halberds and similar weapons are considered to be in the same category). As with hand weapons, we won't worry unduly about the differences – they are fundamentally similar weapons that require a similar approach. Two-handed weapons are difficult to use because they are so heavy. The advantage though is that they are very dangerous – able to smash through armour and crush flesh and bone with horrific ease.

Models armed with two-handed weapons cannot carry pikes, spears, shields, bows or crossbows as they need both hands to carry their weapons. It is also impossible to use a two-handed weapon whilst mounted.

able to support a warrior which is fighting with a two-handed weapon – their long weapons would instantly be knocked aside. So, a spear or pike-armed warrior cannot support a friendly warrior who is fighting with a two-handed weapon.

As you can see, a warrior armed with a two-handed weapon is less likely to win a combat but more likely to inflict a wound. To take full advantage of these weapons, it is a good idea to use warriors armed in this way together with others carrying ordinary swords or other hand weapons, as these more lightly-armed warriors are more likely to win fights than their unwieldy comrades.

ELVEN BLADES

The Elves fight with elegant curved blades of exceptional craftmanship. These weapons are so finely balanced that a skilled Elf warrior can swing their very long blades in a fluid series of cuts and thrusts. Elven blades are hand weapons, but a model wielding one can declare at the beginning of any Fight phase that he is going to use it with both hands. For the duration of that Fight phase, the Elven blade will count as a two-handed weapon. If the warrior also carries a shield or a spear then he cannot use his Elven blade as a two-handed weapon, but models carrying bows can carry Elven blades and use them as two-handed weapons as normal.

LANCES

Heavily armoured horsemen are sometimes equipped with long thrusting spears called lances. These are fixed in place underarm when the warrior is charging, thus allowing the warrior to bring the entire weight and impetus of his charging steed to bear against the enemy.

A cavalry model armed with a lance gets a special bonus when charging, even if it is subsequently charged in the same Move phase. A lance adds +1 to his dice roll on the Wound chart – a roll of 1 counts as 2, 3 counts as 4, and so on. If two rolls are normally required to inflict a wound (eg, 6/4+) the bonus is added to both rolls. The maximum score on a dice is 6, so a roll of 6 still counts as 6.

This bonus is in addition to any other cavalry bonuses for charging cavalry, but it also applies against enemy cavalry and is not lost if the warrior is engaged by enemy cavalry.

If fighting a multiple combat it is necessary to distinguish models that are charging with lances from others – so roll separately or use different coloured dice for them.

If the lance-armed warrior does not charge, he receives no bonus and instead the horseman will have to fight using the butt or shaft of his lance (counts as a hand weapon).

It is impossible to use a lance whilst on foot.

If a model is fighting with a two-handed sword or axe, it automatically suffers a -1 penalty to its dice roll when working out which side wins the fight – a dice roll of 5 counts as 4, a roll of 6 as 5, etc. The minimum possible score is 1, so a roll of 1 still counts as 1 and not as 0. The score can still be enhanced to a maximum of 6 by the use of a Might point as described for Heroes. This penalty reflects that the weapon is heavy and difficult to use.

If fighting a multiple combat, it is necessary to distinguish models that are using two-handed weapons from others – so roll separately or use different coloured dice for them.

By way of compensation, a warrior fighting with a two-handed sword or axe adds +1 to his dice roll on the Wound chart – a roll of 1 counts as 2, 3 counts as 4, and so on. If two rolls are normally required to inflict a wound (eg, 6/4+) the bonus is added to both rolls. The maximum score on a dice is 6, so a roll of 6 still counts as 6. The bonus reflects the fact that the weapon is heavy and very destructive.

There is one further rule – because warriors armed with these weapons must swing them in great arcs it is inappropriate that friendly spearmen or pikemen should be

THROWING WEAPONS

Throwing spears, javelins, and throwing axes are weapons designed specifically to be thrown. Though throwing weapons may appear superficially similar to weapons designed for close combat, they are generally smaller and are balanced for flight. A model that has a throwing weapon can use it in a fight – in which case no special rules apply and it counts just like an ordinary sword or axe. A model armed with a throwing spear cannot fight through another model as can a regular spear-armed warrior.

A model can throw its weapon in the Shoot phase, which works in the same way as shooting a bow or crossbow. Alternatively, a charging model can throw its weapon at the foe it is about to fight. This is an exception to the normal rules as it allows a warrior to 'shoot' as it moves.

A warrior can throw its throwing weapon as it charges. The player moves the model as if it were going to charge the enemy but instead of moving into touch it halts 1"/2cm away. It then throws its weapon at the enemy it is about to fight. The throw is then worked out exactly as if it had taken place in the Shoot phase, even though it is still the Move phase. Once the weapon has been thrown, the charger is moved into contact with the same enemy model or, if the enemy has been slain, the charger completes its move as the player wishes. You will notice that this potentially enables a warrior to slay an enemy as it charges and then charge a different enemy and fight. Note that models armed with throwing weapons are assumed to have enough axes or javelins, etc, to last the whole battle. However only one can be thrown per game turn.

Gimli charges the Orc, stops to throw his axe and then, having failed to kill his enemy, completes his charge.

WHIPS

Whips are often used to distract opponents and create an opening in their guard, but in the hands of an expert they can inflict crippling injuries. Whips are treated exactly like throwing weapons, but generally have a shorter range and lower strength. These vary between different creatures (the whip of an Orc bully being considerably less lethal than the lash of a Balrog), and their characteristic are presented in each model's entry.

BOWS - VOLLEY FIRE

Groups of bowmen can coordinate their fire and loose volleys of arrows into the air in order to rain death on enemies very far away and even out of direct sight! This kind of fire greatly increases the range of the weapon, but it also considerably reduces its accuracy and is effective only against densely packed enemy formations.

Any group of ten or more bow-armed models (not crossbows, thrown weapons, etc.) in base contact with each other and forming an uninterrupted chain of models since the beginning of the Shoot phase, can declare they are going to fire a volley. They can do this as long as they all have the same kind of bow (Elf bow, bow, Dwarf bow, Orc bow etc,) and have all moved no more than half their Move distance in the previous Move phase, as normal for bow-armed models to be able to fire.

The range of bows firing a volley is doubled, but models that are closer than 18"/42cm cannot be targeted, being too close for indirect fire (for example, an Elf bow could hit targets between 18"/42cm and 48"/112cm).

The models in the firing group can pick any enemy model within range as a target for their volley. They do not need to see the target, as long as there is at least one friendly model on the battlefield that is able to see their target.

All models in the firing group that are within range of the target roll a dice. They score a hit only on the roll of a 6, regardless of their Shoot value.

After the number of hits from a volley has been determined, the player controlling the target can pick any model within 6"/14cm of the target (including the target itself) and allocate the hit onto it, even if the model is engaged in combat. Then the player controlling the firing group can do the same with the second hit. The two players continue alternating like this until there are no hits left for that volley or all models within 6"/14cm of the target have been hit once by that volley.

If friendly models are within 6"/14cm of the target, Good models cannot shoot and must choose another target. Evil models can shoot as normal.

Barriers will count as 'in the way' only if they are between the firing group and the model hit, and the model hit is in base contact with the cover. Models inside a wooded area always benefit from an 'in the way' roll because of the trees and models inside buildings or with some other solid protection overhead cannot be hit at all by indirect fire.

Normally, models can be hit only once by volley fire, but extremely large creatures can be hit by more arrows. Models mounted on large bases (with bases of 40mm radius or more) can be hit once per Wound on their profile. This means that, for example, cavalry models can be hit twice (one on the rider and one on the mount), while a Balrog could be hit ten times!

SHIELDS

If a model has a shield, the warrior's ability to defend itself is taken into account by a +1 increase in the model's Defence value.

If a warrior is armed with a two-handed weapon or pike it cannot also carry a shield. It doesn't have enough hands!

If a warrior has both a shield and a bow or crossbow it is assumed the warrior cannot carry both at the same time, so bow/crossbow-armed models receive no increase in their Defence value from carrying a shield but they do still benefit from the following rules for having a shield: a warrior on foot armed with a shield is allowed to fight in a defensive manner by expending its entire effort fending off its foe's attacks. This is called 'defending by shielding' or just 'shielding'. If a player wants a warrior to defend by shielding, he must say it is doing so at the start of a fight.

Note that this cannot be done while mounted on a steed, only models on foot can defend by shielding.

If a warrior is shielding, then two dice are rolled for each Attack he has when determining who wins the fight. So, a warrior that has an Attack value of 1 rolls two dice, an Attack value of 2 rolls four dice, an Attack value of 3 rolls six dice, etc. If the warrior wins the fight then he may not strike any blows against his enemy. His enemies are beaten back the usual distance but he cannot strike against them as they move back.

As you can see, the advantage of shielding is that it makes it more likely for the model to win the fight. The disadvantage is that should he win he strikes no blows. As such, shielding is only a practical response where it is more important for a warrior to survive the turn than it is for him to slay his enemy.

If a warrior is fighting a multiple combat, shielding is only effective if all the warriors on one side do so. In a combat with three models on the same side, for example, all three must decide to use the special shielding rule or none.

A model that is equipped with a spear or pike may not support a warrior who is shielding – the shield and the warrior's efforts to defend himself get in the way of the spear or pike shaft.

A warrior who is lying on the ground can defend himself by shielding if he has a shield. This is the best response to an enemy attack as a warrior who is on the ground cannot strike if he wins the fight in any case.

ELVEN CLOAKS

If the wearer of an Elven Cloak is partially concealed from view, he cannot be seen at all at distances of more than 6"/14cm – the wearer appears to melt into the background. This means that enemies can not charge or shoot the wearer, nor can they target him with magical powers at ranges of greater than 6"/14cm unless they have a completely clear view of the target.

If the model is riding a mount, the cloak has no effect.

BANNERS

Most armies carry to battle banners, standards, icons, totems and other pieces of equipment showing the symbols of their people and leaders. Famous examples of such symbols are the White Tree of Gondor, the Red Eye of Sauron, the Horse of the Rohirrim and the White Hand of Saruman, but many more exist.

EQUIPPING WARRIORS WITH BANNERS

At the additional cost shown in their entry in the Forces section, warriors can be given banners. A force can include a number of banners equal to or less than the number of Heroes it includes.

A model that is given a banner can wear armour and ride a steed, but it cannot use any other kind of weapons/equipment. Any weapons/equipment that the model is already carrying are lost if he is given a banner. Models carrying a banner fight as armed with two-handed weapons, except that they do not get any bonus when rolling on the Wound chart and can fight even when mounted.

If a warrior carrying a banner is killed, a friendly Warrior in base contact can immediately drop all the equipment he is carrying and pick up the banner (effectively, the player must remove the model and replace it with the one carrying the banner). Models cannot pick up a banner while they are engaged in combat. If the banner is not picked up immediately, it is lost in the mayhem of battle.

Heroes can never carry and pick up banners, unless otherwise specified in their entry.

BANNER COMBAT BONUS

All models within 3"/8cm of one or more friendly banner bearers are in range of a banner. If at least one model in a fight is in range of a friendly banner, the entire fight is deemed to be in range of the banner. If a fight is in range of a banner, the side the banner belongs to can benefit from the banner's combat bonus.

Needless to say, in order for the banner to count, the banner bearer must be standing and not lying on the ground (a position which makes the banner rather less visible...).

The combat bonus of the banner allows the player to re-roll one of the dice rolled to determine who wins the fight. The player simply rolls the dice as normal, and can then decide to pick up one of the dice and re-roll it. As normal the second number rolled stands and cannot be re-rolled. Note that this effect does not apply to rolls on the Wound chart.

In a combat where both sides are in range of friendly banners, both players get to re-roll one dice, and they can decide to do so even after seeing the result of their opponent's re-roll. For example: In a fight the Good side's best roll is a 4 and the Evil side's is a 3. The Evil player decides to re-roll one of his dice, obtaining a 5 and taking the lead. At this point the Good player decides he will also re-roll one of his dice and scores a 6, winning the fight!

Might can be used to modify the final result of the dice, after any re-rolls have been used and the final scores established. Players cannot wait to see if the opponent is using Might and then decide to re-roll a dice.

CAVALRY

Mounted troops represent a powerful weapon in the arsenals of any general. This section discusses all the rules for cavalry. We refer to all mounted models as cavalry. Cavalry are usually mounted on horses but Warg Riders are also cavalry.

WHICH MODELS CAN RIDE?

Unless otherwise specified, only Men and Elves can ride horses, while only Orcs can ride Wargs. Other models can ride only the mounts included in their wargear options. Models with a Strength of 6 or more can never ride.

CHARACTERISTICS FOR MOUNTS

A cavalry model comprises a rider and his mount and therefore has two separate sets of characteristics:

	F	S	D	A	W	C
Rider of Rohan	3/4+	3	5	1	1	3
Horse	0	3	4	0	1	3

As you can see horses have no Attacks. When a Rider of Rohan fights an enemy, his horse takes no part in the combat – no dice is rolled on behalf of the horse and if the Rider of Rohan wins the fight, his horse does not strike blows. We'll explain more about how cavalry fight in combat later in this section.

CAVALRY & MOVEMENT

Cavalry models are moved in the same way as models that are on foot, with various additional rules and exceptions. You will find that most of these exceptions are obvious enough – such as horses not being allowed to climb ladders!

WHO SEES – RIDER OR MOUNT?

In the case of a mounted model, the 'model's eye view' is always taken from the perspective of the rider. As the rider is directing his mount it is his ability to see which counts, not that of the horse. This is important for establishing whether a warrior can see an enemy he is about to charge and when shooting (see page 16).

DIFFICULT TERRAIN

Difficult terrain is either too dense or too dangerous for cavalry to move through at full speed. However, a rider can negotiate his way through difficult terrain moving very slowly and carefully. To represent this, all distance moved by cavalry models over difficult terrain counts as four times the actual distance (eg, a rider that moves 2" across difficult terrain counts as having moved 8"). In addition, whilst in difficult terrain, cavalry never gain any of the combat bonuses they normally get when charging, including the bonuses for lances (see page 44).

BARRIERS AND OBSTACLES

When it comes to moving over barriers, always consider the mount's height, not that of the rider. Note that because horses are often modelled in dramatic head-down positions you will have to estimate the horse's true height – easiest by measuring the height of a comparable horse with its head held high. It is the true size of the horse that affects its ability to cross a barrier – not the pose of its head!

Fortunately, most steeds are more or less the same size so we might reasonably assume all to be the same for purposes of our game. We shall assume that all horses and wargs are 40mm tall. All barriers that are less than half this (less than 20mm high or wide) are crossed without penalty. Any barriers between half and equal to the horse's height are counted as obstacles (between 20mm and 40mm) and can be jumped. Any barriers taller or wider are impassable. Note that this is different from infantry models, which can jump obstacles up to twice their height, with a mix of literally jumping and scrambling over the top of the obstacle, but horses are just not too good at that.

JUMPING

A mount cannot jump down a sheer drop more than double its own height.

Cavalry can jump over obstacles as follows: make a roll on the Jump chart (see page 19) in the same way as you would for a warrior on foot. If a 1 is rolled when attempting a jump with a mounted model, then a further attempt can be made. Roll again to see if it successful. However, if a further 1 is rolled then not only does the model fail to jump but the rider is thrown from his mount. See the Thrown Rider chart opposite.

OTHER EXCEPTIONS

Mounted models cannot climb, lie down or crawl. Mounts cannot climb ladders and steep or especially narrow stairs, but steps that are broad and shallow can be moved over at half the mount's usual pace. Eg, a broad flight of stone steps leading up to a building would probably be possible to move over, but a winding stairway in a tower would not. If in doubt about a feature, make sure that both sides are agreed whether steps are accessible to cavalry before the game begins.

MOUNTING AND DISMOUNTING

A model can mount a Warg or similar mount whose height to the saddle is not more than twice the height of the rider. This is treated as a jump and a Jump test is made. If a 1 is rolled, the model fails to mount, a 2-5 is successful but the model cannot move any more that turn, and on a 6, the model's remaining move can be completed by the mount (eg, an Orc moves 3" and gets in base contact with a loose Warg, rolls a 6 for his Jump test to mount and can therefore finish his move by moving another 3").

Dismounting is automatic – the model on foot is simply placed in base contact with the mounted model. The rider can dismount at the beginning of his move, in which case he can move on foot normally. Alternatively, he can dismount at any time during his mounted move, but will be unable to move further that turn and counts as having used up his full move regardless of the distance moved. Once the rider has dismounted, the mount will have to take a Courage test as described in the Courage section.

CAVALRY & SHOOTING

When it comes to shooting at cavalry, we must take into account the chance of a shot striking the mount rather than the rider. The following rules discuss this possibility and what to do when riders and their mounts fall casualty.

MOUNTED TARGETS

When shooting at a cavalry model, the horse is treated as if it were 'in the way' of the rider – a dice roll is made as for any other model partially obscuring the target. Therefore, on a 1-3 the mount is hit, while on a 4-6 the rider is hit.

HITS ON MOUNTS

Hits on mounts are worked out in the same way as hits against warriors on foot. Should the mount be slain, its rider is thrown to the ground. The rider must be replaced with a foot version of the model. Roll a dice on the Thrown Rider chart below to determine if the rider is hurt.

If the rider is slain, the mount runs away and the cavalry model is removed. If the players are using the advanced rules for Courage, there is a chance that the mount can stay and fight on, see the Courage section for more details.

THROWN RIDER CHART

Dice	Result
1	**Knocked Flying.** The rider hits the dirt, suffering a Strength 3 hit. If he survives, he is placed lying down beside his mount and can do nothing else for that turn. If engaged in a combat, he fights lying down
2-5	**Rises from the Dust.** The rider disentangles himself from his mount and dusts himself down. The rider can do nothing else for that turn – if engaged in a combat he cannot strike blows if he wins.
6	**Leaps into Action.** The rider bounds from the saddle of his plunging mount to confront his enemy. The model is replaced by a model on foot and suffers no further penalty.

If a mounted warrior charges a warrior on foot then he receives two special bonuses: 'extra attack' and 'knock to the ground'.

He receives these bonuses regardless of the number of enemy he charges, so long as all his opponents are warriors on foot. The bonuses apply even if the mounted warrior is subsequently charged by other enemy on foot.

These bonuses do not apply to mounted warriors fighting enemy cavalry.

Basically, in order to claim these bonuses, mounted warriors must have charged and be in base contact exclusively with warriors on foot when the fight is resolved.

CAVALRY & FIGHTS

For most purposes, cavalry fight exactly like warriors on foot – the rider and mount fight against enemies in the same combat. Normally, we can assume that it is the rider doing most of the fighting, the mount lending its weight and speed to the impetus on the charge, but that may not always be true. In the case of ferocious beasts like the Wargs ridden by some Orcs for example, the mount is the most lethal of the two and can even continue to fight if the rider is killed.

To represent this in the game, the rider fights as normal and the mount does not fight at all, but the rider can always use the Fight, Strength and/or Attacks characteristics of the mount instead of his own. It can even mix these, using, for example, the rider's Fighting value but the mount's Strength and so on.

For example, compare the characteristics of a Rider of Rohan mounted on a horse with those of a Warg Rider.

	F	S	D	A	W	C
Rider of Rohan	3/4+	3	5	1	1	3
Horse	0/–	3	4	0	1	3

	F	S	D	A	W	C
Warg Rider (Orc)	3/5+	3	4	1	1	2
Warg	3/–	4	4	1	1	2

The Rider of Rohan will use his own characteristics, as they are better than those of the horse he is riding, but the Orc will use the Warg's Strength of 4 if he wins a fight and is rolling to wound his opponents – a considerable advantage!

CAVALRY CHARGE!

The greatest advantage of riding a horse is that a warrior on a charging horse is very difficult to stop – the sheer weight and impetus of the mounted attack will often bowl the enemy to the ground! We have two rules to represent this extra fighting ability.

EXTRA ATTACK
A mounted warrior with this bonus gains one extra Attack. So, a model with 1 Attack would roll two dice in a fight, a warrior with 2 Attacks rolls three dice, and so on.

Note that even if the model is using the Attacks value of his mount because the mount has a higher number of Attacks, he still gets this extra attack. For example, a model riding a Fell beast normally has 2 Attacks and will get 3 when charging!

KNOCK TO THE GROUND
If a mounted warrior with this bonus wins a fight, all his opponents are knocked to the ground, except for models with a Strength of 6 or more. These models cannot be knocked to the ground by cavalry unless the mount itself has a Strength of 6 or more.

A warrior that is knocked to the ground must back away 1"/2cm from his enemy as usual. The model is then placed on its side to show the warrior is lying on the ground. That means he will take double strikes from his enemies just like a model that is fighting whilst lying down. If he is charged in the following turn before he has had a chance to stand up he will have to fight from the ground (see page 21).

A trapped warrior that is knocked down takes double strikes. Note the model does not take quadruple strikes because he is trapped and lying down – the penalty counts for both.

For example, a Rider of Rohan charges two Orcs. He rolls two dice in the Fight (one plus the extra one for the charge bonus) and let's imagine he beats the Orcs. Both Orcs are knocked down and the Rider has the choice of either directing one of his attacks on each Orc (obtaining two strikes on each Orc as the enemies are on the ground), or directing both his attacks on the same Orc (obtaining four strikes on it). The wisest decision is of course to roll to wound with the two strikes from the first attack and then decide where to direct the next attack after seeing if the first Orc has been killed or not.

STRIKES AGAINST MOUNTED MODELS

If a mounted warrior loses a fight, his foes can elect to strike either the rider or mount. This is the choice of the player making the attacks, and if he has several attacks to distribute he can strike against both the rider and mount. Note that a mount isn't considered to be 'in the way' as it is for hits from shooting – warriors are close enough to engage directly so we allow the attacker the choice.

If the mount is slain, after all attacks against the mount and rider have been resolved, the rider must roll on the Thrown Rider chart (shown on page 49).

If the rider is slain, the mount runs away and the cavalry model is removed. If the players are using the advanced rules for Courage, there is a chance that the mount can stay and fight on, see the Courage section for more details.

FIGHTING ACROSS BARRIERS

Cavalry can defend barriers as normal, but they do not receive any of their charge bonuses when charging infantry that are defending a barrier against them.

MONSTROUS MOUNTS

Some mounts are so large and powerful that they can smash through other cavalry with ease, bowling to the ground riders and mounts as if they were foot soldiers. Mounts with a Strength of 6 or higher are classed as Monstrous Mounts.

Monstrous Mounts count as cavalry and follow the same rules for normal cavalry, except that they treat all models on the field as models on foot, with the exception of other Monstrous Mounts, which still count as cavalry. This means that they can use the Extra Attack and Knock to the ground bonuses even when fighting normal enemy cavalry.

When an enemy cavalry model is knocked to the ground, the mount is knocked to the ground and the rider is automatically thrown and knocked to the ground in contact with the mount (placed by the controlling player). The rider immediately suffers a Strength 3 hit as per Result 1 on the Thrown Rider chart – this represents the chance of the rider injuring himself in the fall or even being crushed under the weight of his own steed. The mount is treated exactly like a mount whose rider has been killed (see above), so it will either be immediately removed (mounts with 0 Attacks or Fight value) or it will have to test against its Courage to stay and fight (mounts with an Attack and Fight characteristics).

In addition, when shooting against a monstrous mount, the chance of hitting the mount rather than the rider is higher because of the size of the beast. For each hit against the model, roll a further dice. On a result of 1-4 the mount is hit, on a result of 5-6 the rider is hit.

CAVALRY & MAGIC

If a model employs a magical power (such as *Immobilise* for example) against a mounted model, the rider is always the target of the spell (unless otherwise stated in the spell's description), since we assume he is in control of his own steed's movement. If the rider is affected, then the mount is affected as well (the entire model is immobilised in the case of the above magical power). Of course, if the rider has any Will available and wishes to use it, he gets a chance to resist the spell normally.

The *Sorcerous Blast* power works in a slightly different way. If such power is not resisted, both the steed and the rider are moved back by the blast, both suffer the hit from the blast, both are knocked to the ground and the rider is automatically thrown.

Cavalry models in the path of a model that has been blasted away by a *Sorcerous Blast* (or are fighting it in close combat) suffer a similar fate. Both the steed and the rider are moved aside, both suffer a Strength 3 hit, the rider is automatically thrown and both the rider and his steed are knocked to the ground. The steed and rider are not knocked to the ground if the steed has a Strength of 6 or more, unless the model that is being blasted has itself a Strength of 6 or more.

Note that when a steed is separated from its rider, it will have to take a Courage test in order to continue to fight, as described in the Courage section.

THE MÛMAKIL

Huge war-beasts from the distant south, the Mûmakil (also known as Oliphaunts by some of the people of Middle-earth) were employed by the Haradrim against Gondor and its allies with devastating effects at the Battle of Pelennor Fields. These huge war-beasts carry on their backs a tower of wood and hides, called a howdah, filled with deadly Haradrim archers.

THE HOWDAH

At the top of the howdah is the Commander, who controls the Mûmak with a long set of reins reaching down to the animal's sensitive ears. The Commander is a Haradrim Chieftain wearing armour and armed with a spear, and the Mûmak is effectively his mount. When working out how many models are included in your force (for determining when your force is going to Break, for example), the Mûmak and the Commander count as two models and not as one as is the case with normal cavalry models.

At the start of the game, before beginning deployment, the Evil player can place up to twelve Haradrim Warriors (not Heroes!) from his army into the howdah (we strongly recommend you choose models equipped with bows).

The Haradrim on the Mûmak cannot voluntarily leave the howdah as long as the Mûmak is alive. Models can move normally in the section of the howdah they're occupying. They can also move from one platform to the next (jumping or climbing up/down from one platform to the next is automatically successful, but uses up the entire move of the model, preventing it from shooting).

If the model in the control position at the top is killed, another Haradrim in the howdah will grab the reins and immediately take charge of controlling the beast. From that point on, that model will be unable to shoot his bow and must use his movement to climb to the top of the howdah as quickly as possible.

Note that the Haradrim consider hiding in the howdah extremely cowardly and therefore models in the howdah cannot voluntarily lie down. If forced to lie down in the howdah (by a spell, war machine hit, etc) they must stand up as soon as possible.

If all the models in the howdah are killed, the animal will continue to fight as normal, but it will risk Stampeding (see page 54).

DESTROYING THE HOWDAH OR KILLING THE MÛMAK

If the howdah is destroyed, all the crew suffer normal falling damage and are immediately placed by the controlling player on the nearest point of the table, in contact with the Mûmak's base.

If the Mûmak itself is killed, they suffer normal falling damage and a Strength 9 hit, after which any survivors are immediately placed by the controlling player on the nearest point of the table, in contact with the Mûmak's base. Then the Mûmak model is removed; replace it with an area of difficult ground roughly as wide as its base and 2"-3" high (5-8 cm).

MOVING THE MÛMAK – TRAMPLE ATTACK

A charging Mûmak can cut a bloody swathe through enemy lines, trampling opponents or tossing them aside. To represent this, the Mûmak moves in an entirely unique way.

When you want to move the Mûmak, first rotate its base on the spot, 'aiming' the animal in the direction you want it to move. While rotating, the Mûmak may touch models or terrain. In the case of models, move them out of the way of the rotating animal by the shortest possible route. In case of terrain blocking its rotation, move the Mûmak away from the terrain piece just enough to complete its rotation.

After the Mûmak has been 'aimed' in the new direction, it starts its unstoppable charge. Move the model up to 8"/20cm directly forward, ignoring enemy models' control zones.

If the Mûmak moves into contact with one or more models whilst moving forward, it will Trample them, automatically inflicting three Strength 9 hits on each model. Cavalry models (including monstrous mounts) suffer three hits on the rider and three hits on the mount. If the rider survives but the mount is killed, the rider is thrown and, after testing on the Thrown Rider chart, is placed in contact with the Mûmak. If the rider is killed, but the mount isn't, the animal runs away

in blind panic and is immediately removed (just as if it had been slain by the Mûmak). Mounts which are also Heroes (such as Gwaihir), may of course continue to fight as normal if they survive the Trample.

If an enemy model survives the Trample, the Mûmak stops, exactly like any normal charging model, and will fight the enemy as normal in the Fight phase.

If the model is slain by the Trample, the Mûmak can continue to move, Trampling other models along its way, until it either reaches the end of its 8"/20cm move or it fails to slay an enemy and has to stop.

If the Mûmak moves into contact with a friendly model, the controlling player can choose to either Trample it in order to continue moving if it manages to kill the model (life is hard in the armies of Mordor!), or to stop (you could run into a Nazgûl).

If the enemy wins priority and charges the Mûmak, it can pin it in place and prevent it from moving as normal.

DIFFICULT TERRAIN AND BARRIERS

Mûmakil cannot jump, climb, lie down, or defend barriers. They cannot enter difficult terrain, except for crossing water features at half normal speed as normal. Because of their very limited agility, they cannot cross barriers more than 2"/4cm in height or width. Smaller barriers can be crossed freely.

SHOOTING FROM THE MÛMAK

The Haradrim Warriors can shoot their bows normally, provided that they haven't moved more than half their move in the howdah (the movement of the Mûmak itself does not affect their ability to shoot). It is important to note that the range of their shots (as well as enemy shots, spells directed at them and any other kind of ranged effects) are measured from the bases of the models themselves and not from the base of the Mûmak. The models in the howdah can shoot even if the Mûmak itself is engaged in combat. They can even target the enemies fighting their own Mûmak, but the animal will count as in the way of their shots.

SHOOTING AT THE MÛMAK

Because of the Mûmak's size, the enemy can freely choose to target either the Mûmak, the howdah or any visible Haradrim in the howdah. If targeting a Haradrim, the howdah always counts as an obstacle in the way of incoming missiles, but if the howdah stops the incoming missile then the opponent can roll to wound the howdah itself.

Note that the howdah and its occupants are so high up from the ground that often enemy models will be able to shoot them over friendly models, which should not be in the way of the missiles (but always remember to check from the models' own point of view).

This also means that Good models are allowed to target the howdah and its occupants even while the Mûmak is engaged in close combat by other Good models. On the same account, charging Good models armed with throwing weapons can elect to cast their spears/axes at the howdah or its occupants before completing their charge against the Mûmak.

If targeted by a siege engine or by volley fire from bows, the howdah, the Mûmak itself and each of the crew count as a separate battlefield target. Note that on results of 2-5 on the Scatter chart, hits aimed at the howdah or any of its occupants can always be assigned to the Mûmak itself if the player wishes (even if, technically, this should be impossible because the base of the Mûmak is more than 6" away from them). See the rules for siege engines for more details.

FIGHTING THE MÛMAK

The Mûmak fights as normal, but the Haradrim in the howdah are completely ignored, being too high up to take part. This means that the Commander cannot use his Might to influence the dice rolled in the fight.

If a charging Mûmak wins a fight, all of its opponents are knocked to the ground, regardless of any other factor (this includes monstrous mounts, even if they have charged the Mûmak in the same turn).

Mûmakil themselves can never be knocked to the ground, not by siege engines, monstrous mounts, nor even by another Mûmak!

If a Mûmak loses a fight it does not back away from its opponents, and as a result of this it can never be trapped. It is the opponents that, even after winning a fight, must back away from the Mûmak (after striking their blows against it, of course). Basically it's a case of getting in, striking at the beast and then jumping to safety!

STAMPEDE!

Mûmakil are difficult to control and can sometimes be driven mad by pain. When this happens they are likely to wreak mayhem and destruction among the ranks of their allies as much as the enemy.

Every time a Mûmak suffers a wound, the model controlling it (or the Mûmak itself if all the Haradrim are gone) must immediately take a Courage test. If multiple wounds are inflicted, a separate test must be taken for each one.

A Courage check must also be taken at the beginning of each Evil Move phase if there are no models left on the howdah or if the howdah has been destroyed.

If these tests are passed, all is fine. If any of the tests are failed, the Mûmak will Stampede at the beginning of the next Evil Move phase (still after heroic moves, though). Players might want to place a suitable marker on the Mûmak's base when one such test is failed, to remember it has to Stampede in the next Evil Move phase.

During a Stampede, the Mûmak follows all the normal rules, with the exception that it must always make a full move (the controlling model cannot make it slow down) and that the rotating on the spot to decide the beast's move direction is not done by the Evil player but by the Good player! When 'aiming' the Mûmak, the Good player is free to set it so that it will Trample Good models as well as Evil models during its move. The Good player can 'aim' the Mûmak so that its compulsory full move will carry it off the table (a Mûmak is considered to have left the table if its base moves into contact with the edge of the table), in which case the Mûmak counts as a casualty.

If the stampeding Mûmak moves into contact with another Mûmak, both animals suffer three Strength 9 hits from the impact, but their howdahs are unaffected.

If the Mûmak has Stampeded in the Move phase, the Haradrim in the howdah cannot move, nor can they shoot in the following Shoot phase, as they hang on for dear life. At the end of the Stampede movement, the Evil player must roll a dice for each model in the howdah (this can be modified by Might). On the result of a 1, the model falls to the ground and suffers normal falling damage (see 'Destroying the Howdah').

At the end of the Stampede move, the animal calms down and returns to the full control of the Evil player.

If the Good player gets to move before the Stampede, he can charge the Mûmak as normal, pinning the animal in place and cancelling all the effects of the Stampede.

COURAGE TESTS

Mûmakil themselves and the models in the howdah are, in general, unafraid of things that would scare normal warriors. They always automatically pass any Courage test they need to take (with the notable exception of Stampede tests of course). Note that as long as the Commander is in the howdah, his "Stand fast!" rule cannot affect the models on the ground as they are obviously more than 6"/14cm away from him.

HEROIC ACTIONS

The Commander in the howdah can make heroic moves and heroic shooting, but they only affect the Mûmak itself and the Haradrim in the howdah. He cannot make heroic combats as the Mûmak is too slow for that kind of heroic action.

The Mûmak itself can be only affected by heroic actions made by the Commander and not by other Evil Heroes.

TERROR

In their fury, the Mûmakil are a truly terrifying sight. They evoke Terror in the enemy, as described in the Courage section of the rules.

INSPIRING SIGHT – BANNERS

The presence of the Mûmak has the same effect as a banner on the Haradrim within 3"/8cm of its base. Unfortunately, the beast itself is too dumb to benefit from the rules for banners.

MAGICAL POWERS AGAINST THE MÛMAK

Because of its sheer size and wild animal fury, magical powers that affect the mind cannot affect the Mûmak, only magical powers that deal damage can affect it. Mind control spells can be used against the model controlling the animal though. For example, the Commander can be affected by *Immobilise* (and that would stop the Mûmak from moving) or even *Commanded* to move the animal half a move and Trample friendly models, for example.

Magical powers that inflict damage can be freely directed against the Mûmak, the crew or the howdah itself. The *Sorcerous Blast* spell can inflict damage when cast on the

Mûmak or the howdah, but cannot move them. If a model in the howdah is targeted by a *Sorcerous Blast*, he is damaged normally but is not moved by the spell. If the model survives the damage, the Evil player must roll a dice for it – on a result of 1-3 the model is knocked down in the howdah but otherwise unaffected, but on the result of 4-6 the model falls from the howdah to the ground (see page 52, 'The Howdah').

LIVING SIEGE TOWERS/BATTERING RAMS

If the Mûmak moves into contact with a castle wall or other fortification, all the Haradrim in the howdah except the one that is controlling the animal are free to move onto the defences exactly as if they were coming from a siege tower that has been pushed into contact with the wall (this is an exception to the rule by which the Hardrim cannot leave the howdah, see the rules for siege towers and battering rams later in this book).

The Mûmak can charge fortifications and it will inflict the normal three Strength 9 hits, but if the fortification is Defence 9 or 10, the Mûmak itself will suffer three Strength 9 hits as well. The animal can then attack the fortification it's in contact with once in the Fight phase as normal, but cannot attack models on the walls.

OPTIONAL RULE – TRAMPLING TERRAIN

If the players agree beforehand, they can assign a value of Defence and Wounds (or Batter Points if using the Siege rules) to trees, bushes, hedges, fences, dry stone walls and so on. The Mûmak can then Trample these pieces of terrain as it moves, inflicting three Strength 9 hits on them, and if the terrain piece is destroyed it is removed and the animal can continue with its move normally, levelling the land as it goes.

THE FORTRESS

Moving around in a fortress can often mean negotiating a veritable rabbit-warren of gates, stairs, doors, hatchways, and ladders. Some allow access to towers, turrets and battlements, while others yield passage to the outside world. The extent and purpose of these portals varies from fortress to fortress. Some coastal defences, such as those at Dol Amroth, contain pathways to sheltered subterranean water routes that in turn can be used to reach the harbours. Others, such as the intricate mazes of Dol Guldur, can lead attackers around in circles for hours or even days.

CASTLE WALLS

Generally speaking, castle walls are designed so that attackers cannot scale the outside, forcing them to rely on other methods, such as ladders. To represent this, castle walls may not be climbed unless a scenario specifically says otherwise. (This rule even applies to Moria Goblins – but not to large spiders such as Shelob).

DOORS AND HATCHWAYS

A door or hatch presents no obstacle to movement unless it is too small to allow a model to pass through, or if it is either bolted shut or held by an enemy.

SIZE

A warrior on foot can pass through a door so long as the doorway is no lower than half the model's height. A mounted model can pass through a door if it is at least as high as the mount – the rider can stoop but the mount cannot! If a door is obviously and intentionally supposed to be too small for cavalry to pass through because it is too narrow this must be agreed before the game.

Generally speaking, a warrior can be considered able to move through a hatchway if the hatch is roughly as wide as its base. So, for example, while a warrior on a 25mm base can pass through a hatchway about 25mm wide, a Cave Troll on a 40mm base can only pass through a hatchway that is about 40mm wide or wider.

HOLDING AND BOLTING DOORS & HATCHES

Doors can only be held shut or bolted from the inside. Hatches leading to upper floors can only be held shut from above or bolted from below. If a door or hatch is held or bolted then it must be broken down as described later. Once a door or hatch has been broken down it is destroyed and becomes an open doorway or hatchway.

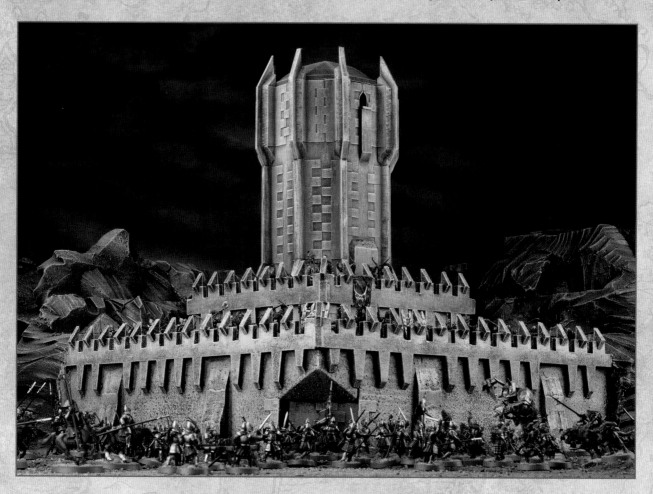

Models on foot touching a door from the inside, or a hatch from above, are considered to be holding it by placing their weight against the door or hatch. Such models cannot shoot, fight or carry ladders or rams. Models can hold a door against any enemies attempting to open it up to a maximum Strength equal to their combined Strength. So, two men with combined Strength 6 can hold a door against one Uruk-hai with Strength 4, but not against two Uruk-hai with combined Strength of 8.

A model that is already holding a door at the start of his move can bolt it shut. A model positioned at the top of a ladder at the start of his turn, and who is beneath a hatch, can close the hatch and bolt it shut. In both cases, the model can then make its move as normal. It is a good idea to place a suitable marker by the door or hatch to show that it is bolted shut.

Any model on the inside of a bolted door or beneath a bolted hatchway can unbolt it and move through without restriction – the door or hatch is then no longer bolted.

GATES

A model touching the inside of a gate may open or close it during the Move phase. The model must remain in contact with the gate as it opens, and may not move further that turn once the gate has been opened. A model opening or closing a gate cannot shoot that turn. A model is not free to open or close a gate if it is fighting an enemy model, or if it is carrying a ladder, ram or comparable burden. Models cannot open or close gates whilst mounted.

STAIRS

Stone or wooden stairways connect the defences together and allow the defenders to move onto ramparts and between different levels. A model that is on foot can move on stairs without penalty – no Climb roll is needed and no movement penalty is applied.

Horses, Wargs, and mounted models cannot normally move on stairs. However, if steps are especially shallow and at least as wide as the model's base, then movement can be allowed – this must be specified before the game.

ACCESS LADDERS

Within a tower, it's quite common for levels to be connected via wooden or rope ladders. Similar ladders might also be used to access battlements from the courtyard.

A model on foot can move up or down a ladder without penalty – no Climb roll is needed and no move penalty is applied. A mounted model cannot use a ladder – and the same goes for any creature obviously incapable of using a ladder, such as a Cave Troll, for example.

REMOVING ACCESS LADDERS

Some strongholds have removable access ladders that extend for a single storey, or the height of a normal wall. Where this is the case, the ladders may be removed by one

or more models to stop enemy models from using them. Once removed, the ladders may be dropped on the floor next to the warrior who removed it, but can be replaced at a later point in the game.

Access ladders can be pulled up, or pulled down to the floor, by a warrior on foot who ends his move touching the ladder (but not actually climbing it). The model must not be touching an enemy, whether on the ladder or otherwise. Note that the warrior forfeits his remaining move and is therefore assumed to have moved his entire move distance and will be unable to shoot.

If no models are on the ladder, it can be automatically pulled up or down. If there is one or more models attempting to climb a ladder then it is much harder to pull it up or down. Roll a D6 and deduct 1 from the roll if there is one model on the ladder and deduct 2 if there are two or more models on the ladder. Add 1 if two or more models have moved so that they are working together to pull the ladder up/down. If the final score is 4 or more, the ladder is pulled up/down and all models on the ladder fall to the ground. Falling models take one Strength 3 hit for each full 1"/2cm of fall.

REPLACING LADDERS

Access ladders can be erected by a simple reversal of the rule described above. A warrior who is free to do so can erect a dropped ladder in base contact, or one that he is still holding from the last turn, expending any remaining movement for that Move phase in the process.

FIGHTING IN THE FORTRESS

In most circumstances, fighting within a fortress is no different to fighting in other situations and therefore very few extra rules are required. However, some fights will take place in confined spaces, often through doorways or hatchways, or along precipitous stairs or battlements. This section deals with these cases. Assaults by troops using siege ladders are described in the section on Besieging a Fortress (see page 59).

DEFENDING

Battlements can be defended from attack from below in the same way as other barriers. The obvious difference is that attackers must use ladders to reach their enemy: this is covered in the rules given under Ladders in the Besieging the Fortress section on page 60.

In addition, fortresses are full of doorways and hatches and very narrow passages. These narrow gaps can also be defended in much the same way as barriers or battlements. This enables a brave warrior to gallantly fight off several times its own number of enemy, either winning time for its comrades, or denying access to its foes.

As doorways and hatches can be different widths we will have to define what 'narrow' means. In gaming terms, a narrow gap is one that is only just large enough for the defender to pass through – typically 25-30mm in the case of a warrior on foot. If a doorway is wider than this a warrior can still position itself in order to block access, but does not benefit from counting as defending.

In some situations you might find it impossible to place the combatants in narrow gaps so that they touch base-to-base. This tends to happen where walls are thick and doors are narrower than the model's base. In these cases, the charger is simply placed as far forward as possible and the models are assumed to be touching in the same way as models fighting over a barrier.

The two models are considered to be touching and will fight across the gap, with the defender counting as fighting behind a barrier.

WORKING OUT DEFENDING FIGHTS

All defending fights are worked out in exactly the same way as fights over a barrier. In the case of fights through gaps, the charger does not actually have to force his way through or over a barrier, but we assume the close presence of stone walls and door embrasures all work to restrict, and therefore disadvantage, the attacker. This means the charger must still roll to see if his blows strike 'the barrier' but in this case the barrier comprises the surrounding masonry and woodwork. Work out the fight as described in the Defending section of the rules for combat.

If the defender is killed, its attacker is immediately moved into the space previously occupied by its opponent in the same way as for defending a barrier (providing there is enough room!). The victor can automatically move through any door or hatchway as it does so.

If the Man defending the gap is slain, the attacker moves into his space.

FIGHTING FROM BOTH SIDES

If a warrior is defending a narrow gap and is attacked from two sides at once then the rules for fighting across barriers apply. If a warrior is defending a doorway or hatchway then work out the fight on the defender's side first.

STUMBLES ON STAIRS

If warriors are fighting on a stair then defeated warriors can move back up the stair without penalty so long as there is room for them to do so. However, warriors moving back down a stair are clearly at a disadvantage – we represent this with the 'Stumble rule'. If a warrior is forced back down a stair make a random dice roll to see if it stumbles. On the roll of a 1, 2 or 3 the warrior stumbles and is knocked to the ground; on the roll of a 4, 5 or 6 the warrior steps down nimbly without stumbling. This makes it much riskier to find yourself fighting an enemy up a stairway than down – as you might expect.

FIGHTING BESIDE PRECIPITOUS DROPS

A fortress has open battlements and stairs that make it quite likely that fights will take place beside precipitous drops. We already have rules to take this into account, but it is worth repeating them here just to remind ourselves of the additional danger of fighting in a fortress.

A warrior who loses a fight must back away 1"/2cm from its enemy and if unable to do so is trapped – trapped warriors take double the usual number of strikes as described in the Fight section. A warrior unable to move back because of a sheer drop can choose to either remain where it is or jump. If it remains where it is the model is trapped and suffers double strikes. If it jumps it is struck normally, but also suffers one Strength 3 hit for each 1"/2cm it falls.

BESIEGING A FORTRESS

The fastest way to resolve a siege is with an escalade. By sending troops with ladders against the walls of the fortress, a general is hoping to buy time with the blood of his own warriors. While an escalade is not a particularly certain way of taking an enemy fortification, if it succeeds the attacker can forgo the long, costly, and tactically vulnerable step of battering his way into the fortress using siege engines.

If an escalade fails, then a commander will have to begin the onerous process of a full siege. Great siege engines are constructed or dragged to the site, lines of supply are laid and the bombardment begins.

The following rules cover everything you need to know about fighting from ladders against troops defending battlements. The most important thing to remember is just how difficult it is to fight whilst standing at the top of a ladder – especially when someone is hitting you back – and especially when that someone is Aragorn! So, as the attacker, be prepared to die in droves. Siege scenarios usually pitch a small number of defenders against a huge horde of attackers – such is the value of stone defences that a tiny number of defenders can hold a fortress against far larger armies.

This section also includes all the rules for breaking down and smashing apart the fortress, including doors, gates, walls, and towers. It includes rules for rams as well as the simple method of hacking apart whatever stands between you and your goal.

All the siege rules assume that warrior models can be placed and moved inside model buildings. If you are unable to move the models inside the buildings then your job becomes a little harder. In this case, you will have to place the warriors aside and note down where they are from turn to turn. This is satisfactory up to a point, but it's much better if you can place the models exactly within the buildings so there is no doubt where they are in relation to doors, windows and each other. As a general rule, most siege scenarios are based around 12"/28cm wall sections (it won't matter if your wall sections are a little longer or shorter than this, although we've found that wall sections between 6"/14cm and 12"/28cm work best).

SIEGE LADDERS

A siege ladder is a very tall and sturdy ladder – and there is no surer way of reaching the top of the enemy's walls! Siege ladders are so much longer and heavier than regular access ladders that different rules apply.

At least two warriors on foot are needed to carry a siege ladder and up to six can do so. Two or three warriors carrying a siege ladder move at half their normal pace. Four to six warriors carrying a ladder move at their normal pace. Note that models with a Strength of 6 or greater count as three models for the purposes of carrying siege ladders.

Warriors carrying a siege ladder cannot shoot that turn and cannot use magical powers. They are not free to carry other burdens, such as rams.

A warrior can drop a siege ladder at any point in his move. A warrior carrying a siege ladder will automatically drop it to fight if he is charged. If the number of warriors carrying a siege ladder is reduced to one, the ladder is dropped immediately.

A siege ladder can be picked up if there are sufficient models in contact with the ladder. Once picked up the ladder cannot move further that turn.

Only warriors on foot can carry and climb a siege ladder, cavalry cannot do so! Only models on 25mm bases can climb a siege ladder. This means that large monsters such as Cave Trolls cannot climb siege ladders – they are just too big and clumsy.

If a siege ladder is moved so that it is touching a wall it is raised immediately. Place the model ladder upright against the wall. No warriors can climb the ladder that turn.

If a siege ladder is in place at the start of the turn attackers can climb it. A model on foot can move up or down a ladder without penalty – no Climb roll is needed and no movement penalty is applied. Models that climb ladders or that start their move on ladders may neither shoot nor cast spells, nor may they carry burdens.

A warrior who climbs to the top of a ladder automatically charges the nearest enemy whose zone of control overlaps the ladder. He stands at the top of the ladder and fights the warrior behind the battlement. If no enemy zone of control overlaps the ladder the warrior can position himself on the rampart – but he cannot charge any other enemy on the rampart as they would not have been visible at the start of his move. Only defenders whose zones of control extend onto the ladder are assumed to be visible as the attacker charges up the ladder.

Designer's Note: *We haven't specified a height for siege ladders because players will make their own fortifications. Ladders must be tall enough so that a model that is standing on the top can convincingly confront an enemy stood on the battlements. However, it is quite important that a model is able to climb all the way to the top in a single turn as otherwise the defenders will simply push the ladders down whilst attackers are climbing up. We found that if the wall height to the level of the rampart is about 140mm and the ladders are about 130mm-140mm high everything works out about right.*

DEFENDING BATTLEMENTS

Models standing on the ramparts of a wall fight by defending the battlements against attackers using siege ladders from below. The rules for defending battlements are based on the rules for defending barriers and are comparable to the rules for defending narrow spaces.

A warrior on the rampart of a wall can be placed immediately behind the battlements and can then defend the battlements immediately in front of him and 1"/2cm either side. This is exactly the same as for defending barriers and is shown on the diagram below. No enemy can attempt to ascend from a ladder onto the rampart if he has to enter the control zone of a model that is defending the battlement. The attacker must fight the defender and kill him in order to climb over the battlement and occupy his enemy's place on the rampart.

The defender is visible and can therefore be charged by the attacker.

A model defending a battlement.

Up to three ladders can be placed into a defender's control zone as shown on the diagram below. If you make your ladders about 20-25mm wide you'll find that this all happens pretty naturally.

All three ladders are in the control zone of the defender.

The rules for defending fights are used to work out the combat. This is exactly the same as for a combat over a wall, hedge, barricade or similar defence-work. The only difference is that the chargers are all stood on top of ladders and so risk falling off if they fail to get onto the ramparts, as noted below.

FALLING OFF LADDERS

The following rules apply to warriors attacking from siege ladders or from access ladders within a fortress. The rules for both are the same.

If a model is fighting from a ladder and is forced to back away 1"/2cm he can only move down the ladder. As he backs away he risks falling from the ladder. If physically unable to back away, for whatever reason, the warrior still risks falling. A model making way down a ladder for a friend who is backing away from a fight does not have to roll – he is not retreating in the face of the enemy.

After the warrior is beaten back, make a random roll to see if he falls. On a 4, 5, or 6 the warrior keeps his footing and backs away as required. On a 1, 2 or 3 the warrior loses his footing and falls to the ground before he can back away. He falls the full distance to the ground and suffers falling damage in the usual way.

If the warrior at the top of the ladder falls then roll a dice for every other model on the same ladder. Any model that rolls a 1, 2 or 3 is also knocked from the ladder by their own friend. Models fall from wherever they are on the ladder – so warriors that are nearer the ground suffer fewer hits.

Warriors that are slain in combat automatically fall in the same way as warriors that lose their footing when backing away. Obviously, as the warrior is already dead he takes no further damage, but there is a chance he will knock other models off the ladder, as described above.

PUSHING DOWN SIEGE LADDERS

A warrior moving behind the battlement so that a siege ladder is directly in front of him can attempt to push the ladder to the ground in the Move phase (as long as there is no attacker at the top of the ladder). This uses up any remaining movement the model may have.

Roll a dice for the model pushing the ladder. Deduct 1 from the result if there is one enemy model already climbing the ladder. Deduct 2 if there is more than one already climbing the ladder (it's harder to push a ladder weighed down by several hundredweight of Uruk-hai!). Add 1 if two or more models have moved so that they are working together to push down the ladder. Add 1 if one or more models that are pushing the ladder have Strength 6 or greater. If you score a 4, 5 or 6 after making any modifications, the ladder topples to the ground and every climbing model takes damage for falling, as described in the Move section. Place the ladder at the foot of the wall.

DOORS, GATES & WALLS

Ordinary houses have only flimsy doors that are easily knocked down by determined warriors. Fortresses, however, are built to withstand sieges – they have doors and gateways made of solid iron-hard oak reinforced with bronze and steel. Because our warriors will be attempting to knock down doors and gates, as well as the walls themselves, we need to allocate suitable Defence values and Batter Points to these structures. Structures do not literally have 'wounds' – instead they have Batter Points. The table below gives the Defence and Batter values for those structures most likely to be found on a battlefield.

KNOCKING DOWN A DOOR, HATCH, OR GATE

A warrior can attack a door, hatch, or gate just like it would attack another warrior – by moving into contact with it. As a door or gate cannot fight back, the attacker will automatically win and may inflict a single strike on the door or gate (regardless of the number of attacks on its profile). If the attacker is also engaged by other enemies in a multiple fight, the fight is worked out as normal. If the warrior wins the fight he can direct a single attack on the

BATTERING CHART

Dice	Result
1	**No effect.** Your blow rebounds uselessly from the hard surface.
2-5	**Damaged.** You have damaged the target and score 1 Batter Point on it (strikes with a Strength of 10 cause 2 Batter Points of damage, not 1).
6	**Broken in.** The target is badly damaged and suffers 2 Batter Points (strikes with a Strength of 10 cause 4 Batter Points of damage, not 2).

gate or his full attacks on enemy models. Roll on the Wound chart as normal to see if the strike would normally inflict a wound. If the roll is not sufficient to cause a wound then the strike has no effect. If the strike would usually inflict a wound then roll a dice and consult the Battering chart. If the door is reduced to zero Batter Points, it is destroyed, and removed from play.

STRUCTURE	DEFENCE VALUE	BATTER POINTS	DESCRIPTION
Internal Domestic Door	5	1	An internal domestic door – the sort of light wooden door you would find in ordinary houses. All wooden hatchways are also Defence Value 5/1 Batter Point.
External Domestic Door	6	2	An external domestic door or internal door in a grand public building or palace. This is a heavier kind of door but still not difficult to break down.
Heavy Door	7	2	A grand external door or an internal door within a fortress connecting one internal space to another, or possibly an external door in a small fortification.
Armoured Door	8	2	An external armoured door – in a fortress this type of door connects any external to internal space on the defender's side of the fortification. It is typical of a door connecting a tower to a walkway, for example. If the enemy breaks into the fortress these doors become the first line of defence.
Heavy Armoured Door	9	2	An external armoured door through the fortification – this is any door that connects to the outside world beyond the fortress. These doors have to be very heavily built, but even so are weak points that have to be guarded day and night.
Fortress Gate	10	3	The main gate to a fortress is as heavily built as possible to withstand the assaults of the enemy.
Access Ladder	5	2	Generally used inside a fortress, access ladders are sturdily built but not proof against solid blows.
Siege Ladder	8	2	Heavier than access ladders, it is still possible to destroy siege ladders with a concerted effort – the high Defence value represents the difficulty of rendering such a ladder irreparable with only a few blows.
Battering Ram	10	2	Because it is little more than a massive timber, a battering ram has few weak spots, and accordingly is hard to destroy.
Wooden Palisade	10	10	Wooden palisades are normally used in temporary fortifications, being quick to build, but not incredibly strong.
Stone Wall	100	12	Stone walls have a nominal Defence value of 100. A wall can only be harmed by strikes of Strength 10, as explained opposite.
Wooden Tower	10	14	Wooden towers are a quick way to expand a fortress, while offering a moderate degree of stability and security.
Stone Tower	100	16	Stone towers have a nominal Defence value of 100 and can only be harmed by strikes of Strength 10, in the same way as walls. Their Batter Points are even greater because these are strongpoints in a fortress's defence.

KNOCKING DOWN PALISADES, WALLS & TOWERS

It is obviously very hard to damage stone walls so we give both stone walls and towers a nominal Defence value of 100, and 12 and 16 Batter Points respectively. Only attacks from an enemy with Strength 10 can harm a stone wall or tower. This will limit the number of things that can harm a wall – as is only right and proper.

Even with attacks with a Strength of 10, a dice roll of 5 or 6 is required to convert a strike into a nominal wound and a roll on the Battering chart. Roll on the Battering chart to determine exactly how many Batter Points have been caused. Remember that strikes with a Strength of 10 or greater cause 4 Batter Points damage, not 2, on the roll of a 6.

Once the wall, palisade or tower has suffered damage, there is a chance that the structure has become sufficiently weakened and will collapse. To represent this, a player rolls a D6 at the start of each turn as soon as priority has been established. If the roll is higher than the number of Batter Points remaining on the wall or tower, it collapses. Note that this means that a wall or tower will never collapse if it has 6 or more Batter Points remaining, and will always collapse if reduced to 0 Batter Points.

Example: A stone wall suffers 8 Batter Points of damage from the explosion of an Uruk-hai Demolition Charge. At the start of the following turn, it will collapse on a roll of a 5 or 6.

If you are playing with a wall made up of several sections, remove that wall section (about 12"/28cm) or replace it

MIGHT POINTS & SIEGES

Heroes can use Might points when attempting to push away a siege ladder as this roll is made on behalf of the warrior himself.

Rolls for stumbling on stairs, falling from ladders when beaten back, or falling because a friend has fallen on top of you are 50/50 random rolls, so Might points cannot be used.

In the case of rolls on the Battering chart, a Hero can only use Might points to affect a roll for 'wounds' he has personally inflicted. If a Hero is striking down a door, for example, then he can use Might to affect his roll to wound and/or his roll on the Battering chart. If a Hero is lending his weight to a battering ram he cannot use Might points.

with a collapsed version of that wall. Alternatively, a piece of black card about 12"/28cm long makes a good representation of the gap. If there are any warriors on the ramparts of a wall when it collapses they are pitched to the ground and take the usual damage for falling. This is one Strength 3 hit per 1"/2cm of fall as described earlier.

When a wall collapses, the area around becomes covered in rubble. Place some rocks or suitable material to represent rubble within 1"/2cm of where the wall originally stood. Any models within 1"/2cm of a collapsing wall take an automatic Strength 3 hit from falling masonry. The area where the wall stood now counts as difficult terrain.

BATTERING RAMS

This is little more than a massive timber – sometimes reinforced with stone, iron or bronze. It can be used to batter either doors/gates or walls. It is exclusively used for battering and cannot be used to attack enemy warriors!

A battering ram can be any length – the larger it is the more models may use it. The minimum number of models needed to carry and use the ram equals the number of warriors whose bases wholly cover at least half the ram's length along both sides as shown opposite.

The maximum number of models that can use a ram equals the number of warriors on foot whose bases can wholly fit along both sides as shown opposite.

Warriors carrying a ram cannot shoot that turn and cannot use magical powers. They are not free to carry other burdens, such as ladders.

A warrior who is carrying a ram at the start of his move cannot charge that turn. A warrior can drop a ram at any point in his move but cannot charge that turn. A warrior carrying a ram will automatically drop it to fight if he is charged.

If the number of warriors carrying a ram is reduced below the minimum number required, the ram is dropped immediately.

A battering ram can be picked up if there is a sufficient number of models in contact with the ram. Once picked up the ram cannot move further that turn. Only warriors on foot

Four Orcs with 25mm bases are needed to use this 75mm long ram.

Up to six Orcs with 25mm bases can use this 75mm long ram.

can carry and operate a ram, cavalry cannot do so! A ram that has reached a door, gate or wall can be used to attack it in the Fight phase, assuming the minimum required number of warriors are still alive to operate it. Remember, warriors fighting other warriors cannot operate a ram.

The ram automatically hits once, causing a single strike with a Strength equal to that of the least strongest crew member, +1 per additional crew member, and up to a maximum value of 9. So, a ram with four Uruk-hai crew has a Strength of 4+3 = 7, a ram with six Uruk-hai crew has a Strength of 4+5 = 9. The maximum possible Strength is 9 regardless of how many crew are manning the ram. Roll on the Wound chart as normal – where a wound would usually be scored, instead roll on the appropriate Battering chart to determine how many Batter Points are inflicted.

Example: Six Uruk-hai reach the fortress gate and begin to pound it with their ram – in the Fight phase the ram makes its strike. With a Strength value of 9 versus a Defence value of 10, a roll of 5 is needed to inflict a 'wound'. A dice is rolled and scores a 5 – sufficient to proceed to the Battering chart (see page 62). The roll on the Battering chart scores a 4 – the gate is damaged and suffers 1 Batter Point. The gate's Batter Points are reduced from 3 to 2. Three such blows will be required to smash the gate apart.

DEMOLITION CHARGES

Uruk-hai demolition charges consist of large chests full of highly unstable blasting powder. It is very destructive but probably just as dangerous to its users as to the foe! Only warriors as heedless of their lives as the White Hand Uruk-hai would contemplate using such an infernal device. No models other than White Hand Uruk-hai are allowed to carry demolition charges.

MOVING THE CHARGE

A demolition charge can be picked up by one or two models that are touching the charge. Once picked up, the demolition charge cannot be moved further that turn. If two models carry a demolition charge they can move at no penalty. If a single model is carrying a demolition charge it moves at half speed. Uruk-hai carrying a demolition charge cannot shoot that turn or cast spells. They are not free to carry other burdens, such as ladders, battering rams or other warriors.

An Uruk-hai can drop a demolition charge at any point in his move. If an Uruk-hai carrying a demolition charge is charged he will automatically drop it to fight. If one carrier is slain, the remaining Uruk-hai can continue to move with the charge at half rate, as described above – an additional Uruk-hai can pick up the charge the following turn if the player wishes but may not move further that turn. If all carriers are slain the demolition charge is dropped immediately.

DETONATING THE CHARGE

To use the demolition charge it must be dropped. A demolition charge cannot be detonated in the same turn that it was dropped. An Uruk-hai model with a flaming brand in base contact with the charge may set it off during the Fight phase. This model must be otherwise unoccupied – a model that is fighting an enemy or operating a battering ram, carrying a ladder or other burden cannot set off the demolition charge. Anyone near the charge when it goes off is almost certain to be killed – so the Uruk-hai attempting to set off the charge must pass a Courage test before doing so. If he fails he cannot detonate the charge. If he succeeds, the Evil player rolls on the following chart to determine the effects:

When it explodes, a demolition charge automatically strikes everything within 2"/4cm of the model – including walls, gates, doors, and, of course, any warriors in range of it. Each target struck automatically takes D6 wounds, regardless of its Defence value. Even walls and towers suffer D6 wounds from demolition charges – roll once on the Battering chart for each wound inflicted. The demolition charge is removed once it has exploded.

DESPERATE DETONATIONS

In dire need, a demolition charge can be detonated without a flaming brand. An Uruk-hai in base contact with a charge may attempt to set it off by hitting the metal casing with his sword. This model must be otherwise unoccupied – a model that is fighting an enemy or operating a battering ram, carrying a ladder or other burden cannot set off the demolition charge – and must pass a Courage test as normal. If the Evil player wishes to do this he must roll a D6 for each Uruk-hai attempting to detonate the charge in this way. On the roll of one or more 6s, the charge is detonated – roll on the Detonation chart as usual.

ATTACKING THE CHARGE

The demolition charge can be shot at normally and has a Defence of 7 and 3 Wounds. If the charge is wounded, roll a D6 per Wound inflicted. On the roll of a 6, the charge is detonated – roll on the Detonation chart as normal. A demolition charge that is wounded by another demolition charge will be detonated on the roll of a 4+ (per wound suffered) rather than a 6. If brought to 0 wounds without explosive incident, the container is shattered and the powder scatters harmlessly on the ground – remove the charge from play. The demolition charge has no control zone and, if an enemy model spends a full turn in base contact with the charge without doing anything else (ie, not shooting, using magical powers, or fighting in combat), the charge is automatically dismantled as described above. Needless to say, Good models may not shoot at a demolition charge, or at a target with a demolition charge in the way, if another Good model is within 2"/4cm of the charge.

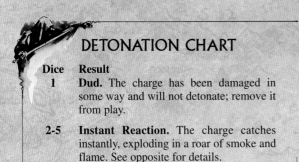

DETONATION CHART

Dice	Result
1	**Dud.** The charge has been damaged in some way and will not detonate; remove it from play.
2-5	**Instant Reaction.** The charge catches instantly, exploding in a roar of smoke and flame. See opposite for details.
6	**Titanic explosion.** The powder in the charge detonates with colossal fury as described opposite, but inflicts 2D6 Wounds rather than D6.

SIEGE ENGINES

Siege Engines have profiles in the same way that Warriors and Heroes do. Understandably, some of the values are simply not relevant to a big, inanimate hunk of metal and wood, and this is reflected in the profile.

	Strength	Defence	Batter Points
Trebuchet	(10)	10	3

MOVING THE SIEGE ENGINE

Siege Engines cannot move themselves, but may be moved by their crew at a rate that varies by the number of models attempting to move it. Three models may move a Siege Engine with them as they move, providing that all three start the Move phase touching the Siege Engine and remain in contact with it throughout their move – the Engine moves at the rate of the slowest model. Two models may move a Siege Engine in this way, but at half

their normal Move rate. A single model may not move a Siege Engine by himself. Models with a Strength of 6 or more (such as Mordor Trolls) count as three models for the purposes of moving a Siege Engine. Siege Engines cannot move through difficult terrain nor cross barriers.

FIRING THE SIEGE ENGINE

A Siege Engine may be fired once each turn provided that it has at least two crew in base contact with it, and that neither it nor they have moved this turn. If there are fewer crew (if the crew are engaged in combat, for example) then the machine cannot fire. Untrained Warriors and Heroes can help to fire the Siege Engine, but reduce its accuracy (see opposite).

All Siege Engines have a Range of 48"/112cm. When firing a Siege Engine, you may either aim at a model (Battlefield target – see opposite) or a point on a fortification (Siege target) exactly in the same way as firing a bow (one or more crew members and the Siege Engine itself must have line of sight to the target).

Roll to hit as normal, using the Shoot value of the crew. If different crew members have different Shoot values, the worst is always used. If you fail to hit, the missile has gone astray of the target or some mechanical error has occurred – either way, the shot misses. If the shot hits you must now roll for scatter if firing at a Battlefield target; if firing at a Siege target no roll for Scatter is required.

SCATTER

If you are firing at a Battlefield target you must roll to see if the shot scatters from your initial target (shots against Siege targets do not scatter). Roll on the Scatter chart (opposite) and apply the result.

Note that neither player may scatter shots onto targets that the Siege Engine could not normally shoot at (they are out of range, there is no line of sight, etc).

FRIENDS IN PROXIMITY AND IN THE WAY

As there is always a fair chance that a Siege Engine shot will scatter up to 6"/14cm from the chosen target, do not make 'In the Way' rolls until you have rolled on the Scatter chart. Determine what, if anything, is in the way, based on the final path of the shot.

Similarly, because of the high degree of inaccuracy, Good Siege Engines cannot shoot at an Evil model if there is a chance of a scattered shot hitting a friendly model. Evil models are unencumbered by such petty morality and may target whatever they wish, whether their friends are close to the target or not.

Note that if a cavalry model is struck, the mount, rider and any passengers are all hit and knocked to the ground – roll to wound for each of them. In the same way, if a model involved in a fight is hit by a Siege Engine shot then all models in the fight are automatically hit.

ROLLING TO WOUND

Once any scatter has been determined, roll to wound as normal using the Strength of the Siege Engine shown in brackets on the profile. If the shot hits a Siege target (whether it was the original target or not) remember to roll on the Batter chart if a wound is caused. Similarly, remember that a Battlefield target struck by a shot from a Siege Engine is knocked to the ground and automatically slain if wounded.

DEPLOYMENT

Because of the size and visibility of Siege Engines, if a scenario requires you to deploy your force in stages you must deploy your Siege Engines first and may not deploy other models until all your Siege Engines (and their crew) have been deployed. In addition, crew must always be deployed in base contact with their Siege Engine and at the same time, unless otherwise stated in a scenario.

TRAINED CREW

Siege Engine crew may operate any Siege Engines that their race may field, ie, Mordor War Catapult crew could skilfully operate any Mordor War Catapult or a Mordor Siege Bow, but not an Uruk-hai Siege Assault Machine or Gondor Battlecry Trebuchet. If they attempt to operate such a machine they count as untrained crew (see below). A crewman may not operate two Siege Engines at once.

UNTRAINED CREW

Warriors and Heroes who are not Siege Engine crew may fire a Siege Engine if the controlling player wishes. If a player chooses to fire a Siege Engine that is being crewed by one or more untrained individuals (ie, not a crewman,

SCATTER CHART

Dice	Result
1	**Wide of the mark.** Your opponent may nominate one of your Battlefield targets or a Siege target within 6"/14cm of the initial target as the new target. If no alternative target is within 6"/14cm, or if the player does not want to do this, the shot misses completely.
2-5	**Slight deviation.** Your opponent may nominate one of his own Battlefield targets within 6"/14cm of the initial target as the new target, if he wishes. If there is no other suitable target within 6"/14cm, the shot misses completely.
6	**Dead on!** The shot lands exactly on target.

or a crewman of a different machine) the Engine will only ever hit on the roll of a 6, regardless of the Shoot value of the crew (even a Siege Engine with a fixed Shoot value, such as a Trebuchet). No Hero other than an Engineer Captain (see overleaf) may use his or her Might to influence rolls to hit, rolls to wound, Scatter chart or Batter chart rolls made by the Siege Engine (see page 36).

A NOTE ABOUT SIEGE AND BATTLEFIELD TARGETS

Most Siege Engines are designed for one purpose and for one purpose only: destroying enemy fortifications. As such they are incredibly powerful machines capable of causing massive damage to their targets but are not easily able to hit smaller quarry, such as individual warriors. To represent this within The Lord of The Rings, we divide potential targets into two types: Siege and Battlefield.

Siege Targets are mostly buildings and fortifications – heavily armoured targets that don't move much (if at all). With targets of this size, precision aiming is not really a factor and even the most unwieldy of machines can easily hit them. The walls and towers of a fortress count as Siege targets, as do all buildings, Siege Engines and Siege towers.

Battlefield Targets are small or comparatively fast-moving targets that Siege Engines have trouble drawing a bead on. This category comprises anything not specifically described as a Siege target – infantry, cavalry, civilians, monstrous mounts, fortress gates and loose mounts all count as Battlefield targets.

Battlefield targets that suffer a hit from a Siege Engine are knocked to the ground and, if they suffer a wound, are killed outright regardless of however many wounds they have on their profile. Fate may be used to save this initial wound, but if the roll is failed then the model is removed as a casualty. The only exception to this is if the model has either 10 or more Wounds on its starting profile, or Defence 10. In this case, the model loses half its initial Wounds (rounding fractions up) and is still knocked to the ground.

COURAGE TESTS

The Siege Engine itself does not need to make Courage Tests and does not count when working out the total size of the force or the break point of the force. The crew of a Siege Engine take Courage tests as normal and count towards the size of the force

ATTACKING SIEGE ENGINES

Siege Engines can be shot at normally. If a wound is scored, roll on the Battering chart to determine the amount of damage caused (see page 62). If brought to 0

Batter Points, the model is disabled for the rest of the game – leave the Siege Engine in place, but it cannot be fired any more.

Siege Engines have no control zone and if an enemy model spends a full turn touching an Engine without doing anything else (ie, not shooting, using magical powers, or fighting in combat), the Engine is automatically dismantled as described above.

Siege Engines count as having a Strength of 6 for the purposes of *Sorcerous Blast* and similar effects.

MODIFYING SIEGE ENGINES

The profiles given for Siege Engines are representative of an average of their type. The truth is that all Siege Engines are slightly different, with each Engine varying in different ways. Gondor trebuchets are often of more efficient construction than Orc catapults, while Orc catapults often fire the severed heads of their enemies, and so on. To allow you to bring more variety and character to your Siege Engines we've included rules for customising them. Each upgrade is available to certain Siege Engines. You may purchase as many upgrades for each engine as you wish (see individual profiles for details). Unless otherwise specified, any Siege Engines included in scenarios are unmodified and have no upgrades. See the individual Siege Engine entries for details.

ENGINEER CAPTAINS

Some Heroes spend their lives training in the art of siege. If you buy this upgrade for your Siege Engine, one of the crew is replaced with a Captain taken from the relevant force list, represent this with a suitable model. Engineer Captains carry a hand weapon, but otherwise have the same equipment as the crew and may not be bought additional equipment (for example, a Minas Tirith Engineer Captain would have a hand weapon and wear heavy armour). However, unlike other Heroes, Engineer Captains may use their Might to influence to hit, to wound, Scatter chart and Batter chart rolls made by the machine. Only a single Engineer Captain can be attached to a Siege Engine.

FLAMING AMMUNITION

For catapults and trebuchets, straw-filled sacks can be soaked in oil and set alight, while on bolt-throwing machines, the projectile itself can be ignited. If a Siege Engine with Flaming Ammunition wounds a Siege target, the firing player may re-roll any 1s on the Battering chart.

SEVERED HEADS

Evil catapults may fire the severed heads of Good Warriors instead of their normal payload. If Severed Heads are fired at a Battlefield target, ignore the normal Strength of the Siege Engine, instead both the initial target and all models within 2"/4cm suffer a single

Strength 3 hit. This shot will neither knock models to the ground nor kill them outright. Any Good models hit must immediately pass a Courage test or retreat (as described in the Courage section). If Severed Heads are fired at a Siege target, they inflict no damage.

SIEGE VETERANS

The crew of this Siege Engine have taken part in countless sieges and are adept at targeting weak spots in constructions. If a Siege Engine crewed by Siege Veterans successfully wounds a target, the controlling player may roll two dice on the Batter chart, not one, and apply the highest result. To receive this bonus, all crew must have the Siege Veterans skill.

SUPERIOR CONSTRUCTION

This Siege Engine is a masterpiece in engineering, granting it enhanced range. This Siege Engine has a range of 60"/140cm rather than 48"/112cm.

SWIFT RELOAD

The crew of this Siege Engine are incredibly fast, aided by several non-standard refinements to its construction. Under optimal circumstances this machine can fire far faster than an unmodified machine. When firing a Siege Engine with this upgrade, the player rolls two D6 and chooses the highest result to determine the number of shots fired.

TROLL

Some Evil Siege Engines can have Mordor Trolls attached to the crew for the purposes of loading and, in extreme cases, defending the construction. Siege Engines that have a Troll crewmember may fire twice each turn provided that the Troll is touching the Siege Engine, has not moved in the preceding Move phase, and is not engaged in combat. The Troll does not count towards the minimum number of crew required to operate the machine, so you must have at least two other crew present. Troll crew carry a huge bludgeoning weapon (not that they really need one to fight effectively). Only a single Mordor Troll can be attached to a Siege Engine.

SIEGE TOWERS

Siege Towers are massive rolling bastions, often constructed of wood. Effectively armoured ladders, an attacker can use such a tower to get his troops directly onto the enemy's battlements whilst the structure of the tower itself defends the warriors within from missile fire. The actual dimensions of a Siege Tower can vary, but it should be tall enough to reach the enemy battlements (normally about 6"/14cm high) and have a ramp just wide enough for two models to stand side-by-side on (about 2"/4cm).

	Strength	Defence	Batter Points
Siege Tower	–	10	4

MOVING THE SIEGE TOWER

Siege Towers cannot move themselves, but may be moved at a rate that varies with the number of models that are pushing it. Six or more models may move a Siege Tower with them as they move, providing that all the models start the Move phase touching the Siege Tower and remain in contact with it throughout their move – the Tower moves at the rate of the slowest model. Between three and five models may move a Siege Tower in this way, but at half their normal move rate. A Siege Tower may not be moved by fewer than three models. Models with a Strength of 6 or higher (such as Mordor Trolls) count as three models for the purposes of moving a Siege Tower. Siege Towers can be turned to face any direction at the start of their move, but cannot change direction whilst moving. Siege Towers may never move through difficult terrain nor cross barriers.

It is possible for some models to be riding the Siege Tower as it is pushed towards the walls so that they are ready to assault the fortification as the Siege Tower hits home. Only infantry models on 25mm bases may ride a Siege Tower in this way. Models can move within the tower or get on/off before, during or after the tower has moved. A player may place as many models on a Siege Tower as will fit. However, each extra model makes the Siege Tower heavier. For each model that is riding the Siege Tower, the models required to push the Tower increases by one.

MOVING WITHIN THE SIEGE TOWER

All Siege Towers consist of one or more platforms (the highest usually being at the level of the battlements of the castle walls) and contain several ladders to allow the attackers to navigate the structure. All ladders within Siege Towers count as access ladders (see page 62). Otherwise models move around the Siege Tower exactly as if it were part of an ordinary tower.

ATTACKING THE SIEGE TOWER

Siege Towers count as Siege targets, and can be shot at normally. They have a Defence of 10 and 4 Batter Points. If a wound is scored, roll on the Batter chart to determine the amount of damage caused. A Siege Tower has no control zone. Enemy models in base contact with the Tower may strike it as if it were a door or gate, rolling on the Batter chart as normal. If brought to 0 Batter Points, the model is destroyed – replace the Tower with a suitable pile of rubble. If a Siege Tower is destroyed, any models riding upon it fall to the ground below, taking a S3 hit for each full 1"/2cm that they fall. Siege Towers count as having a Strength of 6 for the purposes of *Sorcerous Blast*.

ATTACKING FROM THE SIEGE TOWER

Models riding the Siege Tower may shoot or be shot at normally, following the usual rules for Shooting attacks (including line of sight, cover, etc). Models riding the Siege Tower always count as being stationary, regardless of how far the Siege Tower has moved.

ASSAULTING THE WALLS

When the Siege Tower reaches its target, the ramp is dropped and the passengers charge out onto the walls beyond. If a Siege Tower is touching a wall during its Move phase, the ramp can be dropped automatically, creating a bridge to the enemy ramparts. Once the ramp has been dropped, attackers on the upper level of the Siege Tower may move onto the ramparts as if it were open terrain. Defenders charged from the ramp do not get any of the usual bonuses for defending obstacles.

SCENARIOS

A scenario sets the scene for a battle – it describes the circumstances of the encounter, who is involved, and what each side is trying to achieve. Most importantly the scenario describes what the battlefield looks like. Most of the scenarios also include special game rules that apply only for that scenario. Special rules are not a necessary feature of a scenario but they often help to make the game a unique challenge.

SCENARIO FORMAT

Scenarios are normally divided into a number of sections, namely: Description, Participants, Points Match, Layout, Starting Positions, Objectives and Special Rules.

Description describes the incident depicted in the scenario. All the scenarios are based upon or inspired by events portrayed in The Lord of The Rings movies and can be fought as accurate re-enactments should you wish.

Participants explains which characters took part in the incident itself. In most cases, it's impossible to be sure exactly how many Orcs or Uruk-hai fight on the Evil side – there are so many! – so we've estimated a number that gives a balanced game. Where Warriors have wargear options in the Force lists these are specified – otherwise Warriors always have their mandatory wargear as given in the lists.

Heroes can take any options given in the list unless indicated otherwise in the Special Rules.

Points Match provides you with a way of playing the same scenario with any Evil forces versus any Good forces.

Use the Force lists to select your own warriors to take part in the scenario by choosing models as described in the Points Match section. All the scenarios can be fought with any forces. Note that an equal points match won't necessarily enable you to play with the actual participants – which is why we've devised two ways to play each scenario – use either the participants or points match for your game.

The **Layout** section explains how to set up the table for the battle using whatever scenery is required.

Starting Positions describes where the models are placed at the start of the game.

The **Objectives** explains what each side has to do to win the scenario. Every scenario has different objectives and requires you to develop an appropriate tactical approach – what works in one scenario may not work in another!

Special Rules are just that – rules that apply uniquely to that scenario. Most scenarios have special rules of one kind or another to represent the circumstances of the battle.

MAKING UP YOUR OWN SCENARIOS

Once you have played a few scenarios you will want to make up your own. The events in The Lord of The Rings provide plenty of inspiration for you to create your own scenarios, and the same incident can be portrayed in different ways in a tabletop game.

When creating your own scenarios, it's a good idea for the player who has invented the scenario to act as a referee whilst other players take part in the game. The referee foregoes the chance to play – but he is available to adjudicate and interpret the rules as necessary. When you make up new rules for a scenario you'll often find you have to change things a little as you go along the first time you play. If playing a scenario that someone has made up, always be prepared to defer to the referee (even the minions of Evil aren't allowed to argue with the referee!).

EXAMPLE SCENARIO: BALIN'S TOMB

Opposite you will find an example of a normal scenario: Balin's Tomb. More such scenarios can be found in supplement books for The Lord of The Rings Strategy Battle Game, such as The Fellowship of The Ring, in the pages of White Dwarf magazine and on our website.

SCENARIO – BALIN'S TOMB

DESCRIPTION

Travelling beneath the Misty Mountains through the realm of Moria, the Fellowship discovers the tomb of Balin, former lord of the Dwarven kingdom. In a dusty tome clutched in the hands of a skeleton, Gandalf learns of how Moria fell to Goblins and Orcs. Even as Gimli mourns the deaths of his kin, the booming drums of the Goblins echo through the chamber. The Fellowship has been discovered and must ready themselves for battle!

You can play this scenario using just the Basic rules, but will find it more enjoyable if you use the Advanced rules as well.

PARTICIPANTS

GOOD	EVIL
• Frodo Baggins	• 8 Moria Goblins with bows
• Sam Gamgee	• 8 Moria Goblins with shields
• Meriadoc Brandybuck	• 8 Moria Goblins with spears
• Peregrin Took	• 1 Cave Troll with a chain
• Gandalf the Grey	and either a club or a spear.
• Strider/Aragorn	
• Boromir of Gondor	
• Legolas	
• Gimli, son of Glóin	

POINTS MATCH

If you wish to play this scenario as a Point Match the Good side should contain up to 750 points worth of Good Heroes. The Evil player should select 200 points worth of Evil models. Only one Evil model may have more than one wound – this model takes the place of the Cave Troll in the scenario. The remaining Evil forces are divided into three equal groups and take the place of the Moria Goblins. No more than 33% of either side may be armed with bows.

LAYOUT

The scenario is played on a board 18"/42cm x 18"/42cm representing Balin's Tomb. Place the tomb in the centre of the board with the columns and trapdoor placed as shown on the map. The door is placed in the centre of one of the board edges as shown.

STARTING POSITIONS

The Good player can place models anywhere within 3"/8cm of Balin's Tomb.

The Evil player does not set up any models on the table at the beginning of the game, but deploys them onto the table as the game progresses. At the beginning

of the first Move phase, 8 Moria Goblins with shields move onto the table through the door.

OBJECTIVES

The Good side must keep Frodo alive and escape from Balin's Tomb as they make their way to the Bridge of Khazad-dûm. To win this scenario, the Good player must kill the Cave Troll.

The Evil side wins immediately if Frodo is killed.

The game is a draw if any two characters from the Fellowship are killed.

SPECIAL RULES

A Tide of Goblins. At the end of each Evil Move phase after the first, roll a D6. On a 4+ a group of eight Moria Goblins moves onto the table, entering play through either the door or the trapdoor, until all the 24 Moria Goblins are in play. Newly arrived models may act normally, except that they may not charge on the turn they arrive. At the end of the Evil player's third Move phase, the Cave Troll arrives automatically through the door.

During play, the Evil player should place Moria Goblins removed from play to one side, and when these models reach a total of 8, they may be automatically brought back into play through either the trapdoor or the door at the beginning of the Evil player's next Move phase.

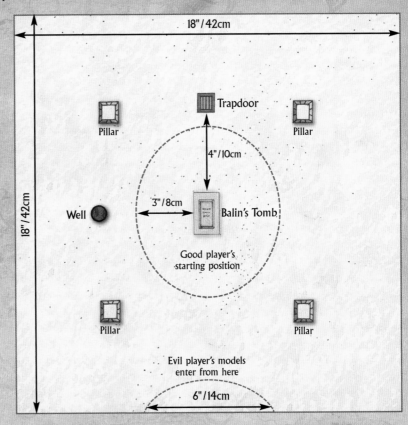

COMMON SCENARIO-SPECIFIC RULES

This section includes some rules that are used in quite a few of our scenarios. Players can of course decide that they want to employ one or more of these rules at any time, perhaps modifying them according to their taste and gaming needs. This can add even more detail to their games and can be great fun, as long as the players agree before the start of the game that they are going to use them!

LOOSE MOUNTS

When a rider is killed, thrown or dismounts and his mount has a Fight and Attacks value of 0, such as a horse, the mount is normally removed automatically. However, there are occasions when it would be useful to be able to remount a loose horse. This can be quite important in some scenarios, but it is a good principle that Good models cannot ride the mounts of Evil models and vice versa.

To take into account situations where representing loose horses is important, we shall say that when a rider is slain, thrown or simply dismounts, the mount must test its Courage as described in the Courage section. If the mount fails the test, it is removed and we assume it runs away and takes no further part in the game. If the mount passes its test, it remains where it is.

A loose mount can be represented by leaving the cavalry model on the tabletop and putting a suitable marker on or next to it. Alternatively, if you do not fix the riders permanently in place you can simply remove the rider. Another option is to have a few separate horse models to be used when the occasion demands.

Loose mounts do not move. They also have no control zone, so other models can move past by them easily.

Loose mounts can still block a warrior's line of sight and might be in the way of a shot. Good models cannot shoot at targets if friendly mounts are in the way – such a thing would be unthinkable! Evil models are under no such obligation, of course.

The enemy might conceivably wish to shoot or attack loose mounts. Loose mounts have no Attacks and so roll no dice in a fight and will therefore lose automatically.

Loose mounts take Courage tests as normal using their own Courage.

LIMITED VISIBILITY

Some scenarios will happen at night, underground, during a sandstorm or in some other situation where visibility is limited (at least for some of the models on the field). This is normally represented by models not being able to charge, shoot or target with magical powers any enemy that is not within a certain distance at the beginning of their move.

LEAVING THE TABLE

Some scenarios require models to leave the table. In this case, if the movement of a model is enough for its base to move into contact with the table edge, the model can immediately leave the table.

PICKING UP WEAPONS

In general, we have not made provision for warriors picking up weapons from other warriors, from weapon stores or discarded weapons that might lie around the battlefield. Keeping track of which warriors have acquired which weapons would be impractical and would make little difference to the battle. However, for players who wish to add a further level of detail, Heroes are allowed to take weapons in some situations.

If a Hero wins a fight and slays all of his opponents he can take one weapon or shield from any of them.

If a Hero does not have a shield and picks one up, he adds 1 to his Defence unless he also has a bow or crossbow. Models who carry pikes or two-handed swords/axe cannot pick up a shield. See the Shield rules on page 46.

If a Hero does not have a bow or crossbow and picks one up, he can shoot and is assumed to also pick up enough arrows to last for the rest of the battle.

If a Hero is already using a shield, then his Defence value is reduced by 1 if he subsequently picks up either a bow or crossbow. See the Shield rules on page 46.

Note that Heroes cannot pick up or use magical weapons or items from their enemy – Good and Evil magic is contradictory in nature and cannot be employed by the foe.

REINFORCEMENTS

Different scenarios have many specific rules to govern when reinforcements turn up during a game, but regardless of that, when a model that didn't start the game on the table enters the game, it can move as normal, measuring from the point it enters the table from. Newly arrived models may act normally, except that they may not charge on the turn they arrive because they couldn't see a target at the beginning of their move (not being on the table…).

CARRYING HEAVY OBJECTS

In many scenarios, models must carry around items, bound prisoners, bodies etc, which we can group together as 'heavy objects'.

For rules on carrying heavy objects, refer to page 65 (moving demolition charges).

CARRYING LIGHT ITEMS

In many scenarios models must carry small precious items, such as Rings of Power, important dispatches and so on.

These do not normally slow the models down and can be passed freely from one model to the next as they move (only once per turn though) by the models just moving into base contact with one another. If the model carrying them is killed, a counter (such as a small coin) must be put in the place where the model was standing before being removed and other models can pick up the item by just moving over the counter during their move. Cavalry must of course dismount in order to pick up an item from the ground.

SENTRIES

Many scenarios include sentries patrolling an area (often with limited visibility) and enemies trying to sneak up on them undetected.

Unless otherwise specified in the scenario, sentries use the following rules. At the start of each Sentry's move, until they are aware of the intruders, roll for each Sentry on the Sentry Movement chart below to see how they move.

The Sentries on the board become alerted to the enemy if:

• A Sentry is hit, but not killed by enemy shooting.

• There is an enemy model within 4"/10cm at the end of the Sentry's move.

If any of the above conditions are met, the Sentries are immediately alerted. From this point onwards they may move, shoot and fight normally.

Note that the distance at which the enemies are spotted can be varied to represent different conditions of visibility.

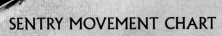

SENTRY MOVEMENT CHART

Dice	Result
1	**Unawares.** The Sentry has seen nothing unusual and, in fact, is more concerned with keeping awake. The model may not move this turn.
2-5	**Suspicion.** The player with Priority may immediately move the Sentry the distance rolled in inches (or twice that rolled in centimetres) in a direction of their choice. Mounted sentries move double this distance.
6	**Patrol.** The Sentry moves normally.

PASSENGERS

Rules for carrying passengers allow for some very dynamic actions where riders pluck their friends from the midst of disaster or carry them towards their goal – just as Legolas carries Gimli and Arwen carries Frodo. Only models specified in the Scenario can be carried as passengers.

The most convenient way of showing that a cavalry model is carrying a passenger is to place the passenger model on the cavalry model's base or as close as possible.

To mount up, either the passenger must move into contact with the cavalry model or vice versa. A standard Jump test is then taken by the passenger. On the roll of a 1, neither model can move further that turn and the passenger does not mount. On a 2-5, the passenger mounts but the cavalry model cannot move further that turn. On a 6 the passenger mounts and the cavalry model can complete its entire move that turn, assuming it's not already done so. Jumping down from a mount is done automatically, no test is required.

A passenger can jump down from a mount before the cavalry model moves, in which case both models can move normally. He can also jump down at any time during the cavalry model's move, but will be unable to move further that turn and counts as having used up his full move regardless of the distance moved.

A passenger cannot shoot with a bow or other missile weapons, cannot make use of magical powers, cannot make heroic actions, and cannot fight in combat. When shooting at a rider/passenger/mount, the shooter declares his target and shoots as normal. If the shot scores a hit then the shooter rolls a further dice to see who is hit: on a 1-3 the mount is hit, on a 4-5 the rider is hit, on a 6 the passenger is hit.

A passenger cannot fight in combat but he can be struck if the cavalry model is beaten. The enemy can choose to strike any or all of his blows against the passenger if he wishes.

If the rider is killed or dismounts, the passenger is automatically thrown.

SWIMMING

Warriors and Heroes may attempt to swim across rivers, lakes or other bodies of deep or fast-flowing waters in some scenarios. Mounted models may not attempt to swim – though they may dismount and attempt to cross without their mount. Models entering such water features do it by moving normally and treating the water as difficult terrain. After this initial move, which represents a dive, they will be swimming (see below).

Swimming models are moved in the Move phase as normal. Roll a D6 for each swimming model and consult the Swimming chart. Swimming models may not lie down, shoot, or carry burdens but will fight as normal.

SWIMMING CHART

Dice	Result
1	**Sink.** The model is overcome by the weight of his wargear and drowns. Remove the model as a casualty.
2-5	**Swim.** The model may move up to half its move through the water. If it reaches the bank it may make a Climb test to pull itself out of the water onto a bank.
6	**Swim strongly.** The model may make its normal move through the water. If it reaches the bank it may make a Climb test to pull itself out of the water onto a bank.

The amount of armour that a model is wearing can adversely affect its ability to swim – this chart represents the ability of a model wearing armour. To represent this, apply the following modifiers to the Swimming chart. These modifiers are cumulative:

• Model is wearing no armour/Mithril armour: +1

• Model is wearing heavy armour/Dwarf heavy armour: -1

• Model is carrying a shield: -1

FORCES

Many people start playing The Lord of The Rings Strategy Battle Game using whatever models they happen to have. This is absolutely fine, because whilst you're learning the rules of the game, it's not such a big deal who wins or whether the forces are exactly matched.

Most players find that once their collection has grown and become more varied, it is more satisfying to fight battles where the sides are equally matched. This part of the rules manual explains how to select balanced forces for a game.

The following pages are divided into twelve sections covering the different lands of Middle-earth – the Shire, Arnor & Angmar, the Elven Havens, Moria, the Woodland Realms, Rohan, Isengard, Gondor (including Númenor), Mordor, the Dwarf Holds, Eastern Realms and Harad. Each section contains Good or Evil forces, or both as appropriate, and includes the warriors and other creatures that are typically found in that land. When selecting your force you may choose to select all your models from one particular section, thereby creating a group of warriors who would be likely to fight together (this is often referred to as a 'themed army'). Of course you do not have to do this – you can pick whatever models you like, as long as they are either all Good or all Evil.

POINT VALUES

The list for each force gives characteristic profiles, weapons, special rules and a points value for every type of model, including warriors and Heroes. The points value is a measure of the model's worth in the game.

It is usual for players to begin the game with an equal points value of warriors. As Good warriors are generally worth more than Evil warriors, this means that the forces of Good will frequently find themselves outnumbered. Most Good warriors are of superior fighting quality compared to the majority of their opponents, so don't despair when you see hordes of Orcs on the other side of the table.

SCENARIOS

Different scenarios employ forces of varying sizes. Inexperienced players are advised to play the smaller encounters before attempting a larger game. As players acquire more models and their collection expands, it will be possible to progress to larger, more demanding scenarios. Though a considerable number of scenarios are available, many players enjoy making up their own scenarios too – taking the events portrayed in The Lord of The Rings as their inspiration.

HOW TO SELECT TROOPS

Begin by choosing which scenario to play. Each scenario can be played with any number of points worth of troops, but we have indicated what we feel is the ideal value for a points matched game. Having decided how many points to choose, each player secretly selects the models they want to use in the game. Use the troop list for your own side to select your force and make a note of the points cost as you do so. You can choose models with a total value up to the points you have agreed, but no more. In most cases you will find that you cannot match the points exactly, but this doesn't matter so long as you do not spend more points than you are allowed.

The scenario you are playing will often limit the number or proportion of Heroes in your force or the number of bow-armed models. This is to ensure that the scenario plays as it is intended even if you choose forces radically different to those portrayed in the actual event.

Oh – in case you were wondering – you can only have one of any named individual in your army. You can't have an army made up entirely of Aragorns, for example!

USING THE RECORD SHEETS

It is a good idea to work out your forces on a piece of scrap paper as you may wish to change your mind, or go back and revise details. Once you are satisfied with your final forces, make sure that you have added up their values correctly. You are then ready to transfer details to a record sheet. You don't need to use a record sheet if you do not wish to, but most players find it convenient to have a handy note of all the characteristics and relevant details for each game – one is provided at the back of this book for you to photocopy.

Simply write down the details for each model onto the sheet. If your force includes several models of the same type, there is no need to make a separate entry for each model; a single entry will suffice in most cases. Once you have copied all the characteristics and made any notes you think will prove useful, your record sheet should be ready for use in your battles.

We have also repeated the Movement chart below for convenience.

MOVE CHART

Type of Model	Maximum move
Man/Woman/Wizard	6"/14cm
Elf	6"/14cm
Eagle	12"/28cm
Ent	6"/14cm
Hobbit	4"/10cm
Dwarf	5"/12cm
Gollum	5"/12cm
Orc	6"/14cm
Moria Goblin	5"/12cm
Uruk-hai	6"14cm
Troll	6"/14cm
Spirit	6"/14cm
Giant Spider	10"/24cm
Fell Beast	12"/28cm
Warg	10"/24cm
Horse	10"/24cm

WARGEAR

Heroes and Warriors have a Wargear section in their entries, where you will find a list of extra equipment that can be bought for them. Sometimes it will be a unique item, maybe of a magical nature, and in those cases the rules are explained in detail in the entry. More often it will be a common piece of equipment, like a weapon or some kind of armour.

The rules for such common pieces of wargear are explained either in the appropriate section of the book (like the Wargear section, in the case of weapons or banners) or here below (as in the case of armour). Their effects are the same for any Hero or Warrior that pays the points for them. Common mounts such as horses and wargs are also listed under the Wargear section.

ARMOUR

If the model wears armour, its Defence value is increased by 1.

HEAVY ARMOUR

If the model wears heavy armour, its Defence value is increased by 2. A model may have either armour or heavy armour – not both. If a model that is wearing armour in his base profile is then bought heavy armour, he will discard the normal armour and replace it with heavy armour, therefore its Defence value will increase only by 1.

SHIELD

If the model carries a shield, its Defence value is increased by 1, unless it also has a bow or crossbow, in which case its Defence does not change. In addition, the model can use the Shielding rule if fighting on foot.

TWO-HANDED WEAPONS

Remember that a model that carries a two-handed weapon cannot also carry a bow/crossbow, a spear or a shield – both hands are needed to wield the weapon.

MOUNTS

Rules for mounts and riders are given in the Advanced rules section. The profiles for horses and wargs are as follows:

	F	S	D	A	W	C
Horse	0	3	4	0	1	3
Armoured Horse	0	3	5	0	1	3
Warg	3	4	4	1	1	2

THE SHIRE

Across Middle-earth, folk are mindful of the shadows beyond their fires, watchful for creatures of evil intent that may be concealed in the darkness. In all these realms, whether in Rohan, Gondor, Dunland, Erebor or a dozen others, strife and danger are constant companions, against whom only hope and forged steel can stand firm. Yet in the centre of Eriador lies a land most unlike all others, a green and idyllic land of cheerful music, swaying crops and long summer days known to its folk as the Shire. Despite being surrounded by all manner of malignant powers left over from the fall of Arnor, the folk of the Shire concern themselves little with that which lies beyond their borders. Instead, they concern themselves as to whether or not the harvest will be plentiful (which it almost always is) and if this year's wine will be as good as the famous Old Winyards (which it invariably is considered not to be).

It may seem strange that such a way of life can survive amongst the stark terrors of the world, let alone that the Hobbits of the Shire are, for the most part, unaware of the perils that surround them. Yet in a very real way they are shielded by that very same innocence, for there are many in the world that believe this carefree way of existence is worthy of protection. Foremost amongst these guardians are the Rangers of the North, the last descendants of Arnor, yet they are not alone in their self-imposed duty. Elves and Wizards are all to be seen lending their aid to the Shire's defence and even Dwarves, self-centred though they often appear, are ready to lend support to this cause should they be able. That so many world-weary folk should defend the Halflings so heedlessly of their own safety might be thought remarkable, yet this pales before the realisation that the Hobbits remain as unaware of their benefactors as they do of potential assailants.

HOBBITS

Though thought to be distantly related to the race of Men, the exact origins of the race of Halflings, or Hobbits, are unknown. They are a physically diminutive people, shorter even than Dwarves, often standing little more than three feet in height, and are generally of slight build – though many of them swiftly put on weight as a result of commonly eating six meals a day, with snacking in between. Oddly, they wear neither boots nor shoes, and instead go about bare-footed in all weathers, their feet protected from the elements by the thick, leathery soles and tightly curling hair.

Like the Men from whom they most have learnt their skills, Hobbits have a great aptitude for all manner of craft and can fashion many useful tools and comely trinkets, though their real skill lies in the cultivation of crops and the tilling of soil. Hobbits have never been a warlike people, yet they are a stubborn folk, capable of great acts of valour that would seem to be at odds with their peaceful, and often lethargic, nature. It is chiefly for this reason that this oft-overlooked folk will one day become the most celebrated people in Middle-earth, for a time will soon come when Hobbits will shape the fortunes of all…

Special Rules

All Hobbits have the following two Special Rules: **Resistant to Magic** and **Throw stones**.

Resistant to Magic. Hobbits are naturally resistant to the influence of magic and the will of others. Every time a Hobbit is targeted by an enemy magical power, he may always attempt to resist it with one dice. This means that even if the Hobbit has 0 Will points on his profile, he can roll one dice to resist all enemy magical powers. If the Hobbit has some points of Will, then he must use those first.

Throw Stones. If a Hobbit does not move at all, he can declare he's 'stooping for a stone', and in the subsequent Shoot phase he can throw it, provided that he is not engaged in combat. This works exactly like a crossbow with a range of 8"/20cm and a Strength of 1.

Pony. A pony has a move of 8"/20cm and follows the normal rules for cavalry mounts (as described in the main rules manual). Ponies may only carry Hobbits and may never carry passengers. In addition, Hobbits mounted on ponies never receive any bonuses for charging. In fact, the ponies are unused to war and inclined to shy away from weapons, and so a model mounted on a pony must take a Courage test to charge any enemy, exactly as if the enemy caused terror.

	F	S	D	A	W	C
Pony	0	2	3	0	1	2

The Ring. If Frodo is included in the force, he carries the Ring. Frodo can put on the Ring at any time during his own Move phase and becomes instantly invisible to all except the Ringwraiths. The model is deemed impossible to see. As the wearer is invisible, he automatically moves through other models and other models automatically move through him (they can't see him so pay no attention to him – we assume Frodo dodges out of the way).

Whilst Frodo is invisible he can neither charge or be charged by enemies who cannot see him – he is effectively ignored. It is best to avoid any potential for confusion by not placing other models in touch if possible. Frodo can even put the Ring on if he has already been charged, in which case he is immediately separated from all enemies that cannot see him.

If the Ring is already being worn then the Good player must roll a dice immediately before he moves Frodo in the Move phase. If the player does not wish to move Frodo he must still roll a dice – but can do so at any time during the Move phase. The roll is made on behalf of Frodo himself so we shall allow the Good player to use Frodo's Might points to modify this dice roll if he wishes to do so. On a score of a 1 or 2, the Evil player moves Frodo instead of the Good player. On a roll of 3, 4, 5 or 6, the Good player moves Frodo as usual. Regardless of which side moves Frodo, he is still part of the Good side and all other actions, such as shooting and fighting, remain under the control of the Good player. This means that when the Evil player moves Frodo, all he can do is move the model, including charging Frodo into any models that can see him (in this case, Frodo does not need to take Courage tests to charge terrifying enemies). He cannot perform heroic actions and cannot pick up or put down other items. He cannot be forced to perform any actions that would cause direct harm to the model (such as jumping down a cliff...) nor be moved off the table if the scenario allows. This represents the struggle between Frodo and the will of Sauron.

If the controlling player wishes Frodo to take the Ring off, he needs to pass a Courage test to be able to remove it. This test can be taken at any point during Frodo's move once it has been established which side has control of his movement. If the test is failed, Frodo must continue to wear the Ring until the next turn, when he will have another chance to remove it.

If Frodo is the only model left on the Good side and he's wearing the Ring, he counts as a casualty – his mind has been taken over by its power. As many scenarios depend on him surviving this is very important! If the Evil side's objective is to kill Frodo this is achieved if he is the only model remaining on the table from the Good side and he is wearing the Ring.

GOOD HEROES

Gandalf the Grey (Wizard)   Points value: 170

	F	S	D	A	W	C	M/W/F
Gandalf	5/-	4	5	1	3	7	3 /6*/ 3

Note: Your force can only include one Gandalf, either Gandalf the Grey or Gandalf the White.

Wargear
Gandalf carries his staff (two-handed weapon), the sword Glamdring (hand weapon) and the ring Narya. At an additional cost, he may have the following:

Horse . . . . .10 pts
Shadowfax . . . . .15 pts

Shadowfax. The great horse Shadowfax may only be ridden by Gandalf. He follows all the rules for horses, except his movement is 12"/28cm.

Of the Order of Wizards, Gandalf the Grey is second only to Saruman the White in power. It is Gandalf who leads the Fellowship until his fall in Moria at the hands of the fearsome Balrog. Gandalf's magical abilities are a great asset to the Fellowship though he is also able to hold his own in a fight.

	F	S	D	A	W	C
Shadowfax	0	4	5	0	1	5

Special Rules
* Staff of Power. Gandalf's staff is not only a symbol of his authority but a potent talisman. To represent his staff's power he can expend 1 point of Will each turn without reducing his own Will store.

Narya. Thanks to the power of Narya, the Ring of Fire, one of the three Elven Rings, Gandalf can re-roll his dice when using Fate points.

Glamdring. Glamdring is a magical sword. When Gandalf fights with Glamdring (rather than his staff), he adds +1 to his Strength characteristic, giving him a Strength value of 5.

Magical Powers
Cast Blinding Light. Dice score to use: 2+.
Command. Range 12"/28cm Dice score to use: 4+.
Immobilise. Range 12"/28cm. Dice score to use: 3+.
Sorcerous Blast. Range 12"/28cm. Dice score to use: 5+.
Strengthen Will. Range 12"/28cm. Dice score to use: 4+.
Terrifying Aura. Dice score to use: 2+.

Bilbo Baggins (Hobbit)   Points value: 90

	F	S	D	A	W	C	M/W/F
Bilbo	3/3+	3	5	1	2	6	1 / 3 / 3

Wargear
Bilbo carries Sting and wears his Mithril coat – both bonuses have been added to Bilbo's profile (without them his Strength and Defence would be 2 each). Note that if Bilbo and Frodo are both included, Bilbo carries Sting and the Mithril coat, whilst Frodo carries the Ring.

Special Rules
The Ring. If Frodo is not in the force, Bilbo can carry the Ring.

Bilbo has lived a great many years and his days of adventure and travel seem far behind him. Though he has grown frail, his strong will and good heart have protected him from the terrible power of the Ring that he has unwittingly guarded and protected for so long.

Frodo Baggins (Hobbit)   Points value: 60

	F	S	D	A	W	C	M/W/F
Frodo	3/3+	2	3	1	2	6	2 / 3 / 3

Wargear
Frodo carries a sturdy blade (hand weapon). At an additional points cost, he can be given the following items of wargear. He can only carry Sting or wear his Mithril coat if Bilbo is not included in the force.

Sting . . . .*.15 pts*
Mithril coat . . . .*.25 pts*
Elven cloak . . . .*.10 pts*

Sting. Sting is a magical blade that shines with a blue light when Orcs are near. When Frodo carries Sting, he adds +1 to his Strength characteristic, giving him a Strength value of 3.

Mithril Coat. Mithril is a rare metal that is as light as a feather, and as hard as dragon scale. The wearer's Defence value is increased by +3, in Frodo's case from Defence 3 to 6.

Special Rules
The Ring. See the full rules for The Ring on page 78.

Frodo has undertaken the quest to carry the Ring to Mordor and cast it into the fires of Mount Doom, thus ending its power forever. Though Frodo is hardly as bold or fierce a warrior as many others in Middle-earth, he alone has the strength of character needed to succeed, for the Ring has a strong and evil will of its own. The Ring wants to be found!

Samwise Gamgee (Hobbit)   Points value: 30

	F	S	D	A	W	C	M/W/F
Sam	3/3+	2	3	1	2	5	1 / 1 / 2

Wargear
Sam carries a sturdy blade (hand weapon). At an additional points cost, Sam can be given the following item of wargear:

Elven cloak . . . .*.10 pts*

Sam is Frodo's stalwart companion and loyal friend – of all the Fellowship only Sam is unable to abandon Frodo to his lone journey to Mordor to destroy the Ring. Stout of heart and determined, Sam remains Frodo's loyal companion throughout all the hardships of their quest.

Meriadoc Brandybuck (Hobbit)   Points value: 10

	F	S	D	A	W	C	M/W/F
Merry	3/3+	2	3	1	1	4	0 / 0 / 1

Wargear
Merry carries a sturdy blade (hand weapon). At an additional points cost Merry can have the following wargear:

Elven cloak . . . .*.10 pts*

Meriadoc Brandybuck, commonly called Merry, is a young hot-headed and meddlesome Hobbit, like his good friend Peregrin Took. It is by chance that Merry finds himself caught up in the greatest adventure of his life. Although he has lived a peaceful and happy life in the Shire, Merry shows a remarkable readiness to adapt to a life of excitement and discovery. Like all Hobbits he is less happy about the necessary culinary deprivations.

Peregrin Took (Hobbit)   Points value: 10

	F	S	D	A	W	C	M/W/F
Pippin	3/3+	2	3	1	1	4	0 / 0 / 1

Wargear
Pippin carries a sturdy blade (hand weapon). At an additional points cost Pippin can have the following wargear:

> *Elven cloak* . . . .*10 pts*

Peregrin Took, commonly called Pippin, is the great friend and companion of the equally young and wild Meriadoc Brandybuck. By a chance encounter, they find themselves propelled from their rustic lives in the Shire into danger of the darkest and most terrible kind. Together Merry and Pippin end up in a dark and dangerous adventure – one that is destined to change them from innocents to heroes.

Frodo of the Nine Fingers (Hobbit)   Points value: 65

	F	S	D	A	W	C	M/W/F
Frodo	3/3+	2	6	1	2	6	1 / 3 / 1

Wargear
Frodo carries a dagger and wears the Mithril coat (included in the profile). He may have the following items at an additional cost:

> *Elven cloak* . . . .*10 pts*
> *Pony* . . . .*5 pts*

Special Rules
It will never really heal. Frodo may never charge an enemy for any reason. He will still fight to defend himself if he is himself charged, but will not strike blows if he wins.

Home is the Hero. When Frodo returns to the Shire in its darkest hour, Hobbits rally to his side, trusting that he will help them cast out their enslavers. Frodo counts as being a Banner (note that he cannot, of course, be picked up and wielded by another model).

Frodo returns from the quest of the Ring changed, much the same as the Shire has changed in his absence. Saddened by the evil and suffering he has seen, and weakened by the burden he has borne, he is no longer so fast to deal out death and judgement. Nonetheless, Frodo has become the greatest hero that the Shire has ever known, and a rallying point for his people.

Samwise the Brave (Hobbit)   Points value: 50

	F	S	D	A	W	C	M/W/F
Sam	3/3+	2(3)	3	1	2	5	2 / 2 / 3

Wargear
Sam carries Sting (the increase in his Strength is shown in the profile above) and may have the following items at an additional cost:

> *Pony* . . . .*5 pts*
> *Elven cloak* . . . .*10 pts*

Sam returns to the Shire a very different Hobbit. Strengthened by the rigours of his journeys and emboldened by the deeds he has done, Sam proves his determination and courage many times over, first during the Scouring of the Shire, but also in the long process of rebuilding in the wake of victory.

Peregrin, Guard of the Citadel (Hobbit)   Points value: 25

	F	S	D	A	W	C	M/W/F
Peregrin	3/3+	2	4	1	1	4	1 / 1 / 2

Wargear

Peregrin carries a hand weapon and wears armour. He may have the following items at an additional cost:

Pony . . . .*5 pts*
Elven cloak . . . .*10 pts*

Special Rules

Guard of the Citadel. Faithful companion of the King Elessar and veteran of Minas Tirith's defence, Peregrin counts as a Hero of Gondor.

Scant trace remains of the foolish and inexperienced Hobbit that Pippin once was. Tempered by the battle-flame that swept across Gondor, the Thain's son is now a leader in his own right, and one who will not be thwarted by Sharkey's rogues.

Meriadoc, Knight of the Mark (Hobbit)   Points value: 25

	F	S	D	A	W	C	M/W/F
Meriadoc	3/3+	2	4	1	1	4	1 / 1 / 2

Wargear

Meriadoc wears armour and carries a hand weapon. He may have the following items at additional cost:

Shield . . . .*5 pts*
Pony . . . .*5 pts*
Elven cloak . . . .*10 pts*
Horn of the Riddermark . . . .*20 pts*

Special Rules

Defender of the Mark. Prepared to defend Éowyn and Théoden to the death, Meriadoc counts as a Hero of Rohan.

Horn of the Riddermark. If Merry carries the Horn of the Riddermark, all Hobbits gain +1 Courage. If Merry is slain, the horn is lost.

Few indeed are those mortals who can claim to have stood firm before the Witch-king of Angmar. Fewer still are they who have dared set their blade upon his undead flesh, yet Merry has done both. His deeds upon the Pelennor have earned him great renown and changed him forever.

Farmer Maggot (Hobbit)   Points value: 50

	F	S	D	A	W	C	M/W/F
Farmer Maggot	3/3+	2	3	1	2	5	1 / 2 / 2

Wargear

Farmer Maggot carries a scythe (two-handed weapon) and is accompanied by his three ferocious dogs: Grip, Fang and Wolf.

	F	S	D	A	W	C
Grip, Fang and Wolf	3/-	3	3	1	1	2

Special Rules

Grip, Fang and Wolf. Farmer Maggot's dogs are a legend unto themselves in the surrounding area. Fast, intelligent and incredibly loyal, they tirelessly guard Maggot's farm, and their presence has convinced more than a few young Hobbits not to steal his crops. Maggot's dogs move 8"/20cm and may always use his Courage while he is still alive and on the battlefield.

Farmer Maggot is a down-to-earth Hobbit, with more than his fair share of stubbornness and common sense, who lives on the border of Buckland. Though some folk in Hobbiton look down on him as a simple farmer, most strangers, be they Hobbits or Big Folk, recognise the shrewdness behind his eyes and the steel in his backbone.

Paladin Took (Hobbit)   Points value: 25

	F	S	D	A	W	C	M/W/F
Paladin Took	2/3+	2	3	1	1	5	1 / 1 / 2

Wargear
Paladin carries a stout walking stick (counts as a hand weapon).

Special Rules
To me Shirefolk! The Thain of the Shire is a symbol of resistance against the ruffians of Lotho and Sharkey. Only Hobbits may benefit from Paladin's Stand Fast! rule. However, the range of Paladin's Stand Fast! is 12"/28cm instead of 6"/14cm.

Paladin Took was the only leader of the Hobbitry to formalise any sort of resistance against the ruffians, fiercely fending off their depredations and protecting the borders of Tookland.

Lobelia Sackville-Baggins (Hobbit)   Points value: 10

	F	S	D	A	W	C	M/W/F
Lobelia	2/3+	1	2	1	1	6	0 / 3 / 1

Wargear
Lobelia carries an umbrella (counts as a hand weapon).

Special Rules
Furious Tirade. No warrior (Good or Evil) may use a Hero's Stand Fast! rule if Lobelia is within 6"/14cm. Warriors cannot benefit from Lobelia's Stand Fast! rule.

The Umbrella is not Mightier than the Sword. If Lobelia wins a combat, she will not strike blows (in actual fact she will still gamely batter her opponent, but with no effect beyond a damaged ego).

While it would be a lie to suggest that Lobelia Sackville-Baggins is popular amongst the other Hobbits, none would deny that she displayed a lot more fire than most when Sharkey's plans became known to the residents of the Shire.

Fredegar Bolger (Hobbit)   Points value: 5

	F	S	D	A	W	C	M/W/F
Fredegar Bolger	2/3+	2	3	1	1	3	0 / 0 / 1

Wargear
Fredegar Bolger carries a variety of Hobbit-sized kitchen implements (counts as being unarmed).

When Frodo moves to Brandy Hall, Fredegar 'Fatty' Bolger assists him and is later driven from the hall when the Nazgûl come searching for the errant Baggins.

Bandobras Took, the Bullroarer (Hobbit)   Points value: 40

	F	S	D	A	W	C	M/W/F
Bandobras Took	3/3+	3	4	2	2	4	2 / 1 / 1

Wargear
Bandobras Took carries a hand weapon and rides a horse.

Bandobras Took, the Bullroarer, is a legend in the Shire for his victory at the Battle of Greenfields.

GOOD WARRIORS

Hobbit Militia   Points value: 3

	F	S	D	A	W	C
Hobbit Militia	1/3+	2	3	1	1	3

Wargear
Hobbit Militia wear everyday clothing and are armed with a variety of common items pressed into service as weapons (count as hand weapons).

The average Hobbit has literally no fighting ability whatsoever. These folk are peaceful and shun all adventure and dangerous living. Their peaceful nature should not be confused for inability to take up arms, however, for it is the combined strength of these good, peaceful folk that drives the bullies off at the Battle of Bywater.

Hobbit Archers   Points value: 4

	F	S	D	A	W	C
Hobbit Archer	2/3+	2	3	1	1	3

Wargear
Archers are armed with knives (count as being unarmed) and short bows (bows with a 18"/42cm range). A Hobbit Archer may carry a signal horn at additional cost:

> Signal horn . . . . .20 pts

Special Rules
Signal Horns – Awake! Fear! Fire! Foes! Signal horns rouse the populace of the Shire to all manner of threats, from wolves to drunken Big Folk. Hobbits take great solace in strength of numbers – something that a fierce blast on a signal horn guarantees. If there is at least one signal horn on the battlefield, all Hobbits gain +1 Courage. If the bearer of the signal horn is slain, the horn is lost.

Protecting the boundaries of the Shire at all times from invasion is a relatively small group of Hobbit Archers, known sometimes as the Bounders. Their sole responsibility is to protect the borders of the Shire from dangerous animals.

Shirriffs (Hobbit)   Points value: 4

	F	S	D	A	W	C
Shirriff	3/3+	2	3	1	1	3

Wargear
Shirriffs are armed with sturdy cudgels and other suitable weapons (hand weapon).

Within the bounds of the Shire there is little need for law keeping and stern discipline. However, the Shirefolk maintain a core of Shirriffs to protect themselves from strife both internal and external. Better trained, with some experience of fighting, the Shirriffs form the core of the Hobbits who rally to the call of Merry and Pippin when the Shire arises to throw off Sharkey's oppression.

EVIL HEROES
Sharkey and Worm (Wizard/Man)　　　Points value: 60

	F	S	D	A	W	C	M/W/F
Sharkey	4/-	4	4	1	2	4	1/4/1
Worm	2/-	3	3	1	1	2	0/0/0

Note: You may only include Sharkey and Worm in your force if Saruman is not present.

Wargear
Sharkey carries a long staff (two-handed weapon) while Worm carries a dagger (hand weapon).

Special Rules
Broken Loyalties. If Sharkey is reduced to one Wound and has no Fate remaining, Worm becomes a Good model and must move towards and attack Sharkey if possible. If Sharkey is slain, Worm reverts to being an Evil model.

Magical Powers
Sharkey may use the following magical powers:
Terrifying Aura. Dice score to use: 2+.
Immobilise. Range 12"/28cm. Dice score to use: 2+.

Sharkey, as he became known in the Shire, was once a power in Middle-earth. As the wizard Saruman the White, he betrayed the White Council to Sauron, but was humbled and his power broken. Escaping the ruin of Isengard, Saruman travelled northwards to the Shire. He had long observed his rival Gandalf's great fondness for the Hobbits, and it seems that there was strength of will in him yet for one final spiteful act. His agent in the court of Rohan, Gríma son of Galmod, went with him for, though he seethed with hatred for his master, he had nowhere else to go.

EVIL WARRIORS
Ruffian (Man)　　　Points value: 4

	F	S	D	A	W	C
Ruffian	3/4+	3	3	1	1	2

Wargear
A Ruffian carries a hand weapon. He may have the following items at additional cost:

Bow . . . . .1 pt
Whip . . . . .1 pt

Special Rules
Whip. Whether a crafted lash of bound leather or simple length of rope, unless it is in skilled hands, a whip's chief power is its ability to cow frightened folk. A whip counts as a throwing weapon with a range of 2"/4cm and Strength 1.

The Ruffians under Sharkey are a violent band of brigands. Originating from the lands around Isengard, they are cruel men willingly drawn into his activities.

ARNOR & ANGMAR

At the time of Gondor's founding in the south of Middle-earth, a second kingdom arose in the north, between the Misty Mountains and the Ered Luin. This was the kingdom of Arnor, over which Elendil ruled until his death at the final battle of the Last Alliance. Arnor was much alike to Gondor, yet its line of kings wavered much sooner and the kingdom found its strength diminished. Such a weakened realm was easy prey for the Witch-king of Angmar, chief amongst Sauron's servants and Lord of the Nazgûl, whose armies ultimately seized and destroyed Arnor's capital of old, Fornost. This single act crushed Arnor forever, despite the best efforts of the north kingdom's allies (the Hobbits of the Shire amongst them).

Nowadays, Arnor is a ghost-haunted land, a place that has seen too much war and known precious little happiness. Ruins of its buildings and statues, testaments to its former glories, can be found in every corner of its old domains. From broken Fornost, to burned Amon Sûl and the Wight-infested downs near Bree, travellers can see the ruin brought to the once-proud kingdom. To stray from the safe pathways of Arnor is to invite great peril, for many evil and unwholesome things survive in the dark forests of Rhudaur, or walk amongst the mists of Evendim. Such creatures vary from savage beasts to malicious and cunning spectres, yet all know little of mercy, and possess cruelty beyond measure. Hope is not unknown even so, for there are many places of a more wholesome power within the boundaries of the old realm, though their numbers are few and their strength fades daily.

THE RANGERS OF THE NORTH

All that remains of the noble houses of Arnor, the Rangers of the North, live within the valleys and hills of Eriador, continuing to defend the common folk from the evils that dwell in the ruins of the north kingdom. Since the fall of Arnor, the Rangers have followed the leadership of chieftains, taciturn and steady-handed Men who can trace their lineage back to Isildur himself, and thence to the blood of lost Númenor. Courageous and determined warriors, the Rangers are masters of all manner of woodcraft and fear neither Man, beast nor unquiet spirit.

Of all the races of Men to remain in Middle-earth, it is the Rangers of the North who earned the most respect from the Elvish peoples, for the Elves perceive the nobility of their calling for what it is. Indeed, several of the Elves of Rivendell, the sons of Elrond amongst them, have taken to spending time in the wilderness alongside the Rangers, lending what aid they can. Many believe that there will come a time when the descendants of Arnor will reclaim their birthright, yet until that day they continue their thankless task, guarding the villages of Eriador from evils unknown to all but they.

GOOD HEROES
Strider / Aragorn (Man)   Points value: 175

	F	S	D	A	W	C	M/W/F
Aragorn	6/3+	4	5	3	3	6	3*/3/3

Wargear
Aragorn carries a sword (hand weapon). At an additional points cost he can be given the following:

Andúril, Flame of the West ....75 pts
Elven cloak ....10 pts
Armour ....5 pts
Bow ....5 pts
Horse ....10 pts

Andúril, Flame of the West. This magical blade has been re-forged by the smiths of Rivendell using the fragments of Narsil, the sword of Elendil. When fighting with Andúril, Aragorn never needs to roll more than 4+ to score a wound, regardless of the opponent's Defence (this rule has no effect against targets that have Batter Points instead of Wounds). His rolls to wound can be modified by using Might as normal.

Special Rules
* Mighty Hero. Aragorn is a mighty hero – the heir of the Kings of Gondor. He may expend 1 point of Might per turn without reducing his Might store. Any additional points of Might expended during his turn will reduce his Might store as normal.

Aragorn, also known as Strider, is a descendant of Elendil and the last heir to the throne of Gondor. His rough and weather-hewn appearance speaks of a hard life spent battling evil in wild places. Aragorn becomes the protector of the Hobbits and the greatest of the heroes of the Fellowship. His fate and that of the Ringbearer are inexorably bound together with the fate of Middle-earth itself.

Halbarad Dunádan (Man)   Points value: 65

	F	S	D	A	W	C	M/W/F
Halbarad Dunádan	5/3+	4	5	2	2	6	3/2/1

Wargear
Halbarad carries a sword (hand weapon), a bow and wears armour. He can be given addition equipment at the following cost:

Spear ....1 pt
Horse ....10 pts
The Banner of Arwen Evenstar ....60 pts

Special Rules
The Banner of Arwen Evenstar. When unfurled by Halbarad as the captured Black Ships approached the Harlond, the Banner of Arwen Evenstar filled the beleaguered hearts of Men with renewed hope and joy. The Banner of Arwen Evenstar counts as a banner but will affect all friendly models within 6"/14cm, not 3"/8cm. In addition, every Good model within 6"/14cm of the banner automatically passes any Courage test they are required to take. Halbarad may still use his bow if he carries this banner.

Kinsman to Aragorn, Halbarad Dunádan is his standard bearer and a fine warrior of courage and nobility who bears the banner of Arwen Evenstar at the Battle of the Pelennor Fields.

Ranger of the North (Men)   Points value: 25

	F	S	D	A	W	C	M/W/F
Ranger of the North	4/3+	4	5	1	1	5	1/1/1

Wargear
The base profile for a Ranger of the North includes armour, a sword (hand weapon) and a bow. He can be given additional equipment at the following extra cost:

Spear ....1 pt
Horse ....6 pts

The Dúnedain, or Rangers of the North, patrol the lands of Eriador and keep them safe from all creatures of Evil.

Tom Bombadil (Spirit) — Points value: 80

	F	S	D	A	W	C	M/W/F
Tom Bombadil	?	?	?	?	?	?	? / ? / ?

Tom Bombadil is a mysterious being that lives in a small cottage past the edge of the Old Forest. Tom's appearance is that of a plump, jolly, little man, always intent on singing nonsensical songs and picking flowers for his beloved Goldberry. Tom seems interested in very little else, but he will never deny his help to travellers in danger, as Frodo and his friends soon find out. Beyond Tom's innocent look though is hidden a being of immense power, to whom all living creatures and even inanimate matter must obey to the letter. Even the Ring has no influence upon him, and the only limit to Tom's powers seem to be his resolution never to cross the borders of his small land, a limit that Tom has imposed upon himself.

Wargear
Tom wears great yellow boots, a blue coat and an old battered hat with a tall crown and a long blue feather stuck in the band. Tom is armed with a large leaf on which he carries a small pile of white water lilies (counts as being unarmed).

Special Rules
Tom is Master. Tom treats all kinds of difficult terrain as open and always gets a result of 6 on the Jump and Climb charts (some say that rocks and trees reverently move aside to let him through...). Tom cannot be harmed by ranged attacks – this means that magical powers have no effect at all on him and missiles that hit Tom disappear and are discarded. No models can move into Tom's control zone unless the Good side player allows them (this includes models moved by a *Sorcerous Blast* spell). Tom can charge enemy models normally and his side will always win any fight Tom is involved in, but neither Tom nor any other Good model involved in the same fight will strike any blows. Tom and all Good models within 6"/14cm of him always automatically pass all Courage tests.

Tom's country ends here: he will not pass the borders. Tom cannot be used in any scenario that does not take place in the Barrow-downs or in the Old Forest.

Magical Powers
Hey! Come merry dol! Range 12"/28cm. Dice score to use: automatic. Tom can instantly heal the body and mind of his friends with a simple act of will and a merry song. This power can be used on a single friendly model. The affected model is instantly restored to the condition he started the game in (getting back all lost Wounds and points of Might, Will and Fate used up to that point in the game, as well as recovering from the effects of any enemy magical power).

Goldberry (Spirit) — Points value: 70

	F	S	D	A	W	C	M/W/F
Goldberry	?	?	?	?	?	?	? / ? / ?

"O slender as a willow-wand! O clearer than clear water!

O reed by the living pool! Fair River-daughter!".

A mysterious creature that lives with Tom Bombadil, Goldberry is a beautiful female spirit. She seems to personify the life-giving and soothing powers of the clearest and purest of waters.

Wargear
Goldberry wears a green and silver gown and golden belt. She has no weapon.

Special Rules
River-Daughter. Goldberry cannot be harmed by ranged attacks – this means that magical powers have no effect at all on her, and missiles that hit Goldberry disappear and are discarded. No Evil models can move into Goldberry's control zone (this includes models moved by a *Sorcerous Blast* spell). Goldberry will never enter the control zone of an Evil model. Goldberry and all Good models within 6"/14cm of her always automatically pass all Courage tests.

Tom has his house to mind, and Goldberry is waiting. Goldberry cannot be used in any force that does not include Tom Bombadil as well.

Magical Powers
Refreshing Song. Range 12"/28cm. Dice score to use: automatic. Goldberry can instantly heal the body and mind of her friends with a simple act of will and a merry song. This power can be used on a single friendly model. The affected model is instantly restored to the condition he started the game in (getting back all lost Wounds and points of Might, Will and Fate used up to that point in the game, as well as recovering from the effects of any enemy magical power).

EVIL HEROES
Barrow-wight (Spirit)

Points Value: 50

	F	S	D	A	W	C	M/W/F
Barrow-wight	3/-	2	7	1	1	6	0 / 5 / 0

Wargear
A Barrow-wight wears heavy armour and carries a sword of great age and exceptional craftsmanship.

Special Rules
Terror.

Magical Powers
Paralyse. Range 6"/14cm. Dice score to use 4+. The affected model is immediately paralysed. A paralysed victim is knocked to the ground and may do nothing until it recovers. If engaged in close combat, the victim rolls no dice (automatically losing any Fight if no other friendly models are involved) and counts as trapped. At the end of the Fight phase, the opposing player must roll a dice for each of his models that are paralysed, on the roll of a 6 that model recovers and immediately stands up. Friendly models that spend the Fight phase in contact with a paralysed model without doing anything else can attempt to revive them. To do so, they roll a dice and need to obtain a 6, as described above. Note that Heroes can use Might to modify this roll.

After the Last Alliance of Elves and Men and the fall of Sauron, the Witch-king fled to the North and there built the kingdom of Angmar. He sent dark spirits south to the Barrow-downs and the skeletal forms of the long-dead rulers walked once more, bedecked with gold and carrying dark blades, their actions directed by the dread will of Sauron's chief servant. In time, the Witch-king was defeated and his kingdom of Angmar destroyed, but the Barrow-wights remain within their tombs, luring the unwary to their doom.

White Warg Chieftains are ferocious and determined beasts, that dwell far to the north of the Shire. Their hunger knows no bounds and often drives them into a maddened state.

White / Wild Warg Chieftain — Points value: 75

	F	S	D	A	W	C	M/W/F
White Warg Chieftain	5/-	6	5	2	3	3	1 / 3 / 1

Wargear
Teeth and claws (counts as a hand weapon).

Special Rules
Terror.

Packlord. A White Warg Chieftain is little more than a cunning beast, and certainly has little or no grasp of tactics and leadership. Only White Wargs may use his Stand Fast! rule or benefit from his heroic actions.

EVIL WARRIORS

Unlike their cousins in the lands to the south, these beasts have never been broken to the service of Orcs and exist solely to roam the plains and hills of northern Eriador, slaking their hunger where they can.

White / Wild Warg — Points value: 8

	F	S	D	A	W	C
White Warg	3/-	4	4	1	1	2

Wargear
Teeth and claws (count as a hand weapon).

THE ELVEN HAVENS

In the early years of the Second Age, the Elves prospered in western Middle-earth, dwelling in great cities scattered across the length and breath of Eriador. With the shadow of Morgoth removed from them, the Firstborn were once more able to enjoy the wonders of Middle-earth. Alas, in time, their reach exceeded their grasp and they were brought low by Sauron's designs. In a series of wars spanning many centuries, the Dark Lord shattered much of the power of the Elves, and many kingdoms and cities were crushed beneath the might of his armies. To this day only a relative handful of Elves remain within western Middle-earth, dwelling in halls either hidden from the eyes of the Lord of Mordor, or protected by power such that even he cannot breach.

Chief amongst these, and well known in the other realms of Middle-earth, is the Haven of Imladris – also known as Rivendell. Founded in the Second Age by Elves fleeing Sauron's assault on the great kingdom of Eregion, Rivendell has ever since been a place of wisdom and healing, a bastion of light in a world

that has dwelt for too long under Sauron's shadow. All beings of good heart are welcome within its walls, whether they be Elves, Dwarves, Men or other, far stranger, creatures. Some such guests are merely travellers passing east over the mountains or west over the hills of Rhudaur who wish to spend a few nights in the safety of the Last Homely House east of the sea and west of the mountains. More often, they come seeking the wisdom to be found within the house of Elrond half-Elven, whose gifts of healing and prophecy are held above comparison.

Further north and west, on the coast of the Great Sea, is the only Elven kingdom to endure the trials of the recent centuries. It is here, at the Grey Havens of Lindon that the ships from blessed Valinor once landed – though they do so no more. New arrivals no longer come to Lindon, for the Elves are slowly departing Middle-earth, carried away into the West by the graceful vessels crafted by the shipwrights of the Grey Havens, seeking to set foot once more upon Valinor's white shores.

ELVES

The Firstborn race, or Eldar, the Elves are the noblest and greatest of all Middle-earth's folk. Immortal and unchanging, Elves suffer not the blight of disease, nor the long slow decay of age, yet they can be slain in battle, or succumb to withering from grief. It is through the Elves that many of the wonders of Middle-earth came to pass, whether they be keen-bladed weapons, songs of great beauty and skill or simply wisdom and knowledge. That which they did not craft themselves is almost always the result of their teachings, for their minds are keen and their hands dextrous beyond the belief of Dwarves or Men. Without the knowledge and skill of the Elves, the great halls of the Númenóreans could never have been crafted, nor the Rings of Power forged – in many ways, they are a light by which the younger races are guided and protected. Yet, as the Third Age passes, so to do the Elves. The ennui that comes with eternal life is a heavy burden for them, and to see the lands they love despoiled by the works of others and corrupted by the evils of Sauron is more than they can bear. Each year, the Firstborn pass away to far-western lands of Valinor in greater numbers, and with each passes a fraction of all that is wondrous in Middle-earth.

GOOD HEROES

Elrond (Elf)   Points value: 170

	F	S	D	A	W	C	M/W/F
Elrond	6/3+	4	7	3	3	7	3 / 3 / 3

Elrond is old even amongst the immortal Elves, having fought against Sauron in an earlier age and seen the Ring taken by Isildur before it was lost. He is the master of Rivendell and the greatest amongst the wise of Middle-earth. He also is the Bearer of Vilya, The Ring of Sapphire, one of the three Elven Rings.

Wargear
Elrond wears heavy armour and carries an Elven blade and the ring Vilya.

Vilya. Thanks to the power of Vilya, one of the three Elven Rings, Elrond can re-roll his dice when using Fate points.

Special Rules
Lineage of the Firstborn; Woodland Creature.

Magical Powers
Nature's Wrath. Dice score to use: 4+.
Renew. Dice score to use: 3+

Glorfindel (Elf)   Points value: 130

	F	S	D	A	W	C	M/W/F
Glorfindel	7/-	4	6	3	3	7	3 / 3 / 3

To those creatures that can see beyond his mortal exterior, Glorfindel appears as a figure of shining white light, a mighty and terrible lord whose powers rival those of Elrond himself.

Wargear
Glorfindel wears light Elven armour and carries an Elven blade. At an additional cost he may have the following:

    Asfaloth (Horse) . . . .*10 pts*

Special Rules
Lineage of the Firstborn; Woodland Creature.

Arwen Evenstar (Elf)   Points value: 60

	F	S	D	A	W	C	M/W/F
Arwen	6/-	3	3	1	2	6	1 / 3 / 1

Arwen is the daughter of Elrond and like her father an Elf of great power and courage. As an immortal she is destined to sail from Middle-earth into the West – yet her love for Aragorn holds her in the mortal realm and leads her towards an altogether different fate.

Wargear
Arwen carries an Elven blade. At an additional points cost, she can be given the following:

    Elven cloak . . . .*10 pts*
    Asfaloth (horse) . . . .*10 pts*

Special Rule
Woodland Creature; Expert Rider. See page 112 for details of this rule.

Magical Power
Nature's Wrath. Range 6"/14cm radius. Dice score to use: 4+.

Special Rules
Lineage of the Firstborn. This Elf Lord is descended from the mightiest of Elvenkind, his power almost beyond reckoning, his appearance enough to strike Terror in the heart of all evil creatures.

Woodland Creature. Elves are perfectly in tune with nature and therefore they never consider areas of wood to be difficult terrain. An Elf can move 6"/14cm in any wooded area classed as difficult terrain just as if he were in the open.

Elladan and Elrohir (Elves)   Points value: 140 for both

	F	S	D	A	W	C	M/W/F
Elladan/Elrohir	6/3+	4	5	2	2	6	3 / 2 / 2

Wargear

Elladan and Elrohir wear light Elven armour. They both carry two Elven blades.

At an additional cost they may have the following:

Elven cloaks . . . . .20 pts for two cloaks
Horses . . . . .20 pts for two horses
Elf Bow . . . . .10 pts for two bows

Special Rules

Woodland Creature.

Twin Elven Blades. Because of their exceptional martial training, the two brothers may, when fighting on foot only, use their swords in three different ways. At the start of the Fight phase, the Good player must declare whether each twin is attacking with two swords, attacking with a single sword, or defending. If he is attacking with two swords he fights as normal, but gains an extra attack (for a total of three) for the duration of the combat. If he is attacking with a single sword he fights with only two Attacks, but counts as armed with a two-handed sword for the duration of the combat. If he is defending, he follows the same rules of a model that is 'shielding' using a shield, obtaining a total of four Attacks, but forfeiting the possibility of striking blows if victorious. Note that the remaining twin cannot defend if his brother has been killed.

Unbreakable Bond. If one of the twins is killed, the other will be driven mad by grief and charge the enemy with fury, abandoning all thoughts of self-preservation. To represent this, immediately after the death of one of the twins, the surviving one's Strength is increased to 5, but his Defence is reduced to 4.

He will always pass any Courage test he is required to take. In addition, he will always move as fast as possible towards the model that killed his brother and will always charge it if possible (even if it means having to make a heroic move). If that model is killed, the surviving twin will then move as fast as possible and charge towards the closest visible enemy for the rest of the game.

The twin sons of Elrond and Celebrian, like their sister Arwen, share their father's half-Elven blood. Because of this, they too will have to choose to follow either the life of the immortal Elves, whose race is nonetheless fading away from Middle-earth, or the life of the mortal Men, whose energetic race is destined to become dominant in the later Ages of the world. It is not known which choice the two are going to take, but so great is their brotherly love that it is sure they will both choose the same destiny. The two brothers are skilled warriors, valorous allies of Aragorn and the other dour-handed Rangers of the North, hunting down and slaying the servants of the Enemy in the vast wilderness surrounding the house of their father.

Gil-galad (Elf)   Points value: 140

	F	S	D	A	W	C	M/W/F
Gil-galad	9/3+	4	7	3	3	7	3 / 3 / 1

Wargear

Gil-galad wears heavy armour and carries the mighty spear Aeglos. At additional cost he may carry a shield.

Shield . . . . .5 pts

Aeglos. The magical spear Aeglos does not follow the normal rules for spears, but instead it confers Gil-galad +1 to his dice roll on the Wound chart.

Special Rules

Lineage of the Firstborn; Woodland Creature.

High King of the Elves. Such is Gil-galad's awesome presence on the battlefield that the range of his 'Stand Fast!' rule is 12"/28cm rather than 6"/14cm.

Gil-galad was the High King of the Elves and mightiest warrior of his age. During this Last Alliance of Men and Elves Gil-galad fought on every battlefield, his bravery and leadership bringing inspiration and hope in those dark days.

Note: *Gil-galad is a mighty Hero who was slain during the Second Age – he does not appear later in the story arc and would not normally feature in any scenarios set in the Third Age.*

Elven Captain

Points value: 65

	F	S	D	A	W	C	M/W/F
Elf Captain	6/3+	4	4	2	2	6	2 / 1 / 1

Wargear

The Elven Captain represented by this profile has an Elven blade. At an additional cost he may have the following:

Heavy armour . . . . .10 pts
Shield . . . . .5 pts
Elf bow . . . . .5 pts
Horse . . . . .10 pts

Special Rule
Woodland Creature.

We have included the option to include Elven Captains as part of your force – note that you can include more than one if you wish. This represents the leaders amongst the Elves who go unnamed in the story of The Lord of The Rings.

GOOD WARRIORS

Elf Warrior

Points value: 7

	F	S	D	A	W	C
Elf	5/3+	3	3	1	1	5

Wargear

The base profile for an Elf warrior does not include any equipment. He can be given additional items at the following cost:

Elven blade . . . .*1 pt*
Spear . . . .*1 pt*
Elf bow . . . .*2 pts*
Heavy armour . . . .*2 pts*
Shield . . . .*1 pt*
Banner (up to one per Hero included in the same force) . . . . .*35 pts*

The Elves are the deadliest warriors in all of Middle-earth, combining skill-at-arms with expertly fashioned wargear. They are proficient with swords, spears and bows, and are the bravest of all fighting troops.

Special Rule
Woodland Creature.

MORIA

Moria was founded in the First Age of the world, long before the forging of the Rings of Power and even before the children of Númenor landed on the shores of Middle-earth. In the east of the Misty Mountains did Durin, the father of the Dwarves, make his home. He and his folk fashioned a mighty underground realm, and Khazad-dûm (as the Dwarves name it) became a testimony to Dwarvish skill and proud splendour. As the numbers of Durin's folk grew, so did they fashion new halls from caverns, span bottomless chasms with bridges of stone and fashion sturdy gates from the very skins of the mountains themselves.

Moria was wealthy because the mountains were wealthy, and the Dwarves delved deep in search of iron, gold, and gemstones of all kinds. These were the toys and servants of the Dwarves, wrought with great skill and cunning to produce all manner of wondrous artefacts that were the envy of the other kingdoms in Middle-earth. Even so, the true riches of Khazad-dûm were not in gold or iron, but in what was called Mithril by the Elves or known as Truesilver in the Common tongue. As hard as dragonscale, it could be polished like silver and wrought like iron.

In the outside world, times changed. The Last Alliance overthrew Sauron and his fortress of Barad-dûr was broken. Unconcerned with the affairs of the outside world, the Dwarves continued to delve below the mountains in search of Mithril. Alas, their greed proved to be their undoing, for as they went ever deeper, they unleashed a terrible power; a creature of shadow and flame, mightier and more terrifying than any Dwarf still living could recall: a Balrog. It slew Durin, the King of Moria, and countless others died at its hand. 'Durin's Bane' the Dwarves named the Balrog and, helpless before its power, they fled in terror. The gates to the once proud realm were closed and the mighty halls fell into ruin.

GOBLINS

In truth, Goblins are not a distinct race but a lesser species of Orcs who made their way to live in the dark caverns below the mountains. There they grew accustomed to the darkness and learned to climb the sheer surfaces of their new homes. The Goblins fear the light and will not leave the shelter of their tunnels during the daytime except in direst need. Cowards at heart, Goblins are nonetheless vicious creatures, who mercilessly attack anything that strays into their realms, nestled in the darkest places of the Misty Mountains. Their hierarchy is anarchy: the strongest and meanest Goblin leads and the others follow. As such, these weak-willed creatures are forever at the mercy of domination at the hands of more powerful evils.

Like all of the evil parodies of the other races of Middle-earth, the Goblins make no beautiful things, but many clever, vicious ones. Without pride and with little notion of honour or courage, Goblins can be considered the antithesis of the Dwarves, with whom they frequently war for control of the deep places of the world. Though a single Goblin is of little threat, when they go to war they do so in massive hordes, using their advantage of numbers to overwhelm the foe.

EVIL HEROES
The Balrog

Points value: 400

	F	S	D	A	W	C	M/W/F
Balrog	10/3+	9	9	4	10	7	0 /10/0

Special Rules

Resistant to Magic. See page 78.

Lash. The Balrog's flaming whip counts as a throwing weapon with a range of 6"/14cm and a Strength of 7.

Terror. The Balrog is a huge terrifying monster and, accordingly, causes Terror.

Ancient Evil. The Balrog's very presence radiates an aura of primeval fear. All Good models within 18"/42cm of the Balrog suffer a -1 penalty to their Courage value until they move out of range (note that this is not cumulative with other rules that confer similar penalties, such as the Moria Goblin Drum).

The Balrog is a mighty creature of great age and power – a monster of a rare and horrific kind. Of all the evil powers in the world it is amongst the most potent and formidable.

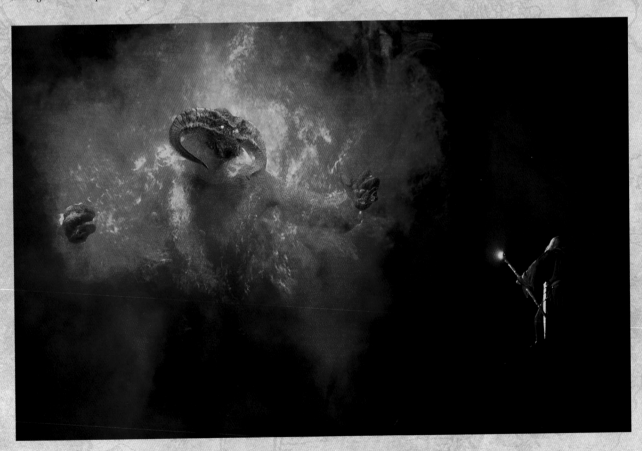

Durbûrz has ruled over Moria for many years. Though not necessarily the cleverest of Goblins, Durbûrz is large and brutal enough to be a successful leader among them. He rules with an iron fist and, as a result, his subjects probably fear him more than any foe.

Durbûrz, the Goblin King of Moria   Points value: 60

	F	S	D	A	W	C	M/W/F
Durbûrz	4/-	4	6	2	2	4	3 / 2 / 2

Wargear
The Goblin King of Moria wears heavy segmented armour and has a sword.

Special Rules
Cave Dweller. The stunted crook-limbed Orcs of Moria, also known as Moria Goblins, are adapted to the underground ruins of the ancient Dwarf stronghold where they live. This allows them to bound across obstacles and gaps effortlessly. Moria Goblins are also able to scuttle up sheer surfaces with the aid of hooks, spines, and spikes incorporated into their armour.

To represent this in the game, no dice roll is required when a Moria Goblin is attempting to jump a gap or obstacle up to double its own height. The jump is made automatically just as if a 6 had been rolled on the Jump chart.

In addition, Moria Goblins can climb up or down vertical surfaces without making a Climb roll – in effect they always count as having rolled a 6 on the chart. However, they're still reduced to half speed whilst climbing – even Moria Goblins can move about more quickly on the ground!

Iron Fist. Such is the fear inspired by Durbûrz in his followers that the range of effect of his Stand Fast! rule is 12"/28cm rather than the normal 6"/14cm.

For centuries untold, the Moria Goblin Shamans have been the tools by which Sauron has enacted his will upon these, the lowest of his minions.

Moria Goblin Shaman   Points value: 45

	F	S	D	A	W	C	M/W/F
Goblin Shaman	2/-	3	4	1	2	3	1 / 3 / 1

Wargear
The Goblin Shaman represented by the profile has a spear and wears armour.

Special Rule
Cave Dweller. See the Goblin King entry above for details.

Magical Powers
Fury. Range 6"/14cm. Dice score to use: 3+.
Transfix. Range 12"/28cm. Dice score to use: 5+.

We have included the option for you to include one or more Moria Goblin Captains as part of your force. This represents the leaders amongst the Goblin soldiery who go unnamed in the story of The Lord of The Rings – the incidental warriors whose role on the battlefield is important in any war. If you choose Captains invent suitable names for each.

Moria Goblin Captain   Points value: 35

	F	S	D	A	W	C	M/W/F
Goblin Captain	3/5+	4	5	2	2	3	2 / 1 / 1

Wargear
The Moria Goblin Captain represented by the profile has a sword and wears spiny segmented armour. At an additional cost he may have the following items:

> Shield . . . . .5 pts
> Orc bow . . . . .5 pts

Special Rule
Cave Dweller. See the Goblin King entry above for details.

EVIL WARRIORS

Moria Goblin Warrior   Points value: 4

	F	S	D	A	W	C
Moria Goblin	2/5+	3	4	1	1	2

Wargear

The base profile for a Goblin warrior includes spiny Goblin armour. Any warrior can be given additional items at the following cost:

Sword or similar hand weapon . . . . .Free
Spear . . . . .1 pt
Orc bow . . . . .1 pt
Shield . . . . .1 pt

Special Rule

Cave Dweller. See the Goblin King entry on page 101 for details.

Goblins are small, mean-spirited creatures that live a troglodyte existence in the numerous delvings beneath the Misty Mountains. The ancient Dwarf tunnels of Moria have become home to these loathsome monsters. They scuttle through the tunnels with amazing dexterity, attacking, destroying and consuming intruders that venture into their dark realm.

Cave Troll   Points value: 80

	F	S	D	A	W	C
Cave Troll	6/5+	6	6	3	3	3

Wargear

The Cave Troll has a club (hand weapon) and can be given additional items at the following cost:

Spear . . . . .1 pt
Troll chain . . . . .5 pts

Troll chain. This is treated as a throwing weapon with a range of 3"/8cm and a Strength of 4.

Special Rules

Terror. Such a huge monster causes Terror in the enemy, as described in the Courage section of the rules.

Throw Stones. If a Troll does not move at all, he can declare he's 'stooping for a stone', and in the subsequent Shoot phase he can throw it, provided that he is not engaged in combat. This works exactly like a crossbow with a range of 12"/28cm and a Strength of 8.

Cave Trolls are large and loathsome creatures that shun the light, preferring to hide away in dark caves and subterranean tunnels. They are slow-witted but nonetheless dangerous creatures once roused to anger.

When Goblins go to war they are often hurried on by the beat of massive drums. Though there is nothing magical about the drums, the sound increases the Goblins' will to fight and the drums themselves can prove a rallying point about which they will fight that much harder. The effect of the drums in the enemy is only slightly less pronounced, as the steady sonorous beat erodes the resolve of even the bravest warriors.

Moria Goblin Drum
Points value: 100

	F	S	D	A	W	C
Drum	-/-	-	10	-	3	-
Goblin Drummers	2/-	3	4	1	1	2

The Drum is accompanied by two Moria Goblin Drummers.

Wargear
The base profile for a Goblin Drummer includes spiny segmented armour and a piece of bone the creature uses to play the Drum (counts as a dagger in combat).

Special Rules
Cave Dweller. See the Goblin King entry on page 101 for details.

Drums in the Deep. At the beginning of the game, deploy the Moria Goblin Drum model following the instructions of the scenario like any other Evil model and place the Drummers in base contact with it. The Drum can be carried by one or two Drummers. If carried by two models it moves at full pace. If carried by one model it moves at half speed.

Drummers carrying a Drum cannot carry other burdens such as ladders.

A Drummer who is carrying the Drum at the start of his move cannot charge that turn.

A Drummer can drop the Drum at any point in his move – but is still not allowed to charge that turn.

A Drummer carrying the Drum will automatically drop it to fight if he is charged or slain. If all Drummers are slain, the drum is dropped immediately.

The drum can be picked up by Drummers in contact with it. Once picked up, it cannot be moved further that turn.

For the Drum to have an effect, at least one Drummer must start the turn in base contact with it and must not move or be engaged in combat. As long as all these conditions are met, the Drum has the following two effects:

- In all fights within 18"/42cm of the Drum which include at least one Moria Goblin, the Evil player can re-roll any one of the dice he rolled when determining who wins the fight. You must stick with the result of the re-roll (you can never re-roll a dice more than once).

- All Moria Goblins on the battlefield (including Heroes) add +1 to their Courage value and all Good models on the battlefield suffer a -1 penalty to their Courage value (note that this is not cumulative with other rules that confer similar penalties).

The Drum can be shot at normally by the Good side, and it has Defence of 10 and 3 Wounds. If brought to 0 wounds, the model is destroyed – leave the Drum in place, but it cannot be played any more. The Drum model has no control zone and if a Good model spends a full turn in base contact with the drums without doing anything else (ie, not shooting, using magical powers or fighting in combat), the Drum is automatically destroyed as described above.

For the purpose of counting the total number of models in the Evil force, only the Drummers count and not the Drum itself.

THE WOODLAND REALMS

In the heart of the land of Rhovanion lies the forest of Mirkwood. In the closing years of the Third Age, Mirkwood, as its name would suggest, is a gloomy and haunted place that only few would dare enter. Those unused to the forest find it oppressive and hateful, thick with a dark and forbidding presence almost without equal, yet more physical threats lurk beneath its branches. Spiders of immense size and appetite spin vast webs between the moss-coated trees, Wargs prowl through the leafy glades and, in the darkest depths, fouler creatures yet wait to ensnare the unwary.

In contrast, the second great woodland realm, Lothlórien, has forever been kept free of Sauron's taint. Here a great Elven realm spans the spaces between the golden Mallorn trees, a sanctuary of peace and healing that can trace its history back to the very earliest of times. Lothlórien has endured the evils that have beset it through the secret strength that is hidden amongst its glades, for some of the greatest and noblest of

Elves dwell within. Most powerful of them all is the Lady Galadriel, kin to the very greatest of the Elves of old. Through the power she wields and that of the Elven ring she is the keeper of, Galadriel has proven a wise protector of her realm and a determined and canny opponent of the Dark Lord and all of his evil schemes.

The third, and final, of the great woodland realms is that of Fangorn, the oldest of all the forests of Middle-earth. When the lands were young, a much greater forest, of which the present day Fangorn is but a part, spread its branches across all of western Middle-earth, flourishing wherever the roots of its trees could draw sustenance. Now, only a few isolated woods remain, the Old Forest in the Shire for one, but Fangorn is by far the largest of these. The forest's name is Elvish in origin, and translates to Treebeard in the common tongue, so named for the eldest of the tree-shepherds, or Ents, that lives beneath its shade.

ENTS

The tree-shepherds of Fangorn are amongst the eldest of all creatures, second only to the Elves in the span of creation. Though Ents vary as much in appearance as the trees that they watch over, all stand many times the height of a man and at rest are commonly mistaken for trees themselves. Called to protect the forest in which they dwell, the numbers of the Ents have dwindled over the years, so now only a relative handful reside beneath Fangorn's boughs. Many more have become 'tree-ish', spending most of their time in slumber and waking only upon the rarest of occasions. Though the Ents mourn the decline of their forest, their greatest sadness is for the loss of the Entwives, who disappeared long ago. Their fate remains a mystery, yet the Ents will never stop searching for them until the world is still and cold.

GOOD HEROES

Galadriel   Points value: 130

	F	S	D	A	W	C	M/W/F
Galadriel	6/-	3	3	1	3	7	3 /6*/ 3

Wargear
Galadriel is unarmed and wears Nenya. At an additional cost she may be given her mirror, an enchanted item of great power.

   Mirror of Galadriel . . . .*25 pts*

Mirror of Galadriel. The visions the mirror shows change with each person, but are always relevant and heavy with much portent. The mirror is deployed within 6" of her at the start of the game – it may not subsequently be moved. At the end of each turn, one Good Hero within 6"/14cm of the mirror may recover their Fate to its starting value.

Nenya. Thanks to the power of Nenya, one of the three Elven rings, Galadriel can re-roll her dice when using Fate points.

* The Lady of Lothlórien. Galdriel may expend a single point of Will each turn without depleting her own store.

Special Rules
Lineage of the Firstborn; Woodland Creature. See page 94 for details

Magical Powers
Command. Range 12"/28cm. Dice score to use 4+.
Cast Blinding Light. Dice score to use: 2+.
Immobilise. Range 12"/28cm. Dice score to use: 3+.

Galadriel is a great sorceress, both mighty and terrifying. Wise beyond mortal measure, her powers are held in awe by lesser folk and her domain is closed to them. By the magics she wields through Nenya – the Mithril ring of adamant – Lothlórien is kept safe from the ravages of time and the assaults of the forces of Evil. So mindful is she of the threats to her realm that it is only due to their exceptional circumstance that the Fellowship are permitted to enter Lothlórien.

Celeborn   Points value: 130

	F	S	D	A	W	C	M/W/F
Celeborn	6/3+	4	4	3	3	7	3 / 3 / 3

Wargear
Celeborn is unarmed. He may have the following:

   Elven blade . . . .*5 pts*
   Heavy armour . . . .*10 pts*
   Shield . . . .*5 pts*

Special Rules
Lineage of the Firstborn; Woodland Creature.

Magical Powers
Immobilise. Range 12"/28cm. Dice score to use: 3+.
Aura of Command. Dice score to use: 2+.

Celeborn is one of eldest of the Elves of Middle-earth, wise and powerful almost beyond comparison. His words have often proved crucial in the councils of the Wise since the Last Alliance of Men and Elves.

Legolas

Points value: 90

	F	S	D	A	W	C	M/W/F
Legolas	6/3+	4	4	2	2	6	3 / 2 / 3

Wargear

Legolas carries two short blades (he counts as being armed with a single hand weapon) and an Elf bow. At an additional points cost, Legolas can be given the following:

Elven cloak . . . . .10 pts
Armour . . . . .5 pts
Horse . . . . .10 pts

Special Rules
Woodland Creature.

Deadly Shot. To reflect his prodigious skills at archery, Legolas is allowed to shoot his bow three times in the Shoot phase instead of once, hitting his targets normally on 3+. Alternatively, he can decide to fire just one arrow, but in this case he will hit automatically, regardless of objects 'in the way' or if the target is in combat.

Legolas is the son of the King of the Wood Elves and like all his people he is a deadly accurate and keen sighted archer. Of the Free Peoples, he represents the Elves as part of the Fellowship.

Haldir

Points value: 70

	F	S	D	A	W	C	M/W/F
Haldir	6/3+	4	4	2	2	6	3 / 1 / 1

Wargear

Haldir carries an Elven blade. At additional cost he can have the following:

Elf bow . . . . .5 pts
Elven cloak . . . . .10 pts
Armour . . . . .5 pts

Special Rules
Woodland Creature.

Expert Shot. Haldir is allowed to shoot his bow twice in the Shoot phase instead of once.

One of the guardians of the forest realm of Lothlórien, Haldir's faith in the alliance between Men and Elves was so great that he willingly led his warriors to stand side-by-side with the defenders of Helm's Deep.

Elven Captain

Points value: 65

	F	S	D	A	W	C	M/W/F
Elf Captain	6/3+	4	4	2	2	6	2 / 1 / 1

Wargear

The Elven Captain represented by this profile has an Elven blade. At an additional cost he may have the following:

Armour . . . . .5 pts
Elf bow . . . . .5 pts

Special Rule.
Woodland Creature.

We have included the option to have one or more Elven Captains as part of your force – note that you can include more than one if you wish. This represents the leaders amongst the Elves who go unnamed in the story of The Lord of The Rings.

Radagast the Brown (Wizard) Points value: 150

	F	S	D	A	W	C	M/W/F
Radagast	5/-	4	5	1	3	7	3 /6*/ 3

Wargear
Radagast carries his staff (two-handed weapon) and a sword (hand weapon). At an additional cost Radagast may have the following:

> Horse . . . . .10 pts

Special Rules
***Staff of Power.** Radagast's staff is not only a symbol of his authority but a potent talisman. To represent his staff's power, he can expend 1 point of Will each turn without reducing his own Will store.

Master of Birds. Radagast is frequently accompanied by a raven that acts as his eyes and ears. To represent the raven scouting the battlefield on his behalf, Radagast is always assumed to have line of sight to any point on the battlefield.

One with Nature. Radagast has a strong connection with nature and through his skills is able to blend with his surroundings and is used to travelling through all manner of terrain. To represent this, whilst on foot he may move through areas of difficult terrain without penalty and always counts as wearing an Elven cloak.

Magical Powers
Terrifying Aura. Dice score to use: 2+.

Immobilise. Range 12"/28cm. Dice score to use: 3+.

Renew. Range 12"/28cm. Dice score to use: 3+.

Panic Steed. Range 12"/28cm. Dice score to use: 2+.

Aura of Dismay. Dice score to use: 5+.

Living on the borders of Mirkwood, Radagast is a member of the Order of Wizards to which both Gandalf and Saruman belong. Less given to displays of power than his fellows, Radagast is a master of hues and shapes and his skill with the birds and beasts of Middle-earth is without equal. Although Saruman derides Radagast's abilities and has never held him in anything other than contempt, Radagast is a dedicated member of the White Council and Gandalf considers him a valuable ally.

Gwaihir (Great Eagle) Points value: 125

	F	S	D	A	W	C	M/W/F
	8/-	6	8	2	3	6	1 / 1 / 1

Special Rules
Fly. Gwaihir moves by flying – his move is 12"/28cm. The Giant Eagle can fly over the top of any models or terrain without penalty. He cannot enter woods, buildings and other terrain that has been deemed impassable, but can land on top of any of these if the players so agree at the beginning of the game. Because it is not possible to fly underground, Gwaihir cannot take part in any scenarios that take place in Moria or other subterranean area.

Terror. Great Eagles inspire Terror in the servants of Evil, as described in the Courage section of the rules.

Lord of the Eagles. Though Gwaihir is a great and noble creature, his keen intelligence is known only to a few. Only Great Eagles may use his Stand Fast! or benefit from his heroic actions.

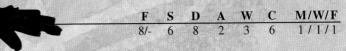

Whilst imprisoned in the Tower of Orthanc Gandalf sought Gwaihir's aid to make his escape. Riding upon the back of the huge eagle, Gandalf fled the clutches of Saruman.

Treebeard (Ent)   Points value: 190

	F	S	D	A	W	C	M/W/F
Treebeard	8/4+	8	8	3	3	7	3 / 6 / 3

Special Rules

Break Stone. Ents are powerful creatures with iron-hard limbs that can smash apart stone just as tree roots can crumble rock. When attacking fortifications, including doors, stone walls, towers and anything else that has Batter Points, Treebeard counts his Strength as 10 and Attacks as 6.

Terror. In their fury the Ents are a truly terrifying sight. Treebeard evokes terror in the enemy, as described in the Courage section of the rules.

Throw Stone. Ents are creatures of great strength, able to tear rocks out of the ground and hurl them across the battlefield with crushing force. To represent this, if an Ent does not move at all he can rip a suitable rock from the ground (provided he's not engaged in combat) and in the subsequent Shoot phase he can throw it. This works exactly like a crossbow with a range of 18"/42cm and a Strength of 10. If the Good player wishes, this rock can be hurled at a castle wall or other building. If this is the case, the Good player nominates a target point and rolls to hit and to wound as normal. If the shot causes sufficient damage to create a breach, the breach occurs at the point the shot was aimed at.

Woodland Creature.

Treebeard is the greatest of all the ancient race of Ents that roamed the forests of Middle-earth before even the Elves came and made their homes. Ents are giants that resemble nothing so much as trees, having lived for so many years in the forests and having become rather like the trees that they love. Ents care little for the world that is beyond the forest realm of Fangorn but the destruction of their beloved woodlands drives them into a raging fury of destruction.

GOOD WARRIORS

Great Eagle   Points value: 90

	F	S	D	A	W	C
Great Eagle	7/-	6	8	2	3	5

Special Rules
Fly; Terror. See the Gwaihir entry for details.

The Great Eagles of the Misty Mountains often hold themselves aloof from the problems of the world, but in times of dire need they will lend aid to those who require it.

Elf Warrior   Points value: 7

	F	S	D	A	W	C
Elf	5/3+	3	3	1	1	5

Wargear
The base profile for an Elf warrior does not include any equipment. He can be given additional items at the following cost:

Elven blade . . . .*1 pt*
Spear . . . .*1 pt*
Elf bow . . . .*2 pts*
Armour . . . .*1 pt*
Banner (up to one per Hero included in the same force) . . . . . .*35 pts*

Special Rule
Woodland Creature.

The Elves are the deadliest warriors in all of Middle-earth, combining skill-at-arms with expertly fashioned wargear. They are proficient with swords, spears and bows, and are the bravest of all fighting troops.

ROHAN

Rohan is a comparatively new kingdom of Men with a history of conflict, whether with the Dunlendings to the west or the Orcs within the White Mountains. Originally called Calenardhon, the starkly beautiful realm was gifted to the sons of Eorl and his folk in recognition of the great service that his people had done for Gondor in a time of peril, despite great hardships of their own. Eternal friendship between the two realms was pledged that day, a bond that would endure through hundreds of years and innumerable wars. Though lasting peace has ever been denied to them, the Rohirrim have always stood firm against the shadow of Sauron and an unflinching friend to Gondor.

Rohan is governed from Meduseld, the Golden Hall of Edoras, and even in the closing years of the Third Age, the line of its kings can be traced back to Eorl, each king as noble and bold as he. Below him serve the Marshals of the Riddermark, brave and canny warriors who captain of the Riders of Rohan, the finest horsemen in the known world. Indeed, the Horse-lords of Rohan are considered without peer, not only for their valour and prowess in battle, but also for their skills at breeding and training horses. The mounts of Rohan are swifter and more obedient than any to be found elsewhere in the kingdoms of Men, and much sought after in the neighbouring realms.

So prized are the horses of Rohan that even the servants of Sauron covet them. Indeed it is far from unusual for Orc raiding parties to launch attacks purely for the purpose of capturing steeds for their master. Such raids are always directed at black horses and provoke great ferocity from the Rohirrim, for the loss of a horse in this way is comparable to the abduction of a family member, so highly do the sons of Eorl regard their steeds.

HELM'S DEEP

One of the greatest Mannish bastions in all Middle-earth, Helm's Deep lies in western Rohan, a great fortress originally constructed when that land was still a province of Gondor. It is named for Helm Hammerhand, the ninth king of the Rohirrim, and arguably the greatest of all its rulers save for Eorl himself. The fortress itself is a mighty castle of cunning stonework, which no foe has taken whilst Men still defended its walls.

Such strength comes at a price; should the battle go ill, escape from Helm's Deep is almost impossible. The only route is one that threads its way through the Glittering Caves of Aglarond, a passage that offers neither safety nor speed. Fortunately, thus far the defenders of Helm's Deep have always prevailed and such a withdrawal has remained unnecessary. This is not remarkable for, in truth, it would take an army of uncommon size, or possessed of some sorcerous devilry, to breach the walls of Helm's Deep.

GOOD HEROES

Théoden, King of Rohan (Man) Points value: 60

	F	S	D	A	W	C	M/W/F
Théoden	5/-	4	4	2	2	5	2/0/2

Wargear
Théoden carries a sword. At an additional cost he may have the following:

Heavy armour . . . . .10 pts
Shield . . . . .5 pts
Horse . . . . .10 pts
Armoured horse . . . . .15 pts

Special Rules
Expert Rider. Models that are expert riders can re-roll the dice on the Jump chart when jumping an obstacle while mounted. In addition, when mounted they benefit from the +1 Defence from their shield even while carrying a bow. If they dismount or are thrown, they must immediately discard either their bow or their shield (in which case their Defence is reduced by 1 point).

Though now old and apparently frail, Théoden is still a great warrior at heart. He is the leader of the brave race of horsemen and doughty warriors that stands between the Tower of Orthanc and Gondor.

Éomer, Marshal of the Riddermark (Man) Points value: 75

	F	S	D	A	W	C	M/W/F
Éomer	5/4+	4	6	2	2	5	3/2/2

Wargear
Éomer carries a sword and has heavy armour. At an additional cost he may have the following:

Throwing spears . . . . .5 pts
Shield . . . . .5 pts
Bow . . . . .5 pts
Horse . . . . .10 pts

Special Rules
Expert Rider. See the rules for Théoden for details.

Éomer is the bravest and most gallant of all the Captains of Rohan – a realm under constant threat from the foul Orcs, Uruk-hai and Wild Men under the leadership of the evil Saruman.

Éowyn, Shield Maiden of Rohan (Woman) Points value: 30

	F	S	D	A	W	C	M/W/F
Éowyn	5/4+	3	3	1	1	5	2 / 2 / 2

Éowyn is the sister of Éomer and King Théoden's niece – and like her kin she is a born fighter. Unwilling to be left behind as her kin ride to battle in Gondor, she disguises herself as a man and joins the host of the Rohirrim.

Wargear

Éowyn has a sword. At an additional cost, she may have the following:

Throwing spears ....5 pts
Armour ....5 pts
Shield ....5 pts
Horse ....6 pts

Special Rules

Expert Rider. See the rules for Théoden for details.

Gamling is a gallant Captain of Rohan, the bearer of the Royal Standard who fights valiantly beside his lord at Helm's Deep.

Gamling, Captain of Rohan (Man)   Points value: 50

	F	S	D	A	W	C	M/W/F
Gamling	4/-	4	6	2	2	4	2 / 1 / 1

Wargear
Gamling carries a sword and wears heavy armour. At the additional points shown he can be given the following:

> *Royal Standard of Rohan* . . . .*50 pts*
> *Horse* . . . .*10 pts*

Special Rules
Expert Rider. See the rules for Théoden for details.

Royal Standard of Rohan. This precious heirloom counts as a normal banner. In addition, any Hero of Rohan who has 0 Might points at the start of the turn automatically adds 1 point Might to his store if he starts the turn within 3"/8cm of the Royal Standard of Rohan. This does not include Gamling himself.

We have presented the option for you include Captains of Rohan. Note that you can have more than one Captain of Rohan if you wish. This represents the leaders amongst the soldiery of Rohan such as Erkenbrand and Grimbold.

Captain of Rohan (Man)   Points value: 45

	F	S	D	A	W	C	M/W/F
Captain of Rohan	4/4+	4	5	2	2	4	2 / 1 / 1

Wargear
The Captain of Rohan represented by the profile has a sword and wears armour. At an additional cost he may have the following items:

> *Heavy armour* . . . .*5 pts*
> *Shield* . . . .*5 pts*
> *Bow* . . . .*5 pts*
> *Throwing spears* . . . .*5 pts*
> *Horse* . . . .*10 pts*

Special Rules
Expert Rider. See the rules for Théoden for details.

GOOD WARRIORS

The land of Rohan lies to the west of Minas Tirith and north of the White Mountains. Allies of Gondor since the earliest days of their realm, the Men of Rohan have ever been ready to go to their aid in time of war.

Warrior of Rohan (Man)   Points value: 6

	F	S	D	A	W	C
Warrior of Rohan	3/4+	3	4	1	1	3

Wargear
The base profile for a Rohan warrior includes armour and a sword or axe (hand weapon). Any warrior can be given additional items at the following extra cost:

Throwing spears . . . . .2 pts
Bow . . . . .1 pt
Shield . . . . .1 pt
Banner (up to one per Hero included in the same force) . . . . . .25 pts

Rider of Rohan (Man)   Points value: 13

	F	S	D	A	W	C
Rider of Rohan	3/4+	3	5	1	1	3
Horse	0	3	4	0	1	3

Wargear
The base profile for a Rider of Rohan includes armour, shield, a bow and either a sword or axe (hand weapon). Any warrior can be given the following:

Throwing spears . . . . .2 pts
Banner (up to one per Hero included in the same force) . . . . . . 25 pts

Special Rule
Expert Rider. See the rules for Théoden for details.

The Riders of Rohan are horse-masters beyond compare, renowned for their great skill and bravery.

Rohan Royal Guard (Man)   Points value: 10

	F	S	D	A	W	C
Royal Guard	4/4+	3	6	1	1	3

Wargear
The base profile for a Royal Guard includes heavy armour, shield and a sword (hand weapon). He can be given the following:

Throwing spears . . . . .2 pts
Horse . . . . .6 pts
Banner (up to one per Hero included in the same force) . . . . . .30 pts

Special Rules
Expert Rider. See the rules for Théoden for details.

Bodyguard. At the beginning of the game choose one Hero of Rohan among those in your force for all your Rohan Royal Guard to protect. As long as this Hero is on the table, the Royal Guard will automatically pass all Courage tests they have to take. If the Hero is killed or leaves the table, the Royal Guard reverts to the normal rules for Courage.

Hand-picked from the very best warriors in all of Rohan, the Royal Guard are sworn to give their lives in the service of their king and to fight without fear. They wear intricately crafted heavy armour and carry the best weaponry that the armouries of Rohan have to offer.

ISENGARD

Lying at the southern spur of the Misty Mountains, Isengard commands a position of great strategic importance, for to its south lies the Gap of Rohan, the only reliable passage from one side of the mountain range to the other. Isengard itself is a fortress of carefully crafted stone, built in the earliest years of Gondor's existence. At its centre stands the tower of Orthanc, a massive edifice of polished black stone, bound tight with sufficient magic to render it indestructible to physical assault. Though originally constructed as part of Gondor's western defences, Isengard is little mentioned in the histories, which would suggest it remained empty for much of the time.

The first notable resident of Isengard was the wizard Saruman the White. Doubtless, the kings of Rohan welcomed this, for they were often embattled and in Saruman they would have had a powerful ally. Though initially Saruman doubtless comported himself merely as a lieutenant in the service of Gondor, he soon became a power in his own right and, before long, threw off any pretence at subservience.

Over the following centuries, the White Wizard's thoughts turned more and more to possession of the One Ring. He began to add to Isengard's defences, recruiting to him an army of all manner of unruly creatures; wild men, Orcs, Uruk-hai, Warg Riders and Goblins. It was in this way that the fortress of Isengard became a threat ever-present upon Rohan's northern border, the caverns below Orthanc given over to the smithying of weapons and armour, the trees upon the mountainside felled and burnt to feed the furnaces of Saruman's army.

THE URUK-HAI

Amongst the most dangerous of all the servants of the dark powers in Middle-earth are the Uruk-hai, a savage race of Orcs who are stronger and immeasurably braver than their smaller cousins. Unusually, the histories of the West are unclear as to how and when these creatures first appeared. Some cite their first appearance at the fall of Osgiliath, whilst others maintain that the Uruk-hai were created by Saruman shortly before the War of the Ring. Of course, while it is true that Saruman created many half-breeds in the caverns beneath Orthanc, it is just as plausible that he was merely shadowing deeds performed by Sauron many centuries earlier.

Whatever the truth behind their creation the Uruk-hai are a force to be reckoned with, bred solely for war, vicious and near fearless. The only loyalty they know is to their master whose commands they carry out unflinchingly – a stark contrast to common Orcs who bicker once the whips are taken from their backs. Like some Trollish breeds, the Uruk-hai are bred to have an increased tolerance against sunlight for, while Orcs do not turn to stone as Trolls do, they are uncomfortable beneath the yellow eye and fight poorly while it is high in the sky. To the Uruk-hai, however, the sun is just another foe at which to snarl in defiance.

EVIL HEROES

Saruman (Wizard)   Points value: 170

	F	S	D	A	W	C	M/W/F
Saruman	5/-	4	5	1	3	7	3 /6*/ 3

Wargear
Saruman carries his staff (two-handed weapon) and a dagger. At an additional cost he may have the following items.

> Horse . . . .*10 pts*

Special Rules
* Staff of Power. Saruman's staff is not only a symbol of his power but a potent talisman. Whilst he wields his staff Saruman can expend 1 point of Will each turn without reducing his own Will store.

Voice of Command. Such is the fear of failure that Saruman inspires in his followers that they will often fight to the last man if his eye is upon them. To represent this, the range of Saruman's 'Stand Fast!' rule is 12"/28cm rather than 6"/14cm.

Palantir. Saruman carries the Palantir, an ancient seeing stone that allows him to spy upon his enemies and form his plans accordingly. Once per game, the Evil player may use the ability of the Palantir to automatically win a Priority roll – he must declare he is using this ability before any dice are rolled for priority.

Magical Powers
Terrifying Aura. Dice score to use: 2+.
Sorcerous Blast. Range 12"/28cm. Dice score to use: 5+.
Immobilise. Range 12"/28cm. Dice score to use: 2+.
Command. Range 12"/28cm. Dice score to use 3+.

Saruman the White is the leader of the Order of Wizards and the most learned in the ways of Sauron the Enemy. But his studies have led him to dream of dominion, and by daring to look into the dread Palantir of Orthanc he has seen many dark and evil things that have stirred his greed and ambition. Now he would dare rise and take even Sauron's crown, but the truth is that his soul is already in thrall to the Evil lord.

Lurtz, Uruk-hai Captain   Points value: 60

	F	S	D	A	W	C	M/W/F
Lurtz	5/4+	5	5	2	2	4	3 / 1 / 1

Wargear
Lurtz is equipped with a sword (hand weapon), armour, shield and an Orc bow.

Amongst a brutal race, Lurtz is a brutal leader, careless of the lives of his warriors, hungry for the blood of his foes. Untiring and determined, Lurtz is a foe to be feared.

Gríma is the treacherous counsellor of King Théoden. Unknown to the King, Gríma is secretly in league with Saruman and has been using every means at his disposal to turn Théoden's mind against his allies. Not only is Gríma a cunning and persuasive advisor, he has poisons, potions and the sorcerous assistance of Saruman from afar to further his evil.

Gríma Wormtongue (Man)   Points value: 25

	F	S	D	A	W	C	M/W/F
Gríma	2/-	3	3	1	1	2	0 / 0 / 0

Wargear
Gríma is armed with a dagger. At an additional cost he may have the following items.

    Horse . . . .*10 pts*

Special Rules
Gríma can be included in the Evil player's force only if Saruman is also included.

Regardless of the scenario you are playing, Gríma is always placed on the table once both sides have placed all their other models. He can be placed in either the Evil side's deployment zone or the Good side's deployment zone.

So long as Saruman is alive no Good model can shoot at or strike blows against Gríma. Good models are allowed to charge Gríma and fight, but will strike no blows if they win because they do not wish to kill Gríma but only to restrain him (being Good can be a pain sometimes you see!).

This restriction ceases to apply if Saruman is slain, if Gríma charges a Good model or if Gríma scores a wound with his dagger (even if the wound is then avoided with Fate). Note that Gríma can decide not to strike blows if he wins a combat in order not to reveal his real allegiance. Once one of these conditions is met, the depth of Gríma's evil is revealed and Gríma becomes an enemy who can be shot and fought in the same way as any other enemy model.

Gríma is always controlled by the Evil player and is moved and fights when it is the Evil side's turn to do so as usual. Although he can fight he isn't very good at it (he's far too sneaky and grovelly) and his chief power is his ability to debilitate enemy Heroes by his endless whining, thereby spreading doubt and misery amongst his foes. This is represented by reducing the effect of Might. If a Good Hero is within 6"/14cm of Gríma then 2 Might points must be expended to modify dice scores or use Heroic abilities instead of 1. As can be readily imagined this is a very powerful ability, and the Good player must try to occupy Gríma and prevent him from using his power to sap the fighting power of the Good Heroes.

Note. For reasons impossible to fathom Gríma is always more effective if the Evil player actually makes an effort to offer bad advice and make pessimistic forecasts of doom to his victims as he follows them about the battlefield.

Uruk-hai Shaman   Points value: 50

	F	S	D	A	W	C	M/W/F
Uruk-hai Shaman	4/-	4	4	1	2	4	1 / 3 / 1

Wargear
The Uruk-hai Shaman represented by the profile has a spear.

Magical Powers
Fury. Range 6"/14cm. Dice score to use: 3+.

Transfix. Range 12"/28cm. Dice score to use: 5+.

The Shamans of the Fighting Uruk-hai normally accompany bands of Uruk-hai on raiding missions and in larger fights, making the presence of Saruman felt at all times through their powers and ensuring that the orders of their master are carried out to the letter.

Sharku, Warg Rider Captain (Orc)   Points value: 55

	F	S	D	A	W	C	M/W/F
Sharku	4/-	4	5	2	2	3	3 / 1 / 1
Warg	3/-	4	4	1	1	2	

Wargear
Sharku wears armour, has an Orc blade (hand weapon) and rides a Warg. At an extra cost he may have the following:

Shield . . . .*5 pts*

Sharku is the chief amongst the Warg Riders, and the boldest of all that murderous horde.

Uruk-hai Captain   Points value: 50

	F	S	D	A	W	C	M/W/F
Uruk-hai Captain	5/4+	5	5	2	2	4	2 / 1 / 1

Wargear
The Uruk-hai Captain represented by the profile has a sword and armour. At an additional cost he may have the following items.

Heavy armour . . . .*5 pts*
Shield . . . .*5 pts*
Two-handed weapon . . . .*5 pts*
Orc bow . . . .*5 pts*
Crossbow . . . .*5 pts*

We have presented the option for you include Uruk-hai Captains. Note that you can have more than one Uruk-hai Captains if you wish. This represents the leaders amongst the soldiery of Isengard and Saruman's domains.

Wild Men Chieftain   Points value: 40

	F	S	D	A	W	C	M/W/F
Wild Men Chieftain	4/-	4	4	2	2	4	2 / 1 / 1

A Wild Men Chieftain carries a crude sword (hand weapon). At an extra cost he may have the following:

Two-handed axe . . . .*5 pts*

The Wild Men of Dunland live upon the borders of Rohan. Like all their kind, the chieftains of the Dunlendings envy and hate the King of Rohan and all his subjects – and are all too ready to take up arms in Saruman's cause to destroy Rohan!

EVIL WARRIORS

Uruk-hai Scout   Points value: 8

	F	S	D	A	W	C
Uruk-hai Scout	4/4+	4	4	1	1	3

Wargear
The base profile for an Uruk-hai Scout includes armour and a hand weapon. Any warrior can be given extra items for the following:

    Orc bow . . . . .1 pt
    Shield . . . . .1 pt
    Banner (up to one per Hero included in the same force) . . . . . .30 pts

The eyes and ears of Saruman's army, the Uruk-hai scouts travel swiftly over all manner of terrain and in all weathers. They also double as hunters, overwhelming any enemy unfortunate enough to encounter them.

Uruk-hai Warrior   Points value: 9

	F	S	D	A	W	C
Uruk-hai	4/4+	4	5	1	1	3

Wargear
The base profile for an Uruk-hai warrior includes heavy armour and a sword. Any warrior can be given extra items for the following:

    Shield . . . . .1 pt
    Pike . . . . .1 pt
    Crossbow . . . . .2 pts
    Banner (up to one per Hero included in the same force) . . . . . .30 pts

The bulk of Saruman's legions are composed of these deadly and savage warriors, clad in plate armour and armed with vicious pikes and powerful crossbows.

Uruk-hai Berserker   Points value: 15

	F	S	D	A	W	C
Berserker	4/-	4	6	2	1	7

Wargear
The Berserker carries a two-handed sword.

Berserkers are the most dangerous of all Uruk-hai; fearless, caring nothing for their own lives, and armed with deadly swords almost as tall as themselves.

Orc Warrior   Points value: 5

	F	S	D	A	W	C
Orc	3/5+	3	4	1	1	2

Wargear
The base profile for an Orc warrior includes crude Orc armour and a hand weapon. Any warrior can be given additional items at the following cost:

    Two-handed sword/axe . . . . .1 pt
    Spear . . . . .1 pt
    Orc bow . . . . .1 pt
    Shield . . . . .1 pt
    Banner (up to one per Hero included in the same force) . . . . . .25 pts

Though he relies upon his Uruk-hai to conduct the bulk of his campaign, Saruman also employs a considerable number of Orcs to support the Uruk-hai in battle.

The Dunlendings, dwellers of the bleak uplands of Dunland, are savage tribesmen who for years have envied the bountiful lands of the Rohirrim.

Wild Men of Dunland   Points value: 5

	F	S	D	A	W	C
Wild Man	3/-	3	3	1	1	3

Wargear

The base profile for a Dunlending warrior includes a sword. At an extra cost he may have the following:

Two-handed axe . . . .*1 pt*

Wargs are gigantic, evil wolves – massive and dangerous creatures with a cunning and carnivorous intelligence. Warg Riders scout far ahead of the main armies of Orcs and other evil creatures, spying out the land and picking off stragglers for interrogation or some far worse fate.

Warg Rider (Orc)   Points value: 12

	F	S	D	A	W	C
Warg Rider	3/5+	3	4	1	1	2
Warg	3/-	4	4	1	1	2

Wargear

The base profile for a Warg Rider includes armour and a hand weapon. Any warrior can be given additional items at the following extra cost.

Throwing spears . . . .*2 pt*
Orc bow . . . .*1 pt*
Shield . . . .*1 pt*
Banner (up to one per Hero included in the same force) . . . . . .*25 pts*

Special Rules

Crude Throwing Spears. The throwing spears carried by the Warg Riders are so heavy and primitive that they can only be used from atop a Warg, so if a Warg Rider dismounts or is thrown, he must immediately discard his throwing spear.

Saruman's devilry has created a primitive explosive charge, able to destroy walls and fortifications as easily as it burns and ruins flesh.

Uruk-hai Demolition Team   80 points

	F	S	D	A	W	C
Demolition charge	-	-	7	-	3	-
Uruk-hai Engineer	4/4+	4	5	1	1	3
Uruk-hai Berserker	4/-	4	6	2	1	8

Crew

An Uruk-hai Demolition Team consists of one demolition charge, one Uruk-hai Berserker armed with a two-handed sword and a flaming brand, and two Uruk-hai Engineers armed with hand weapons. The Uruk-hai Engineers can carry a flaming brand at the following points cost.

Flaming brand . . . .*1 pt*

Special Rules

Flaming Brands. The Uruk-hai accompanying demolition charges can be given flaming brands to assist them in lighting the powder. Uruk-hai warriors equipped in this way cannot be given shields – they need a hand free to carry the brand. Similarly, an Uruk-hai Berserker carrying a flaming brand may not use his sword as a two-handed weapon. They otherwise suffer no penalty. If a model carrying a flaming brand is killed, the brand is extinguished and lost in the chaos of battle.

Alchemical Fury. The demolition charge, as its names suggests, is designed to explode in a burst of heat and flame. See page 65 for details.

In order to raise their ladders more quickly and secure them tightly against the enemy's walls, the Uruk-hai employ a unique engine of war that hurls a massive grapple at the foe's battlements.

Uruk-hai Siege Assault Ballista   65 points

	Strength	Defence	Batter Points
Assault Ballista	(9)	10	4

	F	S	D	A	W	C
White Hand Uruk-hai	4/4+	4	5	1	1	3

Crew

An Uruk-hai Siege Assault Ballista consists of an Assault Ballista and three White Hand Uruk-hai crew armed with daggers and wearing armour. Extra crew can be added at additional cost:

White Hand Uruk-hai crew . . . .*10 pts each*

Special Rules

Raise the Ladders! The Assault Ballista can attempt to raise a ladder to the enemy battlements during the Shoot phase. To do this, the player must first nominate a point on the battlements within range and which at least one crew member and the machine have line of sight to. Roll to hit as usual – if a hit is scored, the grapple has struck home; if the machine misses, there is no further effect. When the grappling hook hits, a single siege ladder within 6"/14cm of the wall base below the target point is moved forward to the wall and raised immediately. All ladder carriers drop their ladder as it is raised. Any one of the carriers can grab the top of the ladder and ride to the top as it ascends. The warrior is then treated exactly as if he had climbed to the top of the ladder that turn.

Piercing Shot. If shooting at a Battlefield target, the missile can conceivably hit several enemies. The target model is struck one blow at the Strength of the Siege Engine, is knocked to the ground, and is flung 2D6"/4D6cm directly away from it. Except as noted below, any other models that lie within the path of the victim suffer a single Strength 6 hit and are knocked to the ground if they have Strength 5 or less. If the propelled model hits an obtacle or Siege target, it immediately stops and inflicts a single Strength 6 upon it.

Upgrades

An Uruk-hai Siege Assault Ballista may be given the following upgrade at additional cost (see page 68 for details).

Flaming Ammunition . . . .*10 pts*
Superior Construction . . . .*15 pts*
Uruk-hai Engineer Captain . . . .*85 pts*

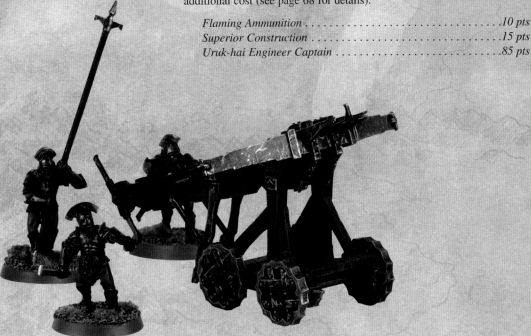

GONDOR

Without doubt the greatest of the Mannish realms of recent history, Gondor stands like a bulwark between Mordor and the rest of the Free world. With every day that passes, it is through the unceasing vigilance and strength of arms that rests within Gondor that peace is bought for many other lands. Such defiance has not been without price, a toll heavily exacted in blood and despair over many long centuries, and Gondor's folk have begun to dwindle while Sauron's forces seem to endlessly replenish their losses.

In these later years, it is from Minas Tirith that the heirs of Anarion, and later the Stewards, have ruled the realm of Gondor. As the last line of Gondor's defence, the Citadel of Minas Tirith is guarded by the finest warriors that Gondor has to offer, tall and mighty warriors in whom the blood of Númenor stills pulses true. It is here, in a small court overshadowed by the Tower of Ecthelion, that the White Tree of Minas Tirith once grew. Its line, like the line of kings, was thought eternal. As time passed, the line of kings all but died out, and so too did the line of the White Tree fail. Now all that stands in the fountain court is a withered husk, a symbol of the early glory of Gondor long since faded.

In the shadow of the White Mountains lie Gondor's fiefs, lesser regions who govern themselves, yet kneel before the throne of Minas Tirith. Arguably the greatest of these is Dol Amroth, the city of the Swan Knights whose name is given for an Elven king long ago lost in the churning seas, yet the other fiefs have traditions and legends all of their own. In Lamedon, tales are told of the Shadow-men who gather deep in Morthond vale, their purpose in this life not yet spent though centuries may pass them by, while the folk of Lossarnach hold their duty to Minas Tirith and Gondor above all else.

THE LAST ALLIANCE

When first the realms of Gondor and Arnor were founded, Sauron hid himself in Mordor, brought low by a previous defeat. Yet the Dark Lord hated the Men of Gondor, descended as they were from the line of Númenor and, in his hatred, Sauron struck against Gondor too soon. Unready though he was, the Lord of Mordor commanded a formidable army, and his will would have prevailed, and Gondor destroyed, but for the intervention of the Elves. The High King of the Elves, Gil-galad, brought his people into the battle against Sauron. Men and Elves fought alongside one another in an echo of earlier days, and many bold deeds and heroic acts were performed. The war, this Last Alliance of Men and Elves, was to last more than seven years and was fought across much of Middle-earth. Before long it had grown into a conflict that touched upon all races, and no realm was left isolated from the strife that had begun along the Anduin. In the final battle on the slopes of Mount Doom, Sauron was cast down – though it cost the lives of many, including those of Gil-galad and Elendil. Alas, Sauron endured through the power of the Ruling Ring he had forged and so did not pass from this life, yet his power was broken for a long while.

GOOD HEROES

Aragorn, King Elessar (Man)   Points value: 260

	F	S	D	A	W	C	M/W/F
Aragorn	6/3+	4	7	3	3	6	3*/ 3 / 3

Note: Your force can only include one Aragorn, either Elessar or Strider.

Wargear

Aragorn carries Andúril (see below) and wears heavy armour. At an additional points cost he can be given the following:

> Armoured horse . . . .*15 pts*

Andúril, Flame of the West. This magical blade has been re-forged by the smiths of Rivendell using the fragments of Narsil, the sword of Elendil. When fighting with Andúril, Aragorn never needs to roll more than 4+ to score a wound, regardless of the opponent's Defence (this rule has no effect against targets that have Batter Points instead of Wounds). His rolls to wound can be modified by using Might as normal.

Special Rules

* Mighty Hero. Aragorn is a mighty hero – the heir of the Kings of Gondor. He may expend 1 point of Might per turn without reducing his Might store. Any additional points of Might expended during his turn will reduce his Might store as normal.

The King of Gondor has finally returned to his people after many centuries, but he must immediately leave his capital on a desperate mission, an apparently suicidal attack on Mordor itself. Not many know that this is a willing heroic sacrifice in order to distract Sauron from the two Hobbbits that are slowly and painfully making their way towards Mount Doom and the destruction of the Ring.

Boromir, Captain of the White Tower (Man)   Points value: 175

	F	S	D	A	W	C	M/W/F
Boromir	6/-	4	6	3	3	6	6 / 3 / 3

Note: Your force can only include one Boromir, either Boromir of Gondor or Boromir, Captain of the White Tower. This profile represents Boromir at his peak, before the Ring cast its influence upon him at the Council of Elrond.

Wargear.

Boromir, Captain of the White Tower carries a sword, the Horn of Gondor, and wears heavy armour. He can be given the following items at additional cost:

> Horse . . . .*10 pts*
> Lance . . . .*5 pts*
> Shield . . . .*5 pts*
> The Banner of Minas Tirith . . . .*50 pts*

Special Rules

The Horn of Gondor. See Boromir of Gondor.

The Banner of Minas Tirith. When held aloft by Boromir, the Banner of Minas Tirith inspires such valour in the Men of Gondor that they fight with renewed skill and vigour. The Banner of Minas Tirith counts as a banner. In addition, if Boromir carries the Banner of Minas Tirith, all Warriors of the realm of Gondor within 3"/8cm receive a +1 bonus to their Fight value. Boromir also receives this bonus, although other Heroes do not. Unlike other banner bearers, such is Boromir's skill in battle he receives no -1 penalty to his dice roll when determining who wins the combat, although he may not also carry a shield or lance.

Boromir, son of Denethor, is Gondor's boldest and most able commander, a master of all the skills of a warrior. As Denethor's heir, Boromir's life has been guided towards the distant day where he will ascend to the stewardship of Gondor, a position that has been held by his family for thousands of years. Wherever he fights, efforts are redoubled, strength rekindled and victory snatched from the very pits of despair – for his fearlessness inspires the people of Gondor, and his voice is able to rally them against the direst threat.

Boromir of Gondor (Man)   Points value: 105

	F	S	D	A	W	C	M/W/F
Boromir	6/-	4	6	3	3	6	6 / 1 / 0

Wargear
Boromir wears armour and carries a sword (hand weapon), a shield and the Horn of Gondor. At an additional points cost he can be given the following:

Elven cloak . . . .*10 pts*
Horse . . . .*10 pts*

The Horn of Gondor. The blast of Boromir's fearsome horn is enough to drain the bravest foe of resolve. Boromir can blow the horn at the start of a fight if he is outnumbered by two to one or more. The enemy combatant with the highest Courage must take a Courage test. If this is passed the combat is fought as normal. If the test is failed Boromir automatically wins the fight and can strike blows against his enemies.

Boromir was a mighty warrior and the son of Denethor, Steward of Gondor. His forefathers ruled Gondor since the long past days of the Kings, protecting the lands of Middle-earth against the evil of Mordor. Boromir was the greatest warrior of the entire Fellowship yet his will was fatally weak and his doubts about their quest almost destroyed its chances of success.

Denethor, Steward of Gondor (Man)   Points value: 30

	F	S	D	A	W	C	M/W/F
Denethor	5/-	4	5	2	2	5	0 / 3 / 0

Wargear
Denethor carries a sword and wears armour.

Special Rule
Broken Mind. Denethor is subject to dangerous fits of madness. At the start of every turn, before players roll for priority, the Good player must take a Courage test for Denethor. If the test is passed, all is fine. If the test is failed, Denethor is controlled by the Evil player as if he was one of his models. The only difference with other Evil models is that Good models cannot target Denethor with missile fire, magical powers that cause damage and cannot strike blows against him if they defeat him in a fight.

Once a great man, the Steward of Gondor is now weary with the responsibility of leading his people during such dark times. The loss of his favourite son Boromir, upon whom the old man had placed what little hope he had left, has proven an almost unbearable pain, seriously threatening the health of Denethor's mind.

Faramir, Captain of Gondor (Man)   Points value: 70

	F	S	D	A	W	C	M/W/F
Faramir	5/3+	4	5	2	2	5	3 / 2 / 2

Wargear
He carries a sword and wears sturdy leather armour. At an additional cost he may have the following items:

Heavy armour . . . .*5 pts*
Bow . . . .*5 pts*
Lance . . . .*5 pts*
Horse . . . .*10 pts*

Faramir is the son of the Steward of Gondor and the younger brother of Boromir – he is also a brave warrior and the leader of the Rangers of Gondor in the disputed border city of Osgiliath. His men are expert forest fighters who are able to merge into and move amongst the undergrowth undetected, ambushing enemy columns and putting the foe to flight with clouds of well-aimed arrows.

After his cataclysmic battle with the Balrog, Gandalf returns to Middle-earth in the new guise of Gandalf the White. Now his powers are greater than ever before, surpassing even his old master Saruman.

Gandalf the White (Wizard)   Points value: 220

	F	S	D	A	W	C	M/W/F
Gandalf	5/-	4	5	1	3	7	3 /6*/ 3

Note: Your force can only include one Gandalf; Gandalf the Grey or Gandalf the White.

Wargear
Gandalf carries his staff (two-handed weapon), the sword Glamdring (hand weapon) and the ring Narya. At an additional cost, he may have the following:

    Elven cloak . . . . .10 pts
    Shadowfax (see Gandalf the Grey) . . . . .15 pts

Special Rules
* Staff of Power; Narya; Glamdring. See Gandalf the Grey on page 78.

The White Rider. When Gandalf unveils his inner light, his presence is enough to steel the resolve of the Good warriors around him. The range of Gandalf's 'Stand Fast!' rule is 12"/28cm rather than 6"/14cm.

Magical Powers
Cast Blinding Light. Dice score to use: 2+.
Command. Range 12"/28cm. Dice score to use 3+.
Immobilise. Range 12"/28cm. Dice score to use: 2+.
Sorcerous Blast. Range 12"/28cm. Dice score to use: 4+.
Strengthen Will. Range 12"/28cm. Dice score to use: 3+.
Terrifying Aura. Dice score to use: 2+.
Your Staff is Broken! Range 12"/28cm. Dice score to use: 3+.

Beregond is a noble and honest man, possessed of an unshakeable honour and a sturdy sword arm. He was promoted to the Citadel Guard after many years of dedicated service on both sides of the Anduin with the Rangers of Ithilien.

Beregond of Gondor (Man)   Points value: 25

	F	S	D	A	W	C	M/W/F
Beregond	4/3+	4	6	1	1	4	1 / 1 / 1

Wargear
Beregond carries a hand weapon, a longbow (counts as an Elf bow) and wears heavy armour. He can be given a horse at additional cost:

    Horse . . . . .6 pts

Special Rule
Bodyguard. At the beginning of the game choose one Hero of Gondor among those in your force for Beregond to protect. As long as this Hero is on the table, Beregond will automatically pass all Courage tests he has to take. If the Hero is killed or leaves the table, Beregond reverts to the normal rules for Courage.

Descended from the nobles of Númenor in an almost true line, Prince Imrahil is the Lord of Dol Amroth. Through times both fair and foul, he has a commanding presence and unparalleled loyalty to the ruling line of Gondor.

Prince Imrahil of Dol Amroth (Man)   Points value: 135

	F	S	D	A	W	C	M/W/F
Imrahil	6/-	4	7	3	3	6	3 / 3 / 3

Wargear
Imrahil carries a sword and shield, and wears heavy armour. He can be given the following items at additional cost:

    Armoured Horse . . . . .15 pts
    Lance . . . . .5 pts

Special Rules
The Lineage of Númenor. Imrahil commands great respect and loyalty from all the free folk of Middle-earth. The range of Prince Imrahil's Stand Fast! is 12"/28cm rather than 6"/14cm.

We have included the option for you to have one or more Captains of Gondor. This represents the leaders amongst the soldiery of Gondor who go unnamed in The Lord of The Rings.

Captain of Minas Tirith (Man) — Points value: 50

	F	S	D	A	W	C	M/W/F
Captain of Men	4/4+	4	6	2	2	4	2 / 1 / 1

Wargear

The Captain of Gondor represented by the profile has a sword and heavy armour. At an additional cost he may have the following items:

Shield . . . .*5 pts*
Bow . . . .*5 pts*
Lance . . . .*5 pts*
Horse . . . .*10 pts*

Damrod is Faramir's trusted right-hand man – a strong arm in a fight and deadly shot with a bow.

Damrod, Ranger of Ithilien (Man) — Points value: 20

	F	S	D	A	W	C	M/W/F
Damrod	4/3+	4	5	1	1	4	1 / 1 / 1

Wargear

Damrod carries a bow and sword, and wears sturdy leather armour.

There are many Kings in Gondor's history – great men who ruled one of the noblest realms in all history.

King of Men — Points value: 55

	F	S	D	A	W	C	M/W/F
King of Men	5/4+	4	4	2	2	5	2 / 2 / 1

Wargear

Kings of Men carry swords. At additional cost they may be given the following equipment:

Armour . . . .*5 pts*
Heavy armour . . . .*10 pts*
Shield . . . .*5 pts*
Horse . . . .*10 pts*
Lance . . . .*5 pts*
Armoured Horse . . . .*15 pts*

We have included the option for you to have one or more Captains of Dol Amroth. This represents the leaders amongst the soldiery of Dol Amroth who go unnamed in The Lord of The Rings.

Captain of Dol Amroth (Man) — Points value: 55

	F	S	D	A	W	C	M/W/F
Captain of Men	4/4+	4	7	2	2	4	2 / 1 / 1

Wargear

The Captain of Dol Amroth represented by the profile has heavy armour, shield and a sword. At an additional cost he may have the following items:

Lance . . . .*5 pts*
Armoured Horse . . . .*15 pts*

Special Rules

Dol Amroth for Gondor! The Captains of Dol Amroth are fantastically skilled fighters, proud of their skills and of their prince – they are the elite warriors of Gondor, and they know it. To represent this, Captains of Dol Amroth always count as being within the area of effect of a banner if Prince Imrahil is within 12"/28cm.

GOOD WARRIORS

Warrior of Minas Tirith (Man)   Points value: 7

	F	S	D	A	W	C
Warrior of Minas Tirith	3/4+	3	5	1	1	3

Wargear

The base profile for a Warrior includes heavy armour and a sword (hand weapon). Any warrior can be given additional items at the following extra cost:

Spear . . . .*1 pt*
Bow . . . .*1 pt*
Shield . . . .*1 pt*
Banner (up to one per Hero included in the same force) . . . . . .*25 pts*

The men of Minas Tirith have lived their whole lives under the shadow in the east, never faltering. It is through their valour that the lands beyond Gondor have been kept safe from Sauron's armies.

Ranger of Gondor (Man)   Points value: 8

	F	S	D	A	W	C
Ranger of Gondor	4/3+	3	4	1	1	3

Wargear

The base profile for a Ranger of Gondor includes a sword (hand weapon), a bow and tough leather armour. Any warrior can be given additional items at the following extra cost:

Spear . . . .*1 pt*

The Rangers of Gondor are hand-picked from the inhabitants of Ithilien for their skill at woodcraft and archery, and are the first line of defence against the hordes of Mordor, holding the crossings of the Anduin against the servants of Sauron.

Tall, stern warriors mounted on swift steeds and bearing keen lances, the Knights of Minas Tirith are truly the pride of Gondor.

Knight of Minas Tirith (Man)   Points value: 13

	F	S	D	A	W	C
Knight of Minas Tirith	3/-	3	5	1	1	3
Horse	0	3	4	0	1	3

Wargear

The base profile for a Knight of Minas Tirith includes heavy armour, a lance and a sword (hand weapon). Any warrior can be given extra items at the following cost:

Banner (up to one per Hero included in the same force) . . . . . .*25 pts*

The Guard of the Fountain Court are selected from the very best warriors in all of Gondor, swearing to give their lives in service to the lords of Minas Tirith and to be fearless in combat.

Guard of the Fountain Court (Man)   Points value: 10

	F	S	D	A	W	C
Guard of the Fountain Court	4/-	3	6	1	1	3

Wargear

The base profile for a Guard includes intricately crafted heavy armour and a spear. Any warrior can be given additional items at the following cost:

Shield . . . .*1 pt*
Banner (up to one per Hero included in the same force) . . . . . .*30 pts*

Special Rules

Bodyguard. At the beginning of the game, choose one Hero of Gondor among those in your force for the Guard to protect. As long as this Hero is on the table, all Guard models automatically pass all Courage tests they have to take. If the Hero is killed or leaves the table, the Guard revert to the normal rules for Courage.

Founded as an order of elite guards answerable only to the king of Gondor, the Citadel Guard are one of the earliest institutions of the kingdom.

Citadel Guard (Man)   Points value: 8

	F	S	D	A	W	C
Citadel Guard	4/4+	3	5	1	1	3

Wargear

A Citadel Guard carries a sword and wears heavy armour. Any warrior can be given the following items at additional cost:

Horse . . . .*6 pts*
Longbow (counts as Elven bow) . . . .*2 pts*
Spear . . . .*1 pt*

Special Rule

Bodyguard. See the guard of the Fountain Court entry for details.

The tall Swan Knights of Dol Amroth are the very elite of the warriors of Gondor, fair and stern of aspect and peerless upon the field of battle, an echo of days long ago lost.

Knight of Dol Amroth (Man)   Points value: 9

	F	S	D	A	W	C
Knight	4/-	3	6	1	1	4

Wargear

A Knight of Dol Amroth carries a hand weapon and shield, and wears finely crafted heavy armour. He can be given the following items at additional cost:

Armoured Horse . . . .*9 pts*
Lance . . . .*1 pt*
Banner (up to one per Hero included in the same force) . . . . . .*30 pts*

Special Rules

Dol Amroth for Gondor! The Captains of Dol Amroth are fantastically skilled fighters, proud of their skills and of their prince – they are the elite warriors of Gondor, and they know it. To represent this, Captains of Dol Amroth always count as being within the area of effect of a banner if Prince Imrahil is within 12"/28cm.

The Avenger is an invention unique to Minas Tirith, a mechanical masterpiece that reloads itself even as it is fired. This efficiency enables the crew of an Avenger to fire many shots in the same space of time that another Engine could fire a single shot.

Avenger Bolt Thrower

Points value: 70

	Strength	Defence	Batter Points
Avenger	(7)	10	3

	F	S	D	A	W	C
Gondor Crewman	3/4+	3	5	1	1	3

Crew

An Avenger Bolt Thrower consists of an Avenger Bolt Thrower and two Gondor crewmen armed with hand weapons and wearing heavy armour. Extra crew can be added at additional cost:

Gondor Crewman . . . . *7 pts each*

Special Rules

Short Range. An Avenger Bolt Thrower has a Range of 24"/56cm rather than the normal 48"/112cm.

Rapid Fire. An Avenger Bolt Thrower fires D6 shots each turn rather than one. Resolve each shot individually, rolling to hit, to scatter, and to wound for each before proceeding with the next. Shots from an Avenger Bolt Thrower do not kill Battlefield targets outright nor knock them to the ground. The usual restrictions on targeting apply. In addition, the second and following shots must be targeted at models within 3"/8cm of the first target.

Accurate. These machines are easier to aim than catapults and other heavy Siege Engines. When firing an Avenger at a Battlefield target the shot will only Scatter 3"/8cm rather than 6"/14cm.

Upgrades

A Bolt Thrower may be given the following upgrades at additional cost (see page 68 for details).

Flaming Ammunition . . . . *15 pts*
Siege Veterans . . . . *15 pts*
Swift Reload . . . . *20 pts*
Minas Tirith Engineer Captain . . . . *75 pts*

The Battlecry Trebuchet flings a huge boulder at the target with terrifying speed, splintering defences and crushing warriors. Though relatively slow to aim and difficult to build, the Battlecry Trebuchet is a machine of frightening power.

Battlecry Trebuchet   Points value: 110

	Strength	Defence	Batter Points
Battlecry	(10)	10	4

	F	S	D	A	W	C
Gondor Crewman	3/4+	3	5	1	1	3

Crew
A Battlecry Trebuchet consists of a Trebuchet and three Gondor crewmen armed with swords and wearing heavy armour. Extra crew can be added at the following cost:

Gondor Crewman . . . . *7 pts each*

Special Rules
Indirect Fire. A Trebuchet always follows the rules for Volley Fire, giving it a range of 18-96"/42-224cm. When firing a Trebuchet, follow the rules on page 45, with the following exceptions. A Trebuchet hits the target on the roll of a 4+ rather than a 6. If a hit is rolled and the target is a Siege target, the shot will hit it automatically (no scattering). If the target is a Battlefield target, roll on the Siege Engines' Scatter chart instead of following the normal rules for allocating hits with a volley.

Area Effect. Trebuchets fire a large stone that shatters on impact, hurling out a wave of debris that is often as deadly as the main projectile. If the Trebuchet scores a hit against a Battlefield target, all models within 2"/4cm of the target take a hit of Strength 5 (this hit does not kill Battlefield targets outright).

Wall-breaker. When a Trebuchet rolls to wound against a Siege target, the controlling player may roll two dice and pick the highest. If a wound is caused, roll on the Batter chart as normal.

Upgrades
A Trebuchet may be given the following upgrades at additional cost (see page 68 for details).

Flaming Ammunition . . . . *15 pts*
Siege Veterans . . . . *15 pts*
Superior Construction . . . . *20 pts*
Minas Tirith Engineer Captain . . . . *75 pts*

MEN OF NÚMENOR
GOOD HEROES

Elendil (Man)   Points value: 165

	F	S	D	A	W	C	M/W/F
Elendil	7/-	4	7	3	3	6	3 / 3 / 1

High King of the Dúnedain and of Gondor, Elendil led his people to Middle-earth where he met and befriended Gil-galad. Elendil's ultimate destiny was to fall before Sauron's might.

Note: *Elendil is a mighty Hero who was slain during the Second Age – he does not appear later in the story arc and should not feature in scenarios set in the Third Age.*

Wargear
Elendil wears finely crafted heavy armour and carries the sword Narsil. At an additional cost he may have the following items:

> Shield . . . .*5 pts*
> Horse . . . .*10 pts*

Narsil. Narsil is a potent blade. Its powers allow Elendil to fight a heroic combat in the Fight phase without expending Might to do so. See page 39 for rules for heroic combats.

Isildur (Man)   Points value: 100

	F	S	D	A	W	C	M/W/F
Isildur	6/-	4	7	3	3	6	3 / 1 / 2

Wargear
Isildur wears finely crafted heavy armour and carries a sword. At an additional cost he may have the following items:

> Shield . . . .*5 pts*
> Horse . . . .*10 pts*

Special Rule
The Ring. If neither Frodo or Bilbo are in the force, Isildur can carry the Ring.

In the final moments of the Last Alliance, Isildur snatched victory from Sauron's grasp and the Ring from his hand. By keeping the Ring, he set events in motion that would not truly conclude for thousands of years.

Note: *Isildur is a mighty Hero who was slain shortly after Sauron's defeat at the close of the Second Age – he does not appear later in the story arc and should not feature in scenarios set in the Third Age.*

Captain of Númenor (Man)   Points value: 50

	F	S	D	A	W	C	M/W/F
Captain of Númenor	5/4+	4	5	2	2	4	2 / 1 / 1

Wargear
The Captain of Númenor represented by the profile has a sword and wears armour. At an additional cost he may have the following items:

> Heavy armour . . . .*5 pts*
> Shield . . . .*5 pts*
> Bow . . . .*5 pts*
> Lance . . . .*5 pts*
> Horse . . . .*10 pts*

This profile represents the leaders amongst the soldiery of Númenor who go unnamed in The Lord of The Rings. If you choose Captains of Númenor invent suitable names for each.

Note: *Captains of Númenor do not appear later in the story arc and should not feature in scenarios set in the Third Age.*

GOOD WARRIORS

Warrior of Númenor (Man)   Points value: 7

	F	S	D	A	W	C
Man	4/4+	3	4	1	1	3

Wargear

The base profile for a Warrior includes armour and a sword (hand weapon). Any warrior can be given additional items at the following extra cost:

Spear . . . .*1 pt*
Bow . . . .*1 pt*
Shield . . . .*1 pt*
Banner (up to one per Hero included in the same force) . . . . . .*30 pts*

The brave Men of Númenor were ever resisting the Dark Lord, meeting his armies with courageous hearts and tempered steel.

Note: *Men of Númenor do not appear later in the story arc and should not feature in scenarios set in the Third Age.*

MORDOR

Sauron's chief stronghold has long been the land of Mordor, a place of ill-fortune and fell reputation that lies between Gondor and Khand. Mordor is a ruined and evil place, a land that has endured too long under the shadow. History does not tell of Mordor before Sauron began to dwell there at the start of the Second Age – no name from earlier times is known. In the years of Sauron's power it became the most feared realm in Middle-earth, a shadow that could stretch across the face of the world. Even its name – literally translated as 'the Black Land'– is a title bestowed as a result of the Dark Lord's presence.

Mordor is ringed on three sides by forbidding mountains. Though they primarily form Sauron's first line of defence, these mountains are also a cage to pen the disloyal and unwilling amongst his servants, as well the innumerable slaves and prisoners interred in the dungeons of the black land. These silent borders are almost unassailable, for in addition to the substantial natural barrier presented by the towering spires of rock, many dread and foul creatures inhabit the tunnels and caverns beneath the peaks – creatures that even the Orcs dread an encounter with.

The only true entrances to Mordor are watched with ceaseless vigilance. Minas Morgul sits like a corrupt spider in Ithilien, above Cirith Gorgor sit the twin towers of Narchost and Carchost, whilst another tower whose true name has been long forgotten rests beside Cirith Ungol. Ironically, these fortresses were built by Gondor in years past, after Sauron fell beneath the Last Alliance. Originally intended to watch Mordor and prevent the Dark Lord from rebuilding his strength, these aged but strong towers have been taken and corrupted. Now infested with Orcs they have been turned to a new purpose – to defend Mordor against their creators – a grim barrier to a forbidden and terrible land.

ORCS

Numerous, cruel and utterly incapable of redemption or compassion, the race of Orcs is nonetheless sprung from the same stock as the immortal and graceful Elves. Indeed, the first Orcs were once Elves, yet their fate was to be a very different one to that of their brothers after Morgoth's taint fell upon them. These ruined beings swiftly multiplied, as all unwholesome things are wont to do, and their numbers fed the armies of darkness, first of Morgoth and then of Sauron.

In the late years of the Third Age, Orcs are to be found in all the dark places in the world, from which they pose a constant threat to the Free Peoples. Fortunately, the fractious and quarrelsome nature of Orcs ensures that without an exceptional leader, or overwhelming numbers, they are a poor match for the well-trained and organised armies of the western kingdoms. It is only when under the command of one of the Nazgûl or another of Sauron's dread lieutenants that the mailed fist of the Orc becomes a thing of power, for Orcs fight with unceasing fury when they fear that which lies behind more than that which stands before them.

EVIL HEROES

The Dark Lord Sauron (Spirit)
Points value: 375

	F	S	D	A	W	C	M/W/F
Sauron	9/-	8	10	3	5	7	3 /6*/ †

Wargear
Sauron carries a mace (hand weapon) and is equipped with heavy armour. At an additional points cost, he can be given the One Ring (if only it was that easy!).

The One Ring . . . . .75 pts

† **The One Ring.** As long as the One Ring is with him, the Dark Lord is all but invincible. Only by taking the Ring from him can he be defeated. This is represented by the fact that Sauron does not have points of Fate as such, but every time he is killed he can roll a dice. On a roll of 2 or more, the power of the Ring sustains him and he is left on the table with only one Wound remaining. Therefore, the only way to take down the Dark Lord is to cause him to lose all his wounds and then hope he rolls a 1 and does not recover his last one. This rare occurrence represents the last wounding strike actually separating the Ring from the Dark Lord (chopping his fingers off, for example).

Note that if Sauron has the Ring, then no Good model can have it. If Sauron does not have the Ring and a Good model is carrying it, if the model puts the Ring on he is immediately removed as a casualty as he falls under the control of the Dark Lord.

Special Rules
Terror. Sauron is the living incarnation of all the fears of the free people of Middle-earth. He evokes terror in his enemies as described in the Courage section.

Ancient Evil. The malign presence of the Lord of the Rings is so overwhelmingly Evil that all Good models within 18"/42cm of Sauron suffer a -1 penalty to their Courage value until they move out of range (note that this is not cumulative with other rules that confer similar penalties, such as the Moria Goblin Drum).

Unstoppable! To face the Dark Lord in combat is almost invariably to face one's death. Every time Sauron wins a fight against multiple opponents, he can choose to strike at the enemy three times as normal or to sweep his mace around in a deadly arc. If Sauron chooses this second option, all the enemies that have taken part in the fight (those in base contact and even those supporting friendly models with spears or pikes) suffer one strike from the Dark Lord.

* **The Lord of the Rings.** So great are Sauron's necromantic powers that he can use 1 point of Will per turn without reducing his own Will store.

Magical Powers
Transfix. Range 18"/42cm. Dice score to use: 2+.

Compel. Range 18"/42cm. Dice score to use: 3+.

Drain Courage. Range 18"/42cm. Dice score to use: 2+.

Sap Will. Range 18"/42cm. Dice score to use: 3+.

Chill Soul. Range 18"/42cm. Dice score to use: 4+.

Sauron is the Dark Lord, the Enemy, the Lord of the Ring. He is driven by a consuming desire to dominate all of Middle-earth and by a burning hatred of Elves, Men and all who stand in his way. In distant times, when he still hadn't revealed his evil nature, he forged the Rings of Power and gave them as gifts to the rulers of the free races of Middle-earth. These kings knew not that Sauron also forged the Ruling Ring for himself, imbuing into it a great portion of his own life force and powers. Through this mighty tool, Sauron could control the other Rings and enslave their bearers to his will. Only the Rings of the Elves could not be dominated, because he had no part in their making. His vast armies of Orcs and other fell creatures were about to subjugate all the Western realms of Middle-earth, but the Last Alliance of Men and Elves defeated his hordes and finally laid siege to his fortress of Barad-dûr in the land of Mordor. There, at a terrible price, the One Ring was cut from the hand of the Dark Lord and he was finally vanquished. But Sauron was not destroyed. As long as the Ring exists, Sauron's spirit endures.

One of the race of those that are named Black Númenóreans, the Lieutenant of the Dark Tower has studied great sorcery under his master and now carries Sauron's word to his servants and enemies alike.

The Mouth of Sauron (Man)   Points value: 60

	F	S	D	A	W	C	M/W/F
Mouth of Sauron	4/-	4	5	2	2	4	1 / 4 / 1

Wargear
The Mouth of Sauron wears armour and carries a sword (hand weapon). At an additional points cost the Mouth of Sauron can have the following:

Armoured dark steed (armoured horse) . . . .*15 pts*

Dark Steed. The Mouth of Sauron rides a huge black horse to carry the word of his dark master to all the peoples of Middle-earth. Only the Mouth of Sauron can ride this evil beast – it will not permit any other creature to mount it. Rules for horses and riders are given in the main rules section.

Magical Powers
Transfix. Range 12"/28cm. Dice score to use: 3+.
Drain Courage. Range 12"/28cm. Dice score to use: 2+.
Sap Will. Range 12"/28cm. Dice score to use: 4+.
Terrifying Aura. Dice score to use: 2+.

Gothmog is the castellan of Minas Morgul and one of the most trusted servants at the command of the Nazgûl. In battle he is fearless, but it is as a commander that he is most dangerous. Unless guided by some other will, it is the way of Orcs to press home an attack until either the enemy is destroyed or their own fragile courage fails them. Such a tactic is not Gothmog's way. He is the master of the battlefield and a truly skilled tactician. He is successful beyond all doubt, for it is the forces under his command that have cast Gondor's armies out of many strongholds along the Anduin.

Gothmog, Lieutenant of Morgul (Orc)   Points value: 135

	F	S	D	A	W	C	M/W/F
Gothmog	5/-	4	6	3	3	5	3 / 3 / 3

Wargear
Gothmog carries a hand weapon and wears heavy armour. He can be given the following items at additional cost:

Shield . . . .*5 pts*
Warg . . . .*10 pts*

Special Rules
Master of Battle. A leader without peer amongst Sauron's minions, Gothmog is a canny opponent, able to read the tide of battle and turn it to his advantage. To represent this, if Gothmog is within 6"/14cm of an enemy Hero calling a heroic action, he may immediately call an action of the same type without expending a point of Might. Note that he may not use this ability to call a heroic shoot or heroic move action if he has already been engaged in combat.

The Witch-king of Angmar (Spirit)   Points value: 70

	F	S	D	A	W	C	M / W / F
Witch-king	5/-	4	8	1	1	6	0-3 /10-20/0-3

Wargear

The Witch-king carries a wicked sword (hand weapon). At an additional points cost he can have the following:

> Dark Steed (horse) . . . .*10 pts*
> Fell Beast . . . .*50 pts*
> Flail (two-handed weapon) . . . .*5 pts*
> Morgul blade . . . .*10 pts*

Morgul Blade. This evil weapon is both magical and poisonous – a deep wound leaves a tainted shard from its blade in the foe's flesh, reducing them to a shattered and helpless wreck. The Morgul blade can only be used once – the Evil player must declare he is using the Morgul blade before rolling to wound. An enemy that suffers a wound from the Morgul blade is automatically slain regardless of the number of wounds on its profile. Heroes can use Fate to avoid wounds suffered from the blade but if this is failed, they are slain.

Special Rules

Might/Will/Fate. See the Ringwraiths for details. Note that the Witch-king starts with a minimum of 10 points of Will at 70 points and can have more Might, Will and Fate than the other Ringwraiths. With all his Heroic stats at full (3 Might, 20 Will and 3 Fate) the Witch-king costs 150 points.

The Will of Evil; Harbinger of Evil, Ringwraiths and the Ring. See the Ringwraiths entry for details.

Terror. The Witch-king is a terrifying supernatural creature. He evokes Terror in his enemies as described in the Courage section.

Fell Beast. Ringwraiths often ride these evil creatures. Rules for monstrous mounts are given in the Advanced Rules section.

	F	S	D	A	W	C
Fell Beast	5	6	6	2	3	3

Fly. A Fell Beast moves by flying – its move is 12"/28cm. It can fly over the top of any models or terrain without penalty. It cannot enter woods, buildings and other terrain that has been deemed impassable, but can land on top of any of these if the players so agree at the beginning of the game. Fell Beasts cannot be used in scenarios that take place in Moria or other subterranean areas.

Feral. If the Ringwraith riding the Fell Beast is killed or dismounts, the creature will automatically fail its Courage test and flee the field.

Magical Powers

Black Dart. Range 12"/28cm. Dice score to use: 5+.

Compel. Range 12"/28cm. Dice score to use: 4+.

Drain Courage. Range 12"/28cm. Dice score to use: 2+.

Sap Will. Range 12"/28cm. Dice score to use: 3+.

Transfix. Range 12"/28cm. Dice score to use: 3+.

Your Staff is Broken! Range 12"/28cm. Dice score to use: 4+.

The Witch-king is the leader of the Ringwraiths. Like the others, he is cloaked and armoured, and has no physical body but only a shadow-like existence held together by the force of his will.

The Ringwraiths (Spirit)   Points value: 55

	F	S	D	A	W	C	M / W / F
Ringwraith	5/-	4	8	1	1	6	0-2 / 7-14 / 0-2

Wargear
Each Ringwraith carries a wicked sword or mace (hand weapon). At an additional points cost, any Ringwraith can have the following:

Dark Steed (horse) . . . .*10 pts*
Fell Beast . . . .*50 pts*

Special Rules
Might/Will/Fate. The Ringwraiths derive their powers directly from Sauron, and the closer they are to their master, the more powerful they will be. At their weakest, such as when they were operating in the Shire, Ringwraiths start the game with no Might, no Fate and 7 points of Will, and cost 55 points. When buying a Ringwraith for your force, decide how many extra points of Might/Will/Fate you are going to give it, up to the maximums shown in its profile. Each extra point of Might, Will or Fate costs an extra 5 points, so a Ringwraith with 2 Might, 2 Fate and 14 Will costs 110 points.

The Will of Evil. Ringwraiths rely on Will far more than other Heroes. It is only by will that they maintain corporeal form. The further they are from Sauron, the weaker is the bond between them and the lower their Will value.

During the game a Ringwraith must give up 1 point of Will at the end of the Fight phase if it has been in a fight. Note that Ringwraiths touching enemy must fight – as all models must – they cannot choose not to fight!

If any Hero should put on the Ring then he becomes part of the twilight world of the Ringwraiths. He is both visible and vulnerable to them! A Hero wearing the Ring is not invisible to a Ringwraith as he is to other models. A Ringwraith does not have to give up Will if he is fighting against a model wearing the Ring – not even if other enemy are included as part of a multiple combat.

Once a Ringwraith suffers 1 Wound or has 0 Will remaining, it is banished. Ringwraiths cannot be destroyed completely in this way – their spirits slowly regenerate – but as this takes several days they are removed as casualties.

Ringwraiths can also employ their Will to use magical powers and to resist the effect of magic just like other Heroes.

Terror. Ringwraiths are terrifying supernatural creatures. They evoke Terror in their enemies as described in the Courage section.

Harbingers of Evil. The malign presence of the Nazgûl is so overwhelmingly evil that all Good models within 12"/28cm of one or more Ringwraiths suffer a -1 penalty to their Courage value until they move out of range (note that this is not cumulative, not even with other rules that confer similar penalties, such as the Balrog's Ancient Evil rule).

Fell Beast. See opposite for details.

Magical Powers
Black Dart. Range 12"/28cm. Dice score to use: 5+.
Compel. Range 12"/28cm. Dice score to use: 4+.
Drain Courage. Range 12"/28cm. Dice score to use: 2+.
Sap Will. Range 12"/28cm. Dice score to use: 3+.
Transfix. Range 12"/28cm. Dice score to use: 3+.

Note on choosing Ringwraiths. As there are eight ordinary Ringwraiths the Evil player can have up to eight ordinary Ringwraiths in his force. The Ringwraiths are not named – we suggest you paint a number under the base of each so that you can readily distinguish them on your record sheet.

The Ringwraiths, or Nazgûl, were once Kings of Men, the bearers of magical rings created by Sauron. Their rings granted endless life but gradually enslaved the Kings to Sauron's will. All that remains of them now are their twisted spirits – their bodies having faded into empty nothingness. Together with their leader, the Witch-king of Angmar, they are known as The Nine and are the most deadly of all Sauron's captains.

Shelob is an evil thing in spider-form, a horror that has haunted Middle-earth for countless years, preying on all living things. It is above the pass of Cirith Ungol that she makes her lair, feeding of those who are foolish enough to step into the caves in which she makes her nest.

Shelob (Giant Spider)   Points value: 90

	F	S	D	A	W	C	M/W/F
Shelob	7/-	7	7	1	6	4	0 / 6 / 0

Special Rules

Movement. Shelob moves 10"/24cm per turn. Like all spiders, Shelob can climb on any surface, regardless of its angle. Shelob therefore can move at full speed over any type of difficult terrain and ignores all obstacles except for water features and gaps such as chasms, ditches and other open spaces, which she has to jump as normal.

Terror. Shelob is a repugnant, terrifying monster! She evokes terror in the enemy, as described in the Courage rules.

Venom. Shelob's sting and fangs are heavy with deadly and incapacitating venoms. If Shelob fails to wound an enemy model, she must re-roll the dice.

Pounce. A deadly hunting spider, Shelob often jumps on her prey using the huge weight of her bloated body to crush them. When charging, Shelob counts as a Monstrous Mount and therefore gets both bonuses that cavalry models get (ie, Extra Attack and Knock to the Ground). As usual with Monstrous Mounts, these bonuses are not lost if Shelob is engaged by enemy cavalry, but are lost if she is engaged by another Monstrous Mount.

Hunting Instinct. Shelob is used to ambushing and dispatching her prey swiftly and effortlessly. If faced with a strong enemy, she is likely to retreat to safety. Every time Shelob suffers a wound, she must take a Courage test. If the test is failed she flees – the model is removed and counts as a casualty.

Though the Orc Shamans worship Sauron without doubt or hesitation, his voice is but one of many that they heed. Many pay homage to the Nazgûl as the heralds of Sauron's coming and worship them as lesser gods in a dark and foreboding

Orc Shaman   Points value: 50

	F	S	D	A	W	C	M/W/F
Orc Shaman	3/-	3	5	1	2	3	1 / 3 / 1

Wargear

An Orc Shaman carries a spear and wears heavy armour. He can ride a Warg at additional cost:

    Warg . . . .*10 pts*

Magical Powers

Fury. Dice score to use: 3+.

Transfix. Range 12"/28cm. Dice score to use: 5+.

Grishnákh leads the Mordor Orcs that catch up with the Uruk-hai carrying Merry and Pippin. He tries in vain to abduct them and take them to his master, Sauron.

Grishnákh (Orc)   Points value: 45

	F	S	D	A	W	C	M/W/F
Grishnákh	4/-	4	5	2	2	3	3 / 1 / 1

Wargear

Grishnákh has a sword and armour. At an additional cost he may carry the following:

    Shield . . . .*5 pts*

Shagrat, Captain of Cirith Ungol (Uruk-hai)　Points value: 55

	F	S	D	A	W	C	M/W/F
Shagrat	5/-	5	5	2	2	4	3 / 1 / 1

Wargear
Shagrat has a sword and armour. At an additional cost he may carry the following:

Shield . . . . .5 pts

The leader of the Uruk-hai garrison of the Tower of Cirith Ungol is as brutal and ferocious as any Uruk-hai captain, but he is also fanatically loyal to the Dark Tower.

Gorbag, Orc Captain　　　　　Points value: 45

	F	S	D	A	W	C	M/W/F
Gorbag	4/-	4	5	2	2	3	3 / 1 / 1

Wargear
Gorbag wears crude armour and has a cruel Orc blade (hand weapon). At an extra cost he may carry the following:

Shield . . . . .5 pts

A classic example of Orc selfishness and greed, Gorbag is prepared to order his warriors to attack the Uruk-hai guards of Cirith Ungol to steal Bilbo's precious coat of mithril.

Orc Captain　　　　　　　　Points value: 40

	F	S	D	A	W	C	M/W/F
Orc Captain	4/5+	4	5	2	2	3	2 / 1 / 1

Wargear
The Orc Captain represented by the profile has a sword and wears crude Orcish armour. At an additional cost he may have the following:

Shield . . . . .5 pts
Orc Bow . . . . .5 pts
Warg . . . . .10 pts

We have presented the option for you to include one or more Orc Captains as part of your force.

Mordor Uruk-hai Captain　　　Points value: 50

	F	S	D	A	W	C	M/W/F
Uruk-hai Captain	5/4+	5	5	2	2	4	2 / 1 / 1

Wargear
The Uruk-hai Captain represented by the profile has a sword and armour. At an additional cost he may have the following items.

Two-handed weapon . . . . .5 pts
Shield . . . . .5 pts
Orc bow . . . . .5 pts

We have included the option for you to include one or more Uruk-hai Captains as part of your force. This represents the leaders amongst the Uruk-hai soldiery who go unnamed in the story of The Lord of The Rings – the incidental warriors whose role on the battlefield is important in any war.

Mordor Troll Chieftain Points value: 140

	F	S	D	A	W	C	M/W/F
Troll Chieftain	7/5+	7	8	3	3	4	2 / 1 / 1

Wargear
Troll Chieftains have crude armour and carry hand weapons.

Special Rules
Terror. Troll Chieftains are so huge and vicious that they evoke terror in the enemy, as described in the Courage rules.

Throw Stones. If a Troll Chieftain does not move at all, he can declare he's 'stooping for a stone', and in the subsequent Shoot phase he can throw it, provided that he is not engaged in combat. This works exactly like a crossbow with a range of 12"/28cm and a Strength of 8.

A small number of the Trolls of Mordor are gifted with a form of primordial cunning and intelligence, which makes them the leaders of their race and a far more dangerous foe than the rest of their kin.

Gollum / Sméagol Points value: 0

	F	S	D	A	W	C	M/W/F
Gollum	4/-	4	4	2	2	4	1 / 0 / 1

Special Rules
Gollum can be included in the Evil player's force if the Ringbearer is included on the opposing side. No points are paid for Gollum – he is 'free'.

Regardless of the scenario you are playing, Gollum is positioned on the table once both sides have placed all their other models. He must be placed within 6"/14cm of the Ringbearer.

So long as the Ringbearer is alive, no Good model can harm Gollum (they cannot shoot, cast *Sorcerous Blast*, or strike blows against him, nor hurt him in any other way). Good models are allowed to charge Gollum and fight, but will strike no blows if they win because they do not wish to kill Gollum. This applies to the Ringbearer himself as well as all other Good models. This restriction ceases to apply should the Ringbearer be slain. Once the Ringbearer is slain, Gollum becomes an enemy and can be shot and fought in the same way as any other enemy model.

Gollum is always controlled entirely by the player who has priority that turn. Whichever side has priority takes control of Gollum and moves him, fights with him, and so on. Regardless of which side controls him, Gollum must always move to within 6"/14cm of the Ringbearer in the Move phase if possible. If this is impossible, he must move as close to the Ringbearer as he can. Note that models can be moved in any order, so the Good player could quite reasonably move Gollum towards Frodo and then move Frodo away all in the same Move phase. When the Good player has priority he can always choose which of the pair to move first and this enables the Good player to keep Gollum at a safe distance from the Ringbearer.

If Gollum attacks and slays the Ringbearer, he automatically puts the Ring on when his opponent is killed. Once Gollum puts the Ring on he will run away and will never ever be heard of again. The model is removed and counts as a casualty.

Cave Dweller. See the rules for Durbûrz, the Goblin King of Moria on page 101.

Many years ago, a small creature called Déagol discovered a ring in the Anduin river. This was, of course, the One Ring, and its evil power began to work at once, for he was murdered and the Ring taken by his companion Sméagol. In time Sméagol became Gollum – a twisted monster, obsessed with the Ring and consumed by his own remorse. But now Gollum has lost the Ring, 'stolen' from him by Bilbo and now borne by Frodo towards its destruction in the fires of Mount Doom. Gollum cannot bear to be separated from his 'precious' and would do anything, endure anything, to possess the Ring once more.

EVIL WARRIORS

Orc Warrior   Points value: 5

	F	S	D	A	W	C
Orc	3/5+	3	4	1	1	2

Orcs are the foulest creatures to walk Middle-earth. They are evil-hearted monsters that rejoice in slaughter and destruction. Orcs bear little loyalty even to their own kind and will readily fight amongst themselves over the spoils of their conquests. Yet they are numerous, and their natural cowardice makes them easy to dominate and so an ideal tool of evil intent.

Wargear
The base profile for an Orc warrior includes crude Orc armour and a hand weapon. Any warrior can be given additional items at the following cost:

Two-handed sword/axe . . . .*1 pt*
Spear . . . .*1 pt*
Orc bow . . . .*1 pt*
Shield . . . .*1 pt*
Banner (maximum one per Hero included in the same force) . . .*25 pts*

Morannon Orc   Points value: 7

	F	S	D	A	W	C
Morannon Orc	3/-	4	5	1	1	2

Wargear
A Morannon Orc carries a crude hand weapon and wears heavy armour. At an additional cost any warrior may have the following:

Shield . . . .*1 pt*
Spear . . . .*1 pt*

Normally, Orcs are not notable for being exceptional warriors, however in recent years the armies of both Mordor and Minas Morgul have been composed of a stronger breed of Orc.

Warg Rider (Orc)   Points value: 12

	F	S	D	A	W	C
Warg Rider	3/5+	3	4	1	1	2
Warg	3/-	4	4	1	1	2

Wargear
The base profile for a Warg Rider includes armour and a hand weapon. Any warrior can be given additional items at the following extra cost.

Throwing spears . . . .*2 pt*
Orc bow . . . .*1 pt*
Shield . . . .*1 pt*
Banner (maximum one per Hero included in the same force) . . .*25 pts*

Special Rules
Crude Throwing Spears. The throwing spears carried by the Warg Riders are so heavy and primitive that they can only be used from atop a Warg, so if a Warg Rider dismounts or is thrown, he must immediately discard his throwing spear.

Wargs are gigantic, evil wolves – massive and dangerous creatures with a cunning and carnivorous intelligence. Warg Riders scout far ahead of the main armies of Orcs and other evil creatures, spying out the land and picking off stragglers for interrogation or some far worse fate.

Orc Tracker   Points value: 5

	F	S	D	A	W	C
Orc Tracker	3/4+	3	3	1	1	2

Wargear
An Orc Tracker carries an Orc bow and a hand weapon, and wears crude Orc armour. At an additional cost any warrior may have the following:

Warg . . . . .6 pts

Orc Trackers are smaller and even less formidable than their brethren. They can cover great distance at speed, however, and are more skilled at archery than other Orcs, able to match the soldiery of Gondor.

Mordor Uruk-hai   Points value: 8

	F	S	D	A	W	C
Uruk-hai	4/4+	4	4	1	1	3

Wargear
The base profile for a Mordor Uruk-hai includes armour and a hand weapon. Any warrior can be given extra items for the following:

Two-handed sword/axe . . . . .1 pt
Orc bow . . . . .1 pt
Shield . . . . .1 pt
Banner (up to one per Hero included in the same force) . . . . . .30 pts

If Orcs are the foulest creatures to walk Middle-earth then Uruk-hai are the most dangerous perversion of the breed. Where ordinary Orcs are crook limbed and timid, the Uruk-hai are strong, muscular, upright warriors of greater skill and courage.

Mordor Troll   Points value: 100

	F	S	D	A	W	C
Mordor Troll	7/5+	7	7	3	3	3

Wargear
A Mordor Troll wears crude armour and carries a hand weapon.

Special Rules
Terror. Mordor Trolls are so huge and vicious that they evoke terror in the enemy, as described in the Courage rules.

Throw Stones. If a Troll does not move at all, he can declare he's 'stooping for a stone', and in the subsequent Shoot phase he can throw it, provided that he is not engaged in combat. This works exactly like a crossbow with a range of 12"/28cm and a Strength of 8.

The Trolls of Mordor have been bred by Sauron so that they can withstand the light of the sun without turning to stone like normal Trolls do. Even bigger and stronger than their subterranean kin, these monsters are amongst the most lethal troops of the armies of the Dark Lord.

Catapults are massive constructions of wood and iron that propel either immense boulders or clusters of smaller rock. Although able to destroy enemy warriors, the true value of catapults is their ability to swiftly break apart enemy defences.

Mordor War Catapult   Points value: 90

	Strength	Defence	Batter Points
Catapult	(10)	10	4

	F	S	D	A	W	C
Orc	3/5+	3	4	1	1	2
Mordor Troll	7/5+	7	7	3	3	3

Crew
A Mordor Catapult consists of a Catapult and three Orc crew armed with daggers and wearing armour. Extra crew can be added at additional cost:

> Orc crewman . . . . .5 pts each

Special Rules
Indirect Fire. A Catapult always follows the rules for Volley Fire, giving it a range of 18-96"/42-224cm. When firing a Catapult, follow the rules on page 45, with the following exceptions. A Catapult hits the target on the roll of a 4+ rather than a 6. If a hit is rolled and the target is a Siege Target, the shot will hit it automatically (no scattering). If the target is a Battlefield target, roll on the Siege Engines' Scatter chart instead of following the normal rules for allocating hits with a volley.

Area Effect. Catapults fire a large stone that shatters on impact, hurling out a wave of debris as deadly as the main projectile. To represent this, if the Catapult scores a hit against a Battlefield target, all models within 2"/4cm of the target take a hit of Strength 6 (this hit does not kill Battlefield targets outright). All models with a Strength of 5 or less that are hit by the shot (either by the initial impact or the debris) are knocked to the ground.

Upgrades
A Mordor Catapult may be given the following upgrades at additional cost.

> Flaming Ammunition . . . . .15 pts
> Orc Engineer Captain . . . . .65 pts
> Severed Heads . . . . .5 pts
> Siege Veterans . . . . .15 pts
> Troll . . . . .90 pts

Mordor Siege Bow   Points value: 50

	Strength	Defence	Batter Points
Siege Bow	(9)	10	3

	F	S	D	A	W	C
Orc	3/5+	3	4	1	1	2

Crew
A Mordor Siege Bow consists of a Siege Bow and two Orc crew armed with daggers and wearing armour. Extra crew can be added at additional cost:

> Orc crewman . . . . .5 pts each

Special Rules
Piercing Shot. If shooting at a Battlefield target, the missile can conceivably hit several enemies. The target model is struck one blow at the Strength of the Siege Engine, is knocked to the ground, and is flung 2D6"/4D6cm directly away from it. Except as noted below, any other models that lie within the path of the victim suffer a single Strength 6 hit and are knocked to the ground if they have Strength 5 or less. If the propelled model hits an obtacle or Siege target, it immediately stops and inflicts a single Strength 6 upon it.

Accurate. Siege Bows are easier to aim than Catapults and other heavy Siege Engines. When firing a Siege Bow at a Battlefield target the shot will Scatter only 3"/8cm rather than 6"/14cm.

This simple Siege Engine is a common sight in the armies of Mordor. The machine flings its payload (either an immense arrow or stone shot) at the target with punishing force.

Upgrades
A Mordor Siege Bow may be given the following upgrades at additional cost.

> Flaming Ammunition . . . . .15 pts
> Orc Engineer Captain . . . . .65 pts

THE DWARF HOLDS

Dwarves can be found in many places throughout Middle-earth. From Ered Luin in the west, to the Iron Hills in the east, Dwarves are to be found wherever there is wealth to be gained, for they love gold above all else, and are craftsmen to rival the skill of the Elves. The greatest Dwarf city was that of Dwarrowdelf, or Moria as the Elves named it, but that has long since fallen into ruin, drowned in shadow and flame. These days, the chief Dwarf hold in Middle-earth is that of the Iron Hills, a great range of craggy peaks to the east of Mirkwood and north of Mordor. Throughout all of the trouble and strife that has befallen Durin's folk, the Iron Hills have remained safe from attack. It can be assumed that this is due chiefly to the skill of the Dwarves in crafting halls that are both wondrous and cannily defensible, though Dwarven secrecy has ensured that little knowledge regarding the Iron Hills has ever entered the histories of Elven or Mannish realms.

Though other Dwarf holds exist far and wide in Middle-earth, most famous is the realm of Erebor that nestles beneath the Lonely Mountain, a singular geographical oddity that rises high above the plains about it. Erebor was possibly the wealthiest of all Dwarf holds save Moria itself, but it too suffered a terrible blow when it was attacked by a great dragon, Smaug, who took its great hoard for himself. In the wake of this tragedy, Erebor was lost to the Dwarves for many long years until fate conspired to leave Smaug slain and the mountain once more in the hands of the Dwarves. As the Third Age closes, Erebor is once more a wealthy place and enjoys friendship with its Mannish and Elven neighbours, remaining one of the greatest of all the bastions of the Free Peoples and a present and redoubtable ally against the forces of Sauron.

DWARVES

Like the Elves, the Dwarves are an elder race whose days are fading as Men come into prominence. In most other ways however, the Dwarves are quite dissimilar from Elves. Where Elves are tall and gracefully spoken, Dwarves are short and gruff. Where Elves prefer to dwell in the forests of Middle-earth, the Dwarves carve their halls deep within the roots of the mountains and have holds in Erebor, the Iron Hills and the Ered Luin. The Dwarves are craftsmen beyond peer, to which their underground halls stand in testimony. Iron and gold are their playthings, and they fashion from them weapons, armour, and jewellery that are admired by all, including the Elves.

Perhaps due to their long span of years, Dwarves can hold grudges for many lives of men and it is perhaps one such grudge, carried forward from a time long forgotten, that has led to the estrangement of the Dwarven and Elven races. Many consider the Dwarves to be selfish creatures, more concerned with wealth than the sufferings of the world, but the truth of the matter is that the Dwarves are too often unaware of happenings outside of their own realms. Even so, the Dwarves have always been staunch allies to those they consider their friends, and the forces of Evil are rightly fearful of Dwarvish fury.

GOOD HEROES

Gimli, son of Glóin (Dwarf) — Points value: 90

	F	S	D	A	W	C	M/W/F
Gimli	6/4+	4	8	2	2	6	3 / 2 / 2

Wargear
Gimli wears heavy Dwarf armour and carries an assortment of fine Dwarf axes (hand weapon), some of which are balanced for throwing (count as throwing axes). He also carries a finely-balanced two-handed axe of exceptional craftmanship.

At an additional points cost, Gimli can be given the following:

Elven cloak . . . . .10 pts

Special Rules
Axes of the Dwarves! At the beginning of each fight, Gimli can choose to either use an axe in each hand, in which case he fights with 3 Attacks, or use his unique two-handed axe, in which case he adds +1 to his dice rolls to Wound, but he does not suffer the usual -1 penalty on the roll to win the fight.

Like all Dwarf-kind Gimli, son of Glóin, is grim and plain-speaking but also a doughty warrior. His courage and his axe are equally valuable additions to the Fellowship on their journey. Gimli is heavily armoured in the fashion of Dwarf warriors and is well accustomed to the rigours of combat. Gimli proves a stalwart warrior during the bitter fighting of the war against Sauron, slaying a multitude of Orcs with his fearsome axe.

Dáin Ironfoot, King of Erebor (Dwarf) — Points value: 125

	F	S	D	A	W	C	M/W/F
Dáin Ironfoot	5/4+	4	9	3	3	7	3 / 3 / 2

Wargear
Dáin wears Mithril armour and carries the great axe Barazantathûl, both heirlooms of his family.

Special Rules
The King under the Mountain. The Dwarves hold Dáin in supreme regard, and will do his bidding without question. Such is Dáin's awesome presence on the battlefield that the range of his 'Stand Fast!' rolls is 12"/28cm rather than 6"/14cm.

Venerable. At the time of the War of the Ring, Dáin is more than 250 years old, and is not as agile as he once was. To represent this, whenever Dáin has to make a Jump or Climb test the Good player rolls two dice and must choose the lowest. This roll can be influenced by Might in the usual way.

Barazantathûl. Although not innately magical, this two-handed axe is of great craftsmanship and possessed of exceptional balance. When Dáin fights with this axe, he adds +1 to his dice roll on the Wound chart, as normal with two-handed weapons, but he does not suffer the usual -1 penalty to the dice for deciding which side wins the fight.

Dáin Ironfoot is the King of Durin's folk and holds court beneath the Lonely Mountain in Erebor. Though burdened by many years, Dáin is a mighty king descended in direct line from Durin, the sire of his race. He has fought many battles across the face of Middle-earth, and grown wise in the arts of leadership and battle. As a result, Dáin commands incredible loyalty from his followers so much so that they will never surrender while he lives.

Dwarf Captain — Points value: 60

	F	S	D	A	W	C	M/W/F
Dwarf Captain	5/4+	4	7	2	2	5	2 / 1 / 1

Wargear
A Dwarf Captain wears Dwarf armour and carries an axe (hand weapon). At an additional cost he may be equipped with the following:

Two-handed axe . . . . .5 pts
Shield . . . . .5 pts
Throwing axes . . . . .5 pts

We have included the option to have one or more Dwarf Captains as part of your force – famous heroes such as Óin and Ori.

Balin (Dwarf)   Points value: 75

	F	S	D	A	W	C	M/W/F
Balin	6/4+	4	8	2	2	6	3 / 3 / 1

Wargear

Balin wears heavy Dwarf armour and carries several axes (hand weapon), one of which is balanced for throwing (throwing axe). He also carries an especially large axe (two-handed axe). At an additional points cost Balin can replace his two-handed axe with Durin's Axe.

Durin's Axe . . . .*20 pts*

Durin's Axe. This ancient heirloom is a deadly Dwarven axe, but it's so light that it can be swung around in deadly arcs with blurring speed. Any Dwarf Hero fighting with this mighty axe adds +1 to his dice roll on the Wound chart. In addition, the wielder of Durin's Axe may re-roll one of his dice when determining who wins a fight, but must accept the result of the second roll.

Balin led a contingent of Dwarves from Erebor in an attempt to reclaim Khazad-dûm. For a short period his mission was successful and the sound of Dwarf hammers echoed once again in the vast subterranean halls. Alas his was a story destined to end in tragedy as Balin was slain by the Goblins infesting the ancient underworld realm.

Dwarf King   Points value: 75

	F	S	D	A	W	C	M/W/F
Dwarf King	6/4+	4	8	2	2	6	2 / 2 / 1

Wargear

A Dwarf King carries a hand axe (hand weapon) and wears Dwarf heavy armour. At an additional cost he may be equipped with the following:

Two-handed axe . . . .*5 pts*
Throwing axes . . . .*5 pts*

Dwarf Kings rule the realms of the Dwarves across Middle-earth, from Ered Luin to beyond the Iron Hills. Gruff and uncompromising, they are firm allies to their friends and death to their foes.

GOOD WARRIORS

Dwarf Warrior   Points value: 8

	F	S	D	A	W	C
Dwarf Warrior	4/4+	3	6	1	1	4

Wargear

The base profile for a Dwarf warrior includes Dwarf armour. He can be given additional items at the following cost:

Axe or two-handed axe (choose one) . . . .*Free*
Dwarf Bow . . . .*1 pt*
Shield . . . .*1 pt*
Banner (up to one per Hero included in the same force) . . . .*30 pts*

The sharp axes of the Dwarves and their stubborn courage are rightly feared among the servants of Evil.

Khazâd Guard (Dwarf)   Points value: 11

	F	S	D	A	W	C
Khazâd Guard	4/-	4	7	1	1	4

Wargear

Each Khazâd Guard wears Dwarf heavy armour and carries an axe (hand weapon) and a two-handed axe.

Special Rules

Bodyguard. At the beginning of the game, choose one Dwarf Hero among those in your force for the Khazâd Guard to protect. As long as this Hero is on the table, all Khazâd Guard models automatically pass all Courage tests they have to take. If the Hero is killed or leaves the table, the Khazâd Guard revert to the normal rules for Courage.

The veterans of the Khazâd Guard, hand-picked from among the strongest Dwarf warriors, are sworn to defend their Lord with their lives. They wear terrifying war-masks and are equipped with the best weapons and armour.

A SHADOW IN THE EAST

Beyond Mordor are a great many realms, largely undocumented by the histories kept in the western lands of Middle-earth. Of these kingdoms, some bow down before Sauron's will, contributing slaves, wealth and warriors to his goals but, even so, there are bastions of the Free Peoples to be found within these lands.

Upon the boundaries of the Sea of Rhûn, lies the mysterious kingdom of Dorwinion. Little is known of the realm save the fact that they are masters of the art of wine-making, capable of blending such heady and flavoursome vintages that even an Elf may lose his wits after a small bowl. Such art is highly sought after in the neighbouring realms – the Elves of Mirkwood are particularly partial to its taste – and Dorwinion has been made rich by trade. Despite this, the inhabitants of the realm remain a mystery, for even the boatmen who ferry their wares labour in ignorance of the nature of their paymasters. Some believe the folk of Dorwinion to be Elves, others consider them to be Men, while others still believe them to be something else entirely, yet none can be sure.

Even further southwards lie the Rhûnish kingdoms, an alliance of warlike and indisputably evil Men whose loyalty has long since been pledged to Sauron – unsurprisingly, as the Dark Lord has invested much time and effort in bringing them under his sway. It is from these lands that now-vanished peoples came to bring ruin to Gondor and Rhovanion, and the ring of iron fortresses that encircle the lands past the mountains of Rhûn haven proven to be a formidable barrier against Gondor's vengeance.

Lastmost, and most southerly, of the eastern kingdoms is Khand, a rolling land of plains and hills. The Khandish folk are as wild and warlike as those of Rhûn, yet their savagery is fuelled by a warrior-code that prizes victory in combat above all else – a trait that makes them highly prized as mercenaries in the neighbouring realms of Harad, Mordor and Rhûn. Skilled horsemen, Khandish warriors are capable of deadly raids, striking without warning and disappearing to the hills from whence they came before the hue and cry can be taken up.

EVIL HEROES

Easterling Captain (Man)   Points value: 50

	F	S	D	A	W	C	M/W/F
Easterling Captain	4/-	4	6	2	2	4	2 / 1 / 1

Wargear

An Easterling Captain has an Easterling halberd (counts as an Elven blade) and wears heavy armour. At an additional cost he may be equipped with the following:

Shield . . . . .5 pts
Horse . . . . .10 pts
Armoured Horse . . . . .15 pts

The Easterlings are the most disciplined and skilled warriors that fight for the Dark Lord. Their captains lead them with a martial prowess that Orcs will never be able to match.

EVIL WARRIORS

Easterling Warrior (Man)   Points value: 7

	F	S	D	A	W	C
Easterling	3/-	3	5	1	1	3

Wargear

The base profile for an Easterling Warrior includes sword and heavy armour. Any warrior can be given additional items at the following cost:

Spear . . . . .1 pt
Shield . . . . .1 pt
Banner (up to one per Hero included in the same force) . . . . . .25 pts

Mysterious human warriors from the remote lands of the East, these are amongst the most well-equipped and disciplined troops available to the Dark Lord, whom they worship with fanatical loyalty.

HARAD

Harad lies far to the south, past the borders of Mordor and Gondor, and covers a greater swathe of land than any other of Middle-earth's kingdoms. In the north, Harad is often thought to be a barren and desolate place, and much of it is, yet some of it has beauty enough to challenge the most verdant realms of the world. This in itself should come as no surprise, for a realm on the scale of Harad will always encompass many different landscapes. As such, Harad's folk have grown accustomed to dwelling within the many varied environs of their land, from the great sandy reaches of the Nâfarat to the dense forests about the ancient city of Kârna.

The people of Harad have grown accustomed to war, for they have long quarrelled amongst themselves, rival chieftains vying for power and privilege wherever they could. Such squabbles serve to strengthen Harad's warriors, which is doubtless what led them to conflict with their neighbouring realms. Chief amongst their foes has been the more northerly realm of Gondor, a land whose fate has been irrevocably entwined with that of their own. Whether the Haradrim should be considered to be aggressors in their own right, or more likened to catspaws of the greater kingdoms of the area, is much debated, yet it cannot be argued that they have been much given to warring with their northern neighbour. Such battles have been ferociously fought on both sides and often end in stalemate – the skill and armour of Gondor matched by the sheer volume of warriors the Haradrim can bring to bear.

THE CORSAIRS OF UMBAR

Along the coasts of Belfalas there are none as feared as the Corsairs of Umbar. Possessed of nautical expertise beyond compare, these raiders prey upon all of the coastlands of southern Middle-earth, taking whatever they can. Descended in equal part from the Black Númenóreans and the indigenous peoples of Harad, the Corsairs hold allegiance only to the Lords of Umbar. Even there, this fealty is mere lip service, for the captains of the Corsair fleets are so rarely to be found within Umbar itself that they remain largely autonomous.

In ages past, the Corsair fleets were composed of great Númenórean frigates, sleek in motion but also strong and unyielding. As time has slipped away, many of the skills to fashion such vessels have been lost, and now many Corsairs put to sea in ships more akin to the traditional Haradrim coastal craft; angular vessels that are all severe silhouettes and pitch-blackened hulls.

EVIL HEROES

Suladân, The Serpent Lord (Man)　　　Points value: 90

	F	S	D	A	W	C	M/W/F
Suladân	5/4+	4	5	3	3	5	3 / 3 / 1

Wargear
Suladân carries a sword and wears armour. He can be given the following items at additional cost:

> Horse . . . .*10 pts*
> Bow . . . .*5 pts*

Special Rules
Poisoned Arrows. The Haradrim always smear the tips of their arrows with the preserved venom of reptiles and scorpions living in their lands. Every time the player hits a model with a Haradrim arrow, but rolls a 1 on the D6 to wound it, he must re-roll the D6.

Ascendant. Suladân's reputation is growing with each victory, making his name commonplace amongst the Haradrim, and his very presence can inspire armies to great deeds. The range of Suladân's Stand Fast! rule is 12"/28cm rather than 6"/14cm.

In truth, Suladân's name passed out of use long ago when he took the name of a revered hero at the time he claimed leadership of his tribe. Since then the name of the Serpent Lord has once more become a famous one throughout Harad, and his own legend grows with each victory.

Haradrim King (Man)　　　Points value: 60

	F	S	D	A	W	C	M/W/F
Haradrim King	5/4+	4	5	2	2	5	2 / 2 / 1

Wargear
A Haradrim King wears armour. At an additional cost he may have the following items:

> Hand weapon . . . .*Free*
> Spear . . . .*1 pt*
> Bow . . . .*5 pts*
> Lance . . . .*5 pts*
> Horse . . . .*10 pts*

Special Rules
Poisoned Arrows. See the rules for Suladân above.

Harad was once ruled by great kings, whose whims fashioned the destiny of the realm. Though all royal lines have now long since died out, we have included the option for you to include such mighty leaders in your forces if you wish.

Haradrim Chieftain (Man)　　　Points value: 45

	F	S	D	A	W	C	M/W/F
Haradrim Chieftain	4/4+	4	5	2	2	4	2 / 1 / 1

Wargear
A Haradrim Chieftain wears armour. At an additional cost he may have the following items:

> Hand weapon . . . .*Free*
> Spear . . . .*1 pt*
> Bow . . . .*5 pts*
> Lance . . . .*5 pts*
> Horse . . . .*10 pts*

We have included the option for you to include one or more Haradrim Chieftains as part of your force.

Special Rules
Poisoned Arrows. See the rules for Suladân above.

Hâsharin (Man) — Points value: 90

	F	S	D	A	W	C	M/W/F
Hâsharin	5/3+	4	4	3	2	4	1 / 1 / 3

The despotic lords who rule Harad exercise their will through the Hâsharii, an order founded in Sauron's name. Any decision taken by the Lords of Umbar, no matter how trivial, must be ratified by a member of the Hâsharii order, and any attempt to skirt their authority is always noticed and remembered. To frequently question or contradict the will of a Hâsharin leads to death, whether by public execution, or through the quiet application of their murderous skills.

Wargear
A Hâsharin carries a wide array of poisoned blades (count as a hand weapon), throwing daggers, and a blowpipe (treat it as a bow with a range of 12"/28cm).

Special Rules
The Bane of Kings. The weapons of the Hâsharii are coated with a deadly poison, far more potent than that commonly used by other warriors. Each time a Hâsharin strikes a model with a shooting or close combat attack, but fails to wound, he must re-roll the D6.

Stalk Unseen. Hâsharii learn to walk silently and stealthily through all manner of terrain. A Hâsharin always counts as wearing an Elven cloak

Preternatural Agility. Hâsharii are graceful and elegant fighters, able to dart aside from the thrust of a blade with ease and strike through the gaps in a foe's armour with pinpoint accuracy. To represent this dexterity in gaming terms, a Hâsharin can never be trapped whilst still standing.

The Mûmakil are not native of the arid land of Harad, but come from the savannahs even further afield. The Men that live there, a mysterious and fierce race of deadly hunters known in Harad as 'the Mahûd', were the first to tame the Mûmakil. Through centuries of trade and war, the Haradrim learnt how to use these, the Mûmakil, as beasts of burden and war, but the Mahûd are still the best at controlling these mighty creatures. The tribal leaders of the Mahûd can develop such a strong empathy with these animals that they are said to even be able to talk to them. For this reason, the wealthiest Haradrim leaders go to great lengths to hire the services of a Mahûd Chieftain to command their Mûmak into battle.

Mûmakil of Harad Points value: 275

	F	S	D	A	W	C
Mûmak	4/-	9	7	3	10	2
Howdah	-	-	9	-	5	-

The Mûmak automatically comes with a Commander (Haradrim Chieftain armed with a spear and wearing armour).

The Mûmak may have the following upgrades at additional cost:

> *Tusk Weapons* . . . . *20 pts*
> *Mahûd Chieftain* . . . . *25 pts*

Wargear

Tusk Weapons. Sometimes the Haradrim attach long chains, spikes and other lethal implements to the tusks of the Mûmakil, in order to make it even more difficult for unfortunate victims to escape the fury of their charging war-beasts. If given this upgrade, the Mûmak inflicts four Strength 9 hits rather than the normal three when Trampling.

Mahûd Chieftain. The Mahûd Chieftain carries a hand weapon and wears armour. He replaces, in all respects, the Mûmak's Commander, except that he always stands on the bi-forked wooden structure at the front of the Mûmak (the position at the top of the howdah can be freely filled by a normal Haradrim). In such a position, the Mahûd Chieftain receives less cover against incoming missile fire than the Haradrim in the howdah. The howdah counts as in the way of an enemy shot only if some part of it is physically between the shooter and the Mahûd Chieftain (following the normal rules for cover).

	F	S	D	A	W	C	M/W/F
Mahûd Chieftain	4/-	4	5	2	2	5	3 / 2 / 2

EVIL WARRIORS

Haradrim Warrior (Man)   Points value: 5

	F	S	D	A	W	C
Haradrim	3/4+	3	4	1	1	3

Wargear
The base profile for a Haradrim warrior includes armour and a dagger (hand weapon). Any warrior can be given additional items at the following cost:

Spear . . . .*1 pt*
Bow . . . .*1 pt*
Banner (up to one per Hero included in the same force) . . . . . .*25 pts*

Special Rules
Poisoned Arrows. See the rules for Suladân on page 156.

Life amongst the perpetually warring tribes of Harad has always been hard, for even when there is no greater conflict, the inter-tribal raids grant little peace, and such continual warfare has left the menfolk hardened to the arts of battle.

Haradrim Raider (Man)   Points value: 11

	F	S	D	A	W	C
Haradrim	3/4+	3	4	1	1	3
Horse	0	3	4	0	1	3

Wargear
The base profile for a Haradrim Raider includes a bow, armour and a dagger (hand weapon). Any warrior can be given additional items at the following cost:

Lance . . . .*1 pt*
Banner (up to one per Hero included in the same force) . . . . . .*25 pts*

Special Rules
Poisoned Arrows. See the rules for Suladân on page 156.

Among the Haradrim tribes are accomplished horsemen who roam the desert and savannah alike, conducting unrelenting raids upon their neighbours.

THE WAR FOR MIDDLE-EARTH

The main section of this rules manual covers the most common ways of playing the game, that of narrative, or story-driven, scenarios. Though these alone will give you many hours of gaming pleasure, the extent of The Lord of The Rings goes much deeper. In this section you'll discover many more ways to play The Lord of The Rings, as well as finding helpful advice on building up your forces and expanding your gaming horizons.

So far you've learnt how to play The Lord of The Rings Strategy Battle Game as well as all the different forces to collect. By now, you'll probably have played through several scenarios and acquired a burgeoning collection of miniatures. Whether you are just starting out or are a battle-hardened general, this section of the book contains a wealth of advice on how to get more involved in The Lord of The Rings hobby.

ASSEMBLING MINIATURES

This section comprises all the basics you'll need to get your miniatures assembled and into the fray in short order. You'll be walked through basing and assembling your metal and plastic models, as well as learn some top tips. It won't be long before you're ready to tackle a multi-part model from the range, such as the Cave Troll.

PAINTING THE MODELS

The models don't have to be painted in order to enjoy playing The Lord of The Rings but there's nothing like gaming with a set of fully painted gaming miniatures. In this section, you'll see how to prepare miniatures for painting, and applying the first coats of paint. In addition, there are a few painting effects that can be used to add the appearance of light and shade to models, which are shown in close-up detail. These include applying extra layers of paint and ink, as well as how to paint specific areas of the

model that benefit from extra attention, such as the face. We finish off with stage-by-stage painting guides, covering Hobbits and Dwarves.

MAKING TERRAIN

The more exciting your battlefield looks, the more enjoyable the game will be. A gaming table looks better straight away by adding just a few pieces of terrain to it, and in this section you'll learn how to build your own scenery. You'll be shown how to make small terrain features from everyday objects (as well as collecting pieces of ready-made scenery) and putting them on simple surfaces, as well as the more challenging project of making a gaming board.

BATTLE SCENARIOS

For those times when you don't want to play games based on specific narratives, this section contains more general encounters, called Battle Scenarios, which represent snapshots of the action that takes place throughout the story of The Lord of The Rings. Unlike story-driven scenarios, this allows any Good force to be pitted against any Evil force, presenting you with an almost unending degree of variety to your games.

MUSTERING THE FORCES

This section offers a guide to how two very different forces, one Gondor, the other of Mordor, were collected, as well as expounding the painting and modelling techniques that were used to get them onto the gaming board.

PREPARING FOR A SIEGE

Some of the most exciting games you can play in The Lord of The Rings, siege games also require a fundamental piece of terrain: a castle. This section shows you how to make a simple set of fortifications over which you can play your games as well as a scenario to get you started.

RIVER ASSAULT RULES

Rivers can make for excellent gaming terrain and so, in this section, we show you how to make simple boats, as well as presenting rules for how to use them in your games.

COASTAL RAIDS

By now, you should be a veritable painting and modelling powerhouse, so here you'll find a section to pull everything together. Coastal raids not only offer you a wide variety of scenarios to play, but also the opportunity to use the boats you've made and the forces you've collected. Also in the section are guidelines for making a coastline for your troops to assault and defend.

ASSEMBLING MINIATURES

The Lord of The Rings gaming miniatures are made from either rigid plastic or high quality pewter. The plastic models are an ideal starting point for a collection – they provide the player with a core of warriors at relatively little cost. The metal models are hand-cast pieces available either as boxed sets or in display packs.

ASSEMBLING PLASTIC MODELS

Pieces can be removed from the sprues using modelling clippers or a suitable craft knife. If desired any attachment scars can be gently pared away with a craft knife or filed smooth by means of a file. Some plastic models come in two or more parts, and all will need affixing to their base. You can assemble the components using a polystyrene cement or plastic glue.

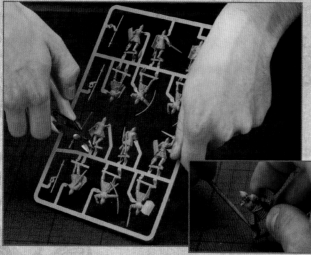

ASSEMBLING METAL MODELS

The Lord of The Rings miniatures range includes both small and large models. Some are cast in a single piece whilst others come as kits of several components. Generally speaking, most of the man-sized creatures are single-piece castings whilst the largest monsters, such as the Shelob, are multi-piece models.

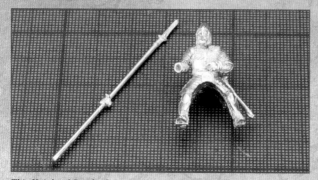

This Knight of Gondor has a separate spear that will need carefully fixing in place with superglue.

MODELLING TIP

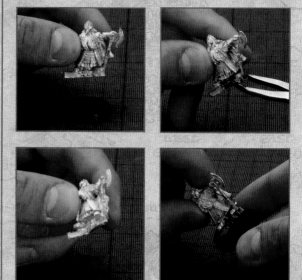

Hand-cast metal models will naturally vary slightly and it is quite common for a model's base rail to sit loosely in the plastic base. This is not usually a problem as the models will be glued to their bases anyway – but a firm fit can be created by taking a small pair of pliers and kinking the base rail slightly.

Remove any stray metal vents or casting marks from the model before assembling. Vents are cut into the moulds to allow air to escape – this leaves a thin spur of metal that often falls away when the model is removed from the mould. If not this can be removed with a modelling knife or clippers, and any resultant scar can be filed flat using a small modelling file.

If a model comes in two or more metal parts some extra work is required. Test the pieces for fit before assembly and use a file to smooth out any notable blemishes or high points that prevent alignment. Don't worry if the fit is not perfect – hand-cast parts vary slightly and it is usual to find slight gaps that will require filling later. Once you are satisfied with the fit assemble the pieces using superglue.

FILLERS

Slight gaps and joins will tend to disappear under a coat of paint, or can be filled with a dab of glue. Larger gaps however will need to be filled. There are many types of modelling putty available for this, such as Green Stuff. Most come as a two-part epoxy putty that hardens once mixed.

GLUE

Glues commonly used for modelling include liquid polystyrene, PVA glue and superglue.

ASSEMBLING MULTI-PART MINIATURES

A Cave Troll.

GETTING STARTED

Within The Lord of The Rings range there are a number of large creatures for you to add to your force. These are normally multi-part figures, designed for more advanced modellers, but do not be put off by this. Here are a few of the tools that you'll need to assemble multi-part models:

Superglue
A craft knife
A selection of needle files
A pair of clippers
A pin vice and drill bits
A cutting board

Safety is a very important consideration when undertaking modelling work of any kind. All of these tools are potentially dangerous and need to be used with care. Blunt blades are dangerous, as far more force is required to make a cut.

l. Using a pair of clippers, carefully remove the tabs from all the component parts.

2. The next stage is to smooth the surface down with a needle file and remove any rough edges.

3. Some multi-part models come with a pin in one of the legs. A hole should be cut onto the base and the pin glued into it. In the case of the 40mm round base, the underside

has a set of specially located holes; turn the base upside down so you can see a suitable hole that matches the model's stance. Drill a small guide hole directly through its centre, using a pin vice.

4. Hold the base firmly and twist the knife gently into the guide hole until it bores through the plastic.

5. The legs are then attached to the base using superglue.

PINNING

In the case of multi-part models, such as the Cave Troll, Balrog and Fell Beast, pinning the different pieces together gives a stronger fit. The model is also less likely to break due to handling during a game. To pin a model, the two joining parts have a matching hole drilled into them into which a small metal rod is glued, adding strength to the joint.

1. Two holes are drilled into the join, approximately 5mm deep.

2. A short length of wire is inserted into each of the holes and a small blob of paint applied to the end of each.

3. Whilst the paint is still wet the two parts are carefully aligned and pressed together. When the two parts are separated the paint leaves two marks where matching holes need to be made. Once they are drilled, slightly longer pieces of wire are glued into the holes and the join completed.

You can pin any parts you feel need strengthening like this.

DETAILING BASES

Larger models naturally have bigger bases and it's a good idea to add some scenic decoration such as a small rock, plants or bushes. Bear in mind that one or two well-placed areas of detail will work far better that overloading the base with too much material.

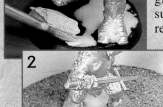

1. A small pebble is first glued to the base using superglue. Once dry, the remaining surface of the base is painted with PVA.

2. Dip the base in sand and, once the material is dry, it is ready for painting.

LARGE CREATURES

Quite often bodies such as the Balrog's come in two halves. To ensure a good join between the two pieces, you may need to file them down a little or fill in any tiny gaps. Apply a thin layer of black paint to the rim of one of the

body halves, and when the paint is dry press the two halves together and give a very slight twist.

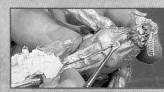

When the two halves are pulled apart, paint will have worn away where the pieces need to be filed down. File away small areas of metal, repeating the whole process until a good fit is achieved.

FILLING GAPS

When the model is assembled, some joins may still be

visible. Roll Green Stuff into a long sausage and lay it along the line of the join. Smooth the putty into shape using the blunt end of a sculpting tool dipped in water.

Details such as scales or fur require a little modelling work to blend the modelling putty so that it matches the detail. Using the sharp end of the sculpting tool, follow the pattern and lines of the model as closely as possible.

PAINTING YOUR MODELS

Most players will want to assemble their models right away so that they can learn the game or take part in a new scenario. Other players feel that models are only really 'finished' once painted and would never dream of bringing a warrior to battle without its requisite coat of paint. The Lord of The Rings battle game works perfectly well whether the models are painted or not. If you are learning the game you certainly won't want to wait until you have painted an entire army before playing. On the other hand, most players enjoy the spectacle of painted models and usually get round to painting at least some of their collection.

WHAT YOU WILL NEED

You will need somewhere to paint, such as a desk or table placed by a window so you can see what you are doing. Good lighting is important and if you want to paint in the evenings you will need a desk lamp or something similar.

Once you have cleared a space to paint, put a good thick layer of newspaper onto the surface to protect it from spills and being scratched. It's a good idea to back this up with a piece of heavy card or board on the area where you will be working directly, but an extra layer of newspaper will do just as well.

Finally, make sure your work area is as comfortable as possible. If you can adjust the height of your chair or the table itself so much the better. Put on some music – listen to the radio – relax and enjoy spending time painting.

BRUSHES

Citadel Colour brushes are made specifically with painting our kind of models in mind. They are made from quality sable and sized according to function.

Different painters will favour different sizes of brush depending on their style and subject, but most people find the Standard brush is ideal for most purposes. After that, the most useful is the Detail brush for intricate work, and a Basecoat brush for larger areas. One each of Detail, Standard and Basecoat will provide all you need for most tasks.

If you prefer, other makes of quality sable artist brushes can be used. You can find a selection in any specialist art suppliers. In addition, the The Lord of The Rings paint set comes with a Starter brush which is halfway between a Standard and Detail in size and is an ideal compromise for most functions, especially for beginners who often find a slightly smaller brush easier to handle.

Looking After Brushes – Brushes are not cheap so it is worth looking after them. They will last longer and serve you better. Try to avoid getting the brush so overloaded that the paint runs into the metal part of the handle (the ferrule) where it will dislodge the glue and unseat the bristles. When you have finished a painting session rinse out your brush carefully in clean, cold water, and repoint the bristles between thumb and forefinger. Store the brushes point-upwards in an old mug or similar container – they will retain their points for longer.

Old Brushes – As brushes wear they gradually lose their points and develop stray bristles. Pinch off any bristles that become bent or stick out at an angle. Once the brush becomes too worn for general use it can be employed for gluing, painting bases, or for other rough work where it would be a waste to use a good brush.

Above is a range of paints and brushes available from Games Workshop for painting your The Lord of The Rings miniatures.

PAINT

Citadel Colour paint is designed for painting plastic and metal miniatures. It is non-toxic and water based but waterproof once dry. You can also use other water-based acrylic modelling or artists' paints, although you will find colour and consistency varies somewhat from one manufacturer to another. To begin with you'll need a small selection of colours to which you can add different shades as required.

WATER

You will need clean water to rinse brushes between colours and to thin down paint. A low, sturdy container is essential to avoid accidentally knocking over your water.

TISSUE

This is useful for wiping paint and excess water from brushes. Also useful for dealing with the occasional spillage.

PALETTE

A fancy word for an old white plate, saucer, glazed tile, or something similar – although an expensive artists' palette is fine too. Whilst it is sometimes convenient to use paint straight from the pots, on the whole it is better to avoid doing so as it is all too easy to mix the colours or introduce dirty paint water. The palette forms a reservoir of colour and a surface to mix paint and water as needed.

UNDERCOATING MODELS

It is recommended that models are primed before painting. This is simply a matter of applying an undercoat – usually white – over the entire model. The undercoat provides a better surface for the paint and ensures that bare metal or plastic doesn't show through.

Even when spraying outside, put plenty of paper down to contain the spray.

There are two basic methods for undercoating. Most experienced painters use a spray can of matt white undercoat or primer such as the Citadel Skull White undercoat. The spray makes an especially good surface finish for the paint.

A more convenient method for beginners is to apply a brush-on undercoat using either Citadel Smelly Primer or Skull White paint. This is nothing more than a coat of white over the entire model.

Colour of Undercoat – Some experienced painters prefer to work off a black primer rather than a white base. This can be more difficult to work with because colours always look different when applied over black and coverage may be more patchy. Painters who use this method usually leave the primer uncovered in the deepest recesses of the model, and work up the paint with progressively lighter colours. This can be very effective in the hands of experts but it is by no means a superior method – many experts prefer to work from white.

MAKING A START

As any experienced artist will tell you there is no right or wrong 'look' when it comes to painting. Even a simple coat of paint will vastly enhance the appearance of your collection.

If you want to become a real expert then you will have to practice, watch other painters, and take the time to develop your skills. Most importantly, don't feel that you have to produce a masterpiece each and every time you paint. Now and again you might want to paint a model specifically as a display piece, but such models are best kept away from the gaming table and preserved from constant handling and wear.

FLAT COLOUR

When you apply a single solid colour onto your undercoat, the result is a flat colour – an even coverage with no shading, highlighting or other effects. In some cases two light coats of paint may be needed to achieve a uniform flat colour – this gives better results than a single very heavy coat, which may obscure detail.

When you're starting out painting miniatures in flat colours will be the natural thing to do. However, after you've gained some confidence you might want to start adding little tricks such as a 'wash' or 'drybrushing', which will transform a model's appearance dramatically.

WASHES

Traditionally a 'wash' is a mix of paint and sufficient water to give a fluid consistency. This mixture is applied over a light base colour and, depending on how much wash is used, will tend to run into the cracks and crevices. The result is an overall 'stain' that is stronger in the recesses where the wash gathers. This introduces a level of naturally gradated shading onto the model and breaks up the overall colour into subtle patches of dark and light. The surface finish will be slightly mottled and therefore appears more natural in the case of organic surfaces such as flesh, leather, and cloth.

The Citadel Colour range includes acrylic inks that are designed to be used with washing and glazing techniques. The darker ink colours are ideal for washes, and black can be mixed in to make them even darker. Because ink contains an intense pigment in a transparent medium, it gives different results to a mix made up of paint and water.

Apply Chainmail paint over the whole suit of armour. *Apply a wash of Black Ink over the Chainmail areas.*

Paint the skin Bronzed Flesh. *Apply a diluted mix of Flesh Wash, Scorched Brown and PVA glue to the skin.*

Paint the hair Bubonic Brown, leaving the Chaos Black undercoat in the deepest recesses. *Apply the same mix used for the face to the hair.*

By adding some PVA glue you can change the effect of an ink wash. The PVA glue enhances the way in which the wash gathers in the crevasses of the model, and produces a stronger contrast once dry. You will have to experiment to judge the effect for yourself. Conversely, if you want to reduce the gathering quality of an ink wash, producing a more even overall tone, add a little liquid soap, such as washing up liquid. This breaks the surface tension so the ink stains the surface more uniformly without forming patches.

If you wish to make washes using paint, it is worth experimenting by adding Citadel Colour Varnish to the mix. This makes paint behave much more like ink and strengthens the contrast compared to paint and water alone. Again, as with all wash techniques, you will need to experiment to gauge the result. Some courage is called for!

Paint the cloak Goblin Green.

If you use too much wash, or if the wash is settling where you do not want it, it is easy to draw away the surplus using either a brush or tissue. If bubbles form in the wash they will usually disperse quickly, but sometimes they will dry within the recesses of the model leaving clean patches. Blowing briskly on the model will help to disperse any bubbles whilst the wash is still wet.

Paint a mix of Golden Yellow and Bestial Brown over Skull White. *Apply a watered down wash of Scorched Brown over the hair.*

Apply a dilute mix of Dark Green Ink, Scorched Brown paint, and PVA glue.

Washes seem to work better over pastel colours as this emphasises the contrast. Add a little white to the basecoat and observe the effect of a wash.

> *The Citadel Colour inks, paints, varnish and PVA glue can be mixed together to vary the properties of a wash. As with all techniques, improvement comes with practise, and in the case of washes it is worth performing a few tests so that you can judge the results for yourself. You can do this by taking a white undercoated figure and experimenting with the different effects of using inks, diluted paint, and paint and varnish.*

DRYBRUSHING

The drybrush technique is a fast and attractive way of adding highlights to areas of raised detail. It can also be used to apply a fine texture to large flat areas such as armour plating to create a realistic effect. A light drybrush over an entire model can give it an overall dusting that draws the colours together and gives a natural appearance.

Drybrushing is most easily demonstrated by painting hair or fur texture. Begin with a suitable base colour that has been shaded with a wash if required – the drybrushing is added at the final stage to provide highlights.

Take the brush (preferably an old brush) and mix up a lighter shade of the base colour. The paint needs to be fairly dense. If the paint is a little thin, let it dry slightly on the palette. Work the colour into the brush and then wipe any excess back onto the palette.

Now – most importantly – run the brush over a tissue or newspaper, or some similarly absorbent surface, until the strokes leave almost no mark even when applied with pressure. Depending on the effect you want, you can make the brush more or less dry.

Begin by stroking the brush gently over the surface that you wish to highlight. If done properly the brush should leave no discernible strokes, but only deposits a fine, even dusting of colour over the high points on the model.

The drier the brush, the more the effect will appear as a dusting of even colour. Build up the highlights gradually and notice how repeated dusting gives naturally gradated highlights. The longer you work at the result, the more intense the effect.

Several progressively lighter layers of drybrushing can be applied to increase contrast – the final layer can be white. When you drybrush over a fairly bright colour, the result can sometimes look very chalky. If you want to restore colour while retaining the highlighting, apply a wash of ink mixed with a lot of water to bring some of the colour back into it.

Drybrush Scorched Brown straight onto the black undercoated fur.

Apply a lighter drybrush of Snakebite Leather on top.

Give the fur a final drybrush of Bleached Bone.

First, apply a basecoat of Tin Bitz to the Uruk-hai's armour.

Then drybrush over the armour with Mithril Silver.

Drybrush the cloak with Shadow Grey.

Lightly drybrush Bestial Brown on the edge of the cloak to resemble dirt.

LAYERING

Layering is a technique of representing shade and highlights by painting successive gradations of a colour from dark to light. Two-tone layering over a black undercoat provides shading and highlighting and looks effective from any reasonable distance. In principle, the technique can be used with any undercoat and can be refined to the point where individual layers become indistinguishable even from very close up. A multi-tone layering technique taken to its ultimate form gives results that are comparable to a fully blended technique, but there are many situations where an extra layer will help to pick out details.

Basic colour   *First layer*   *Second layer*

Layering can be used to produce a dramatic contrast. Many people find this 'stripy' style very pleasing when well executed. That means choosing colours that work together despite the differences in shade. Dramatic layering rarely uses more than three layers and some examples of useful colour combinations are shown below.

Paint a layer of Dwarf Flesh over a basecoat of Bestial Brown, leaving the deepest recesses dark.   *Apply a lighter layer of Elf Flesh over the previous one, concentrating on the highest points of detail.*

If you look at the Citadel Colour range you can work out dramatic contrasts by taking a root colour and picking out the midtone and one of the lightest colours in the series.

A sophisticated multi-layer technique relies on mixing the colours together in different proportions to produce intermediate shades. The colour samples shown below illustrate this quite well. In our samples the effect is a succession of stripes, but if the stripes are sufficiently narrow then the eye ceases to distinguish the individual shades even from close up.

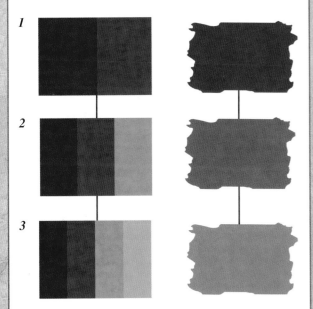

The samples above show how an Orc's flesh was painted using this layering technique.

1. The first layer was painted with a base colour mixed from equal amounts of Terracotta and Snakebite Leather.

2. The flesh was highlighted by adding increasing amounts of Dwarf Flesh to the base colour.

3. Once a layer comprising roughly equal parts of the three colours was achieved, progressive amounts of Rotting Flesh was added to any further layers.

Give Saruman's robes a basecoat of Bestial Brown.   *Layer Kommando Khaki on top of the folds of the robe, leaving the base colour in the recesses.*

Apply a lighter layer of Bleached Bone over the previous one.   *Finally, apply a layer of Skull White on the top of the sharpest folds.*

Hair and Fur – *Hair and fur textures can be brought to life by means of brushing a lighter colour over the raised detail to create highlights. The less paint you use the more subtle the effect – experiment to get a look which you like. You may find it helps to actually wipe most of the paint from the brush, leaving only a little dry residue. Then brush over the areas to be highlighted, depositing a fine dusting of paint to the raised areas.*

Base colour

First layer

Final layer

Painting Faces – *Beginners often find faces daunting but it is quite easy to get a realistic effect using the method shown here. In this case the artist is working over a black undercoat – but the technique will work perfectly well over white. The base colour is Dwarf Flesh. Once this is dry, Brown Ink has been painted over and allowed to gather into the creases. Once this is dry, the artist has mixed Dwarf Flesh and Elf Flesh and repainted the face*

Base colour

Ink stage

Highlight stage

but leaving the Brown Ink showing around the eyes, nose, and other recessed areas. Finally, Elf Flesh has been used to paint the high points on the face – the bridge of the nose, cheeks, and brow ridges. This can be seen more clearly in the accompanying diagram.

Detail – *The amount of detail you include is up to you, but don't feel you have to add every fingernail or dot the pupil of each eye. Our models are generally seen at arm's length or greater and will appear very much like real people at 50 to 100 paces away. At those kinds of distances eyes, nails, teeth, and details of clothing don't really stand out. Trying to paint eyes onto models an inch tall is not only taxing, but tends to look unrealistically starey. Such levels of detail are best reserved for those models you want to display, where you might happily spend an hour getting the face 'just right'.*

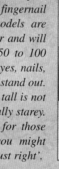

Button, rivets, and small details – *Imagine you are painting a coat with a row of buttons and you have painted the coat colour. Now you want to make the buttons really stand out from the coat. First paint each button black, allowing the paint to cover the entire button and slightly overlap onto the coat. Wait until this is dry and then paint each button with silver, leaving the overlap showing black. Result – a silver button outlined in black. You can use the same technique to outline any small area of raised detail to make it really stand out.*

Varnish – *Some people like to apply a coat of varnish to their model once it is finished. This protects the paint from chipping or wearing away whilst the miniature is being used in a battle.*

Should you wish to varnish your models use either a brush-on polyurethane varnish or a spray can. Some people like the highly shiny finish of protective varnish – but others hate it!

If you prefer a non-gloss finish, satin varnishes are available too!

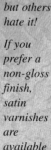

CONVERSIONS

Some modellers create entirely new miniatures by cutting, transplanting, and remodelling the standard pieces. Hobbyists usually refer to these special models as conversions – you'll find much more about painting, modelling and converting in Games Workshop's monthly magazine White Dwarf.

This nicely converted Gondorian Captain started life as a Spearman – the sword has been carefully cut from another model and repositioned.

The Elven Captain conversion is based on the Elrond model but has been given a different head and a shield slung on his back.

This Rohan warrior has had his spear replaced with an axe.

This splendid Rider of Rohan started life with a bow but has been converted to carry a sword and shield – his mount has also been changed into a rearing pose.

This Rohan warrior's right arm has been repositioned to make a more dramatic pose.

This Mordor Orc was originally armed with a sword. The hand was drilled through and a piece of wire inserted. An axe head was cut from another Orc and attached to make a long-hafted axe.

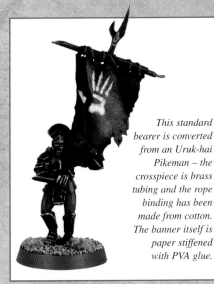

This standard bearer is converted from an Uruk-hai Pikeman – the crosspiece is brass tubing and the rope binding has been made from cotton. The banner itself is paper stiffened with PVA glue.

Riding down his Uruk-hai foe, this Rider of Rohan was originally converted to feature his spear pointing downwards. Then the modeller decided to add an Uruk-hai being ridden down by the mounted warrior. The final touch was to cut and turn the rider's head towards his victim.

MAKING FLAGS

You can add a flag to a spear to make a suitable banner or substitute a weapon for a length of wire to make a flag pole. The best material for flag poles is brass rod as this is quite rigid. To add a flag pole to a model it is necessary to cut away any weapon and drill out the fist so that it can carry the wire pole.

A flag can be made from paper. A piece of newsprint devoid of ink, such as can be found along the edges of any newspaper, is ideal for this as it is absorbent but reasonably stiff. Cut the flag shape leaving an extra 5mm towards the pole. Wrap the flag round the pole and check for fit. Using PVA 'white woodworking glue', glue along its extreme edge and allow to dry. Now wrap the flag round the pole and apply more PVA glue thinned with water, allowing the glue to soak into the part of the flag around the pole. Once this is dry paint the entire flag with a mixture of PVA glue and water, arrange into a dramatic shape, and allow to dry. As the PVA dries out it stiffens sufficiently so the flag can be coated overall with white, ready to paint with your preferred design.

Remove the model's weapon with clippers.

File the hand flat.

Drill a hole through the hand with a pin vice.

Cut the flag from a piece of paper.

Push a piece of brass rod through for the banner pole.

Use PVA to fasten the flag.

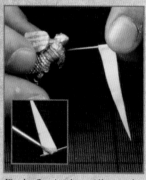
Fix the flag in place. Allow to dry.

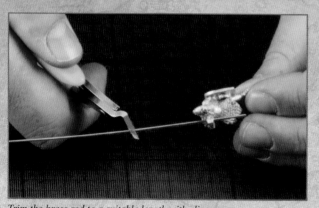
Trim the brass rod to a suitable length with clippers.

Apply a good coat of PVA, shape as desired and allow to dry.

Rohan banner

Eomer's banner

Rohan banner

Elven banner

Gondorian banner

Isildur's banner

Gondorian banner

Aragorn's banner

Orc banners

PAINTING DWARVES

Throughout this book there are photographs of superbly painted models on the tabletop. Here we show you how easy it is to get a good result yourself. To paint your models you don't need many tools either; just a few paints, a brush, a space to work on with newspaper to protect the surface and a little patience.

This painting guide shows how to paint a Dwarf. By applying just a few quick and effective techniques, you'll be able to to recreate the same colour scheme we used on Balin's Dwarves.

Textured areas such as metal can be brought to life by brushing Chainmail over the raised detail to create highlights. You may find it helps to actually wipe most of the paint from the brush, leaving only a little dry residue. Then brush over the areas to be highlighted, depositing a fine dusting of paint to the raised areas.

The model is undercoated Chaos Black.

2
Using the same approach as for painting the metal, apply Bestial Brown to the strands of beard and hair. To finish off the beard, paint the clasps with Chainmail.

3
Dwarf Flesh is applied to the face and hands. Try not to paint into the recesses of the eyes and fingers – you want to keep the undercoat showing to define the shape.

3
If you get paint between the fingers or into eyes, slightly thin down some Chaos Black paint and, following the shape of the model, line-in the recesses.

4
Apply a base colour of Snot Green to the Dwarf's tunic and sleeves. To make a solid colour you may have to apply several thin coats of paint.

5
Bubonic Brown is painted onto the boots.

6
To finish off, an equal parts mix of Flesh Wash and water is applied to the boots to create shading effect.

7

The axe handle and helmet are painted a basecoat of Dark Flesh.

8

Bestial Brown is applied to the belt and pouch.

9

To finish off the Dwarf's tunic, you may want to paint a stripe of Golden Yellow around the hem. You may have to apply several coats of paint to produce a solid colour.

10

Drybrush Chainmail onto the metal on the shield.

11

Re-undercoat the centre of the shield Chaos Black.

12

To finish off the shield, apply a coat of Snot Green over the black undercoat. Paint several coats to get a strong flat colour.

This approach to painting a Dwarf demonstrates how flat colours, when neatly applied to a model with a few painting effects, can really bring a model to life. When painted onto Balin's Dwarfs, this simple colour scheme creates a unified look to the force which is effective on the tabletop.

PAINTING HOBBITS

Unlike many of the other races of Middle-earth, the Hobbits have no armies. While this means that they don't wear a uniform and each Hobbit's choice of clothing is different, they tend to share a love of natural colours. On these pages, you'll find a guide to painting a selection of colours, commonly worn by Hobbits. When you come to painting your own models, simply select a few of these, and combine them as you wish.

WHITE APRON

Apply a basecoat of Fortress Grey.

Add a layer of Skull White.

Finally, stain the apron with watered down Vermin Brown.

LIGHT BROWN UNDERSHIRT

Begin with a basecoat of Snakebite Leather.

Apply a layer of Desert Yellow.

Highlight the undershirt with Kommando Khaki.

BEIGE HAT

Give the hat a basecoat of Snakebite Leather.

Apply a layer of Desert Yellow.

Highlight with a mix of Kommando Khaki and Bleached Bone.

ORANGE HAT

Use Vermin Brown as the basecoat for the hat.

Apply a layer of Vomit Brown.

Highlight the hat with Bleached Bone.

LIGHT GREEN JACKET

Paint the coat with a layer of Catachan Green.

Add a second layer of Catachan Green mixed with a little Fortress Grey.

Highlight the coat with pure Fortress Grey.

BLUE SMOCK

Paint the model with a mixture of Regal Blue and Chaos Black.

Add Fortress Grey to the mix for the next layer.

Finish off the smock with a highlight of Fortress Grey.

BROWN JACKET

Begin with a basecoat of Scorched Brown.

Apply a layer of Scorched Brown mixed with a little Bleached Bone.

Add more Bleached Bone to the mix for the final highlights.

DARK GREEN COAT

Apply a basecoat of Dark Angels Green, mixed with Chaos Black.

Add a little Skull White for the second layer.

Add more Skull White to the mix for the final highlights.

MAKING TERRAIN

To fight a battle with miniature warriors it follows that you'll need a miniature battlefield. Some players enjoy creating accurate scale scenes to stage their games, others are happy to improvise around a few basic pieces and let their imaginations do the rest; either way works just as well.

If you enjoy scenery making then you'll probably want to devote more time and attention to the appearance of your battles. If you don't, then you'll still want to know how you can create useful terrain relatively quickly. Whatever your skill level or needs – this section of The Lord of The Rings rules manual is all about making scenery for your battlefield.

THE TABLE

A typical kitchen table will be more than big enough to stage all except the largest battle but a bigger table gives you the flexibility to create grander and more ambitious battlefields. Many enthusiasts make their own dedicated games table by taking a large sheet of chipboard, plywood, or medium density fibre-board (MDF) and fastening it over the top of an old table, desk or cupboard. The standard size for these materials is 8' x 4' (about 240cm x 120cm). This is big enough for staging large battles and about the greatest width that most people can comfortably reach and move models that are in the middle of the table.

Most players don't have the room to leave such a large table set up all the time, so they keep the board separate to the base, storing it elsewhere when not in use. Depending on the material used it may be necessary to provide some bracing underneath to prevent the board bending under its own weight.

If you don't have room for a large table then the kitchen or dining room table can be pressed into service – unless of course your family's needs dictate otherwise. Valuable antiques and prized polished surfaces should be avoided at all costs. If you have no other option there is always the floor – which has the benefit of being flat and large, and should you accidentally drop a model it won't have far to fall!

A CLOTH BATTLEFIELD

One of the quickest and easiest ways of making a battlefield with a landscape of rises and falls is to use a large piece of cloth. You'll need a piece of cloth that's a suitable colour to represent the ground – ideally green or brown – and of a fairly heavy weight. A blanket is ideal.

Spread the blanket over the table's surface and place books, magazines, or something similar underneath to create hills and valleys. With a little care it is possible to make the battlefield interesting by introducing cover that will restrict visibility and provide shelter. With the cloth in place you can add further scenery such as scrub, trees, buildings, and ruins to complete the scene.

COMMERCIAL SCENERY

Most people will be familiar with the kind of detailed scenery available for model railway enthusiasts. A battle scene is very similar in many ways and you can use many of the same items and materials. Most model railway buildings, fences, and actual constructions are a little small, but trees and foliage have no obvious scale and can be used to good effect.

Games Workshop's attractive range of tabletop scenery includes Battle Mats, trees, hedges, walling, and various set pieces such as ruins, all of which are similar in concept to those you'll find in railway hobby stores.

The most useful purchase you can make is a bag of lichen. Lichen, or reindeer moss as it is also known, is a natural product that you can buy in model railway stores and sometimes from craft or gift shops as it is also used by flower arrangers. Lichen can be used to represent scrub, bushes, or any kind of similar vegetation, and can be re-used time and time again to create different layouts.

Lichen, or reindeer moss, makes an excellent hedge or line of scrub.

Larger rocks make for ideal instant terrain.

A few small rocks and a scatter of sand produces an instant scene.

MAKING A GAMING BOARD

Battles fought over a plain featureless tabletop soon lose their edge. There are only so many times you can face your opponent's force with nothing between you except a wide open space. Terrain adds an extra level to a battle and making best use of it can mean the difference between victory and defeat for a general.

Free-standing terrain pieces such as hills and buildings are great if you want to have a few items scattered about but if you want to fight on a more realistic and permanent battlefield, modelled terrain boards and, in particular, modular terrain is the way to go.

Modular terrain boards are best made from polystyrene sheets which are lightweight and easy to sculpt to whatever features you want. Hills and valleys can be created by carving into the polystyrene or adding additional layers until the feature is the height you're after.

THE PLAN

As with all projects it's best to have an idea of what the finished item will look like. This is especially true if you are going to build modular terrain because then you can see the different battlefields you can create by turning the boards around and fitting them together in different combinations. To the right are some examples.

 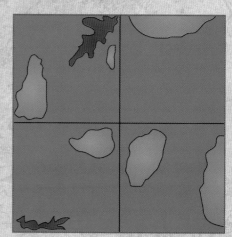

BUILDING THE BOARDS

1. Begin by drawing your plan onto the polystyrene sheets. Then carefully cut away thin slivers of the polystyrene with a craft knife or hot wire cutter – make sure you cut away from yourself to avoid accidents. Features such as valleys or rivers should be cut deep enough so that they are still apparent when covered by paint or battle mat.

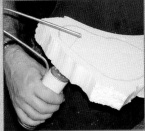

2. Cut out hills with a hot wire cutter. If you want some of the hills to be taller, cut out a second layer of polystyrene to glue on top of them.

3. Glue hills and other such features to the board using PVA glue and then apply filler to cover up any gaps.

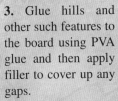
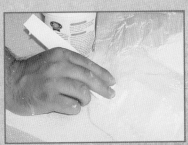

4. Using a Battle mat is an easy solution for adding texture to large areas. By applying a watered down solution of PVA glue and allowing it to soak in, you can mould the mat into the contours and features you have created.

5. Textured paint is another good way of covering parts of your board.

6. Rocky areas can be created using sand, small stones or slate. Adding a coat of textured paint helps to stop bits falling off in transit and applying some of the paint to the surrounding mat helps to blend the areas together.

PAINTING ROCKS

Rocks can be painted in many different ways. This is the method used on the boards on these pages.

1. First apply a Chaos Black undercoat. Then paint the whole surface with Dark Flesh and drybrush with Bestial Brown and then Vomit Brown.

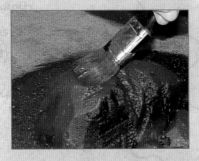

2. To stop the rocks looking too regular, drybrush small sections with Codex Grey and then Bleached Bone.

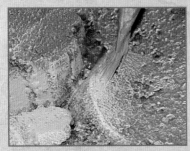

3. Static Grass, sand or small stones are great for covering up gaps.

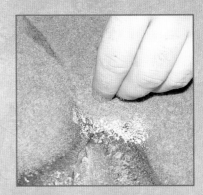

4. To finish off the board, add a strip of duct tape to strengthen the polystyrene against damage. For extra stability, you could always glue the boards to MDF cut to the required size.

BATTLE SCENARIOS

This section of the book introduces a different way of playing The Lord of The Rings Strategy Battle Game – Battle Scenarios. These scenarios are different from normal ones because they set more generic conditions, allowing players to collect one or more forces and then pitch these forces against those of their friends.

THE FORCES

Players first need to agree how big a force they want to use in the game. This normally depends on how long a game they are prepared to commit to. As a rough average, every 100 points equals to around ten models, but this can vary enormously if the force includes very powerful Heroes, which are worth hundreds of points on their own. A game with 500 points a side takes normally a couple of hours to solve, and we find that this time gets longer and longer if players have to control more models. Moving a lot of models one by one takes a lot of time, and that means that the opponent has to wait before he gets to move his own troops, resulting in a very slow game. To reduce this problem we've arbitrarily set the maximum number of models in each force.

Below are the set of limitations we recommend for a good force to be used in a 500 points game:

- Each force can include up to 500 points of either Good or Evil models.

- Each force can include a maximum of fifty models.

- Each force must include at least one Hero to lead it into battle. There is no limit on the points that can be spent on Heroes, so each force can be entirely made up of Heroes if the player wishes.

- Evil Forces cannot include Gollum. Good forces cannot include Tom Bombadil or Goldberry.

- No more than a third (33%) of each force's models can be armed with bows/crossbows. (IMPORTANT: only the Riders of Rohan and Haradrim Raiders models that are actually firing a bow count as armed with bows. All the Riders and Raiders that are carrying a bow on their back do not count as armed with a bow. Note that their points cost remain the same).

- Remember that named Heroes (Gandalf, Lurtz, the Witch-king and the other eight Ringwraiths, etc.) can only be taken once.

- Whenever any rule is repeated in several publications, the most recent version always takes precedence.

SCENARIOS

In the following pages can be found four examples of Battle Scenarios, which make for interesting games to be played with the forces selected according to the guidelines given above. Players can agree which scenario to play or they can roll a dice and consult the following chart:

Dice	Scenario
1	Scenario 1 – The Relief Force
2	Scenario 2 – Take and Hold
3	Scenario 3 – Cornered!
4	Scenario 4 – Pitched Battle
5	The player controlling the Evil force chooses the scenario.
6	The player controlling the Good force chooses the scenario.

Of course players are free to create their own battle scenarios and to change the guidelines regarding the selection of the forces, to experiment, adapt the game to their needs and find new ways to have fun with The Lord of The Rings Strategy Battle Game!

SCENARIO 1 – THE RELIEF FORCE

DESCRIPTION

A group of noble heroes is leading a detachment of warriors of the Free Peoples to reinforce a garrison besieged by the forces of the Dark Lord, and to reach their beleaguered friends they have to cut their way through the enemy lines. This could happen around a small fort on the borders of Gondor or it could even be a minor episode during the great siege of Minas Tirith. Will the forces of Good make it across the enemy defences or will the servants of the Enemy manage to stop them?

STARTING POSITIONS

Both players roll a dice, the player who scores highest can choose the side of the table in which to deploy and consequently play from. The Evil side deploys half of his force (round fractions up) no more than 12"/28cm from his own edge of the table. The Good side then deploys half of his force no more than 12"/28cm from his edge of the table. After these initial deployments the Evil side will then deploy the rest of his force using the same restrictions as before. Finally the Good side deploys the remainder of their force adhering to the deployment restrictions.

OBJECTIVES

The Good side must attempt to break through, by reaching the opposite side of the board and moving off the table with as many models as possible, including at least one Hero. The Evil side must try to slay as many of their enemies as possible before they can escape.

The game is played until the end of the turn in which all of the Good force has been destroyed/has broken through, or the time available for the game expires. At this point, check the victory conditions. Remember that models that retreat off the table because of a failed Courage test, count as slain.

Major Good Victory / Evil Defeat
More than half of the Good force (including a Hero) has moved off the Evil side's table edge.

Minor Good Victory / Evil Defeat
More than a third of the Good force (including a Hero) has moved off the Evil side's table edge.

Minor Evil Victory / Good Defeat
A Good Hero has moved off the Evil side's table edge.

Major Evil Victory / Good Defeat
None of the above conditions have been met.

SPECIAL RULES

Strength in Numbers. As the Evil force is just a part of a larger force scattered around a vast area to search for the Good forces, the Evil force does not need to take tests for being Broken.

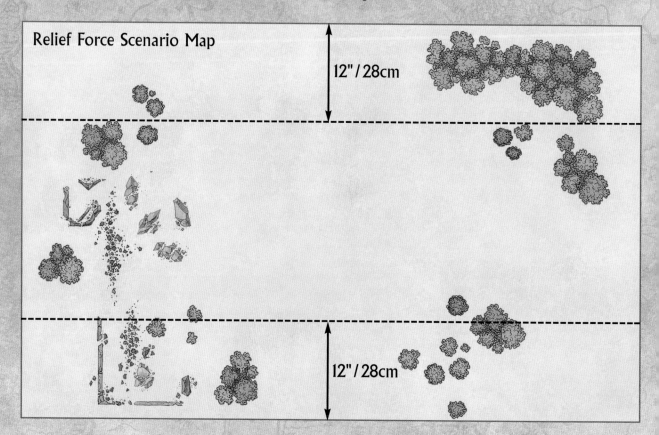

Relief Force Scenario Map

12"/28cm

12"/28cm

SCENARIO 2 – TAKE AND HOLD

DESCRIPTION
At the height of battle, a strategic opportunity presents itself, and suddenly an otherwise unremarkable area becomes vitally important to the cause of the war. One force pounces on the objective and attempts to secure it, leaving their adversaries with an uphill battle to reclaim it.

STARTING POSITIONS
At the start of the game place a marker in the centre of the table. This is the objective and can represent a strategic hill, the resting place of an important artefact, or even the hiding place of a critically wounded hero. The players then roll off to decide which table edge they will play from.

No models are deployed at the beginning of the game. They will enter the table following the Reinforcements special rule (see below).

OBJECTIVES
Once a force has been reduced to half its original numbers, the game might suddenly end. At the end of each turn after this condition is met, roll a dice: on a result of 1-2 the game ends (Might cannot be used to influence this dice roll). When the game ends, count the number of models from each side whose bases are entirely within 3"/8cm of the table's centre and refer to the victory conditions.

Major Victory / Defeat
Only one side has models in the area.

Minor Victory / Defeat
A side has double or more models in the area than the enemy has.

Draw
Time expires in any other situation.

SPECIAL RULES
Reinforcements. At the end of each player's Move phase, after finishing to move their models, players must roll a dice for each model not yet on the gaming table and consult the chart below (Heroes can use their Might to influence their dice roll):

Dice	Result
1-2	The model is delayed and doesn't move onto the table yet. These delayed models count as being on the table for the purpose of determining when the game might end and the entire force needs to start taking Courage tests.
3	The model moves on the table from any point of either short table edge (both the edge and the entering point are chosen by the opponent) at least 6"/14cm from any table corner.
4	The model moves on the table from any point of either short table edge (chosen by the controlling player) at least 6"/14cm from any table corner.
5-6	The model moves on the table from the controlling player's table edge.

Newly arrived models act normally but may not charge. Roll for each model separately, deploy the model and then roll for the next one. Do this each turn until all models have arrived.

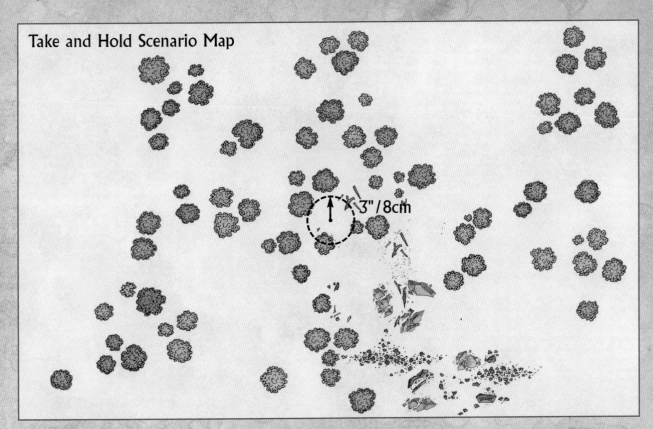

Take and Hold Scenario Map

3"/8cm

SCENARIO 3 – CORNERED!

DESCRIPTION

A marauding band of Evil creatures has been rampaging through the land, burning, pillaging and murdering innocent civilians. A detachment has finally managed to corner them and bring them to battle, with the intention of killing the leader of the raiding party, eliminating the cunning monster responsible for this horror.

STARTING POSITIONS

Before the start of the game the Evil player divides his/her force into two groups. The Good player then picks one of the two groups to be the Evil force used for this scenario. The other group is put aside and is not used at all. The most expensive model in the Evil force is the one that the Good side is trying to kill. If two or more models cost the same amount of points and are the most expensive in the force, then the Good player must declare which model he is going after.

The Evil player deploys his entire force first, within 6" of the table's centre point.

The Good player can then deploy his force anywhere on the table more than 12" away from any Evil model.

OBJECTIVES

The Good force is trying to kill the designated model and the Evil force is trying to protect it until it escapes by moving off the table edge.

Major Good Victory / Evil Defeat
The designated model is killed.

Minor Good Victory / Evil Defeat
The designated model escapes by leaving the table (voluntarily or as a result of failed Courage test), but has suffered two or more wounds.

Minor Evil Victory / Good Defeat
The designated model escapes (voluntarily or as a result of failed Courage test), but has suffered one wound.

Major Evil Victory / Good Defeat
The designated model escapes (voluntarily or as a result of failed Courage test) without suffering any wounds.

Draw
Time expires in any other situation.

SPECIAL RULES

Trap! The Evil side has priority in the first turn of the game.

Desperate! Realising that the enemy will give them no quarter, the Evil force does not need to take Courage tests when Broken.

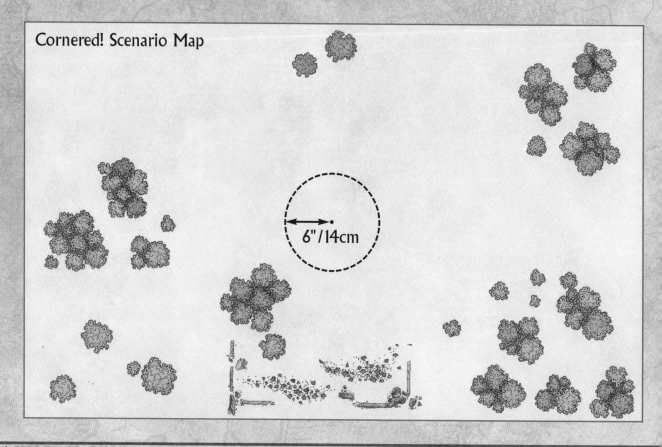

Cornered! Scenario Map

6"/14cm

SCENARIO 4 – PITCHED BATTLE

DESCRIPTION
Once more Good and Evil face each other on the field of battle. Only the Valar know who will win the day!

STARTING POSITIONS
Both players roll a dice, the player who scores highest can choose the side of the table to play from. The side with the most models in his force starts deploying. If the forces are equal, roll a dice, the highest scoring player can decide who starts to deploy.

When deploying, the first player chooses half of his force (rounding up), and rolls a dice. On a 1-3, the models can be deployed no more than 12"/28cm from his edge of the table. On a 4-6, the models can be deployed no more than 18"/42cm from his edge of the table.

Then the other player does the same with half of his force.

The first player then deploys the remaining half of his force as described above, followed by the other player.

OBJECTIVES
The game is played until the end of the turn in which one force is reduced to a quarter of its original number or the time expires.

Major Victory / Defeat
There is only a quarter of the enemy force left and there is at least one surviving Hero on the winning side.

Minor Victory / Defeat
There is only a quarter of the enemy force left, but there are no surviving Heroes on the winning side.

Draw
Both forces are brought to a quarter of their initial strength at the end of the same turn, or the time expires before the victory condition is achieved.

SPECIAL RULES
In this game, the first turn's priority does not go automatically to the Good side, but is determined by rolling a dice: the player that rolls highest gets priority for the first turn (re-roll any ties).

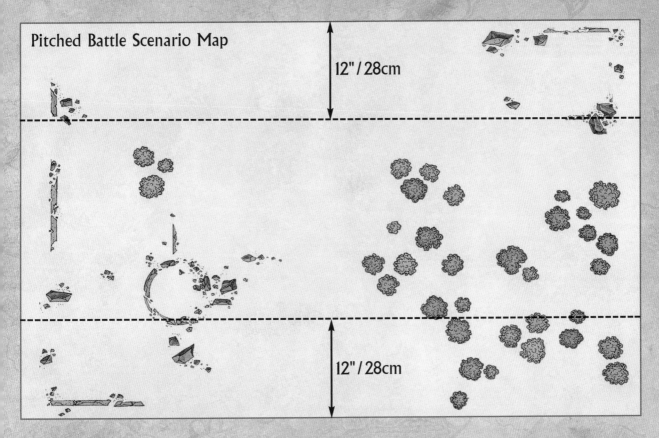

Pitched Battle Scenario Map

12" / 28cm

12" / 28cm

Collecting your forces is probably the most important and enjoyable part of this hobby. There are many different ways to go about mustering your warriors and heroes, so much so that it can seem a little challenging to start with, but with a little thought and planning you can get a force up and running in no time at all.

There are two main ways to build up your The Lord of The Rings forces, and these tend to be defined by the style of game you prefer. If you play lots of 'narrative' scenarios that recreate events from the book or film, the best way is to collect your models as you work your way through the narrative arc. Most supplements for The Lord of The Rings start you with a small selection of models that gradually build into much larger collections for some truly epic battles. If you play more battle scenarios, however, you'll be more likely to want to develop a themed force. This can be based on models you've already collected, although it is sometimes more rewarding to build a themed force from scratch.

Over the next few pages, you'll see how two very different forces were put together for the purpose of playing battle scenarios. Painting tips and modelling guides show how the two armies were given a unified look and a personal touch. It's worth remembering that even though these forces were assembled for battle scenarios, they form a great basis for narrative-style scenarios as well.

WARRIORS OF MINAS TIRITH

Who could forget the brave defenders of Minas Tirith battling against impossible odds in The Return of The King movie, their bodies and armour battered by numerous encounters with the Mordor Orcs of Sauron. Having decided what to collect, the best place to start is with the backbone of any force – the basic troops. For a Gondor force, this is the Warriors of Minas Tirith. Over the following pages is a stage-by-stage painting guide taking you through the different stages of painting a the force. All of the techniques can easily be applied to other forces from The Lord of The Rings.

<table>
<tr><td colspan="4">COLOUR CHART</td></tr>
<tr><td>Bestial Brown</td><td>●</td><td>Chainmail</td><td>●</td></tr>
<tr><td>Dwarf Flesh</td><td>●</td><td>Mithril Silver</td><td>●</td></tr>
<tr><td>Elf Flesh</td><td>●</td><td>Chaos Black</td><td>●</td></tr>
<tr><td>Tin Bitz</td><td>●</td><td>Codex Grey</td><td>●</td></tr>
<tr><td>Boltgun Metal</td><td>●</td><td>Scorched Brown</td><td>●</td></tr>
</table>

THE SKIN

On armoured models such as these, it's best to paint any areas of skin first as it can be difficult to reach them once you have painted the armour.

After undercoating the model, paint any skin areas with Bestial Brown.

Then add a layer of Dwarf Flesh.

Follow with highlights of Elf Flesh around the mouth and chin.

THE ARMOUR, WEAPONS & SHIELD

The armour of a Warrior of Gondor has seen many a battle in recent times so is painted to look slightly worn and dirty.

First apply a layer of Tin Bitz to all areas of the armour.

Next, drybrush a layer of Boltgun Metal – Tin Bitz will show in the recesses to give a worn effect.

Pick out the raised areas on the armour and the sword with Chainmail.

Finish off by applying Mithril Silver, and to the tree of Gondor symbol on the shield and breastplate.

CLOTH & SHIELD FACE

Mix Codex Grey with Chaos Black to produce a flat, dusty basecoat. Although it would originally have been black when new, this mixture adds to the effect of the armour looking battle-worn.

Begin with a dark mix on the shield.

Add more Codex Grey to the mix and highlight the raised areas.

Highlight the cloth with Codex Grey.

HAIR

Paint a basecoat of Scorched Brown on the hair, then drybrush with Bestial Brown.

BASE

The Men of Gondor spend most of their time in the film fighting the Orcs in the ruins of Osgiliath and the White City. We chose to represent this by adding sand and small stones to their bases and painting them the same colour as the terrain they would be fighting on.

RANGERS OF GONDOR

Once you have a basic force and have played a few battles, it's time to start thinking about adding additional troops. To complement the close combat ability of the Warriors of Minas Tirith, the Rangers of Gondor bring to battle their skill with the bow. Either by launching a deadly rain of arrows at a distance or picking off individual Orcs clambering amongst the ruins, they too have their part to play in the defence of the White City.

PAINTING CLOAKS

Paint a layer of Catachan Green as the main colour of the cloak.

Follow this with a layer of Catachan Green mixed with Graveyard Earth.

Then highlight with a mixture of Graveyard Earth and Bleached Bone.

Tip: To add to the appearance of the Rangers being in the city rather than the countryside, drybrush some of the colours from the base onto their boots and the bottom of the cloaks.

COLOUR CHART

Catachan Green	●
Graveyard Earth	●
Bleached Bone	●
Dark Flesh	●
Vermin Brown	●
Blazing Orange	●

BASING THE RANGERS

Although the Rangers would normally be found in the depths of the wilderness, this small detachment is operating within the ruins of Osgiliath. To represent this on the models, they were based in exactly the same way as the rest of the force to maintain coherence.

RANGER CONVERSION

It is always worth putting a little more effort into some models to make them stand out. One way to achieve this is to use a basic model from the force and change its equipment or pose. Another is to use a completely different model and add detail so it has something in common with your warriors.

This is a quick and simple conversion to the Aragorn model.

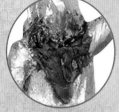

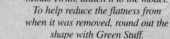

Remove the head and replace with one from a Ranger model. Add Green Stuff in the form of a hood to raise the head above the shoulders slightly.

Remove the left hand and replace with one carrying a Ranger bow.

Using the quiver from a Warrior of Minas Tirith, attach it to the model. To help reduce the flatness from when it was removed, round out the shape with Green Stuff.

The sword is a swap from a Knight of Gondor model.

PAINTING THE RANGER

The model was painted and based in the same style as the other Rangers but with some additional touches.

First the coat was painted with a basecoat of Catachan Green, followed by Catachan Green mixed with Graveyard Earth. This was then highlighted with a mixture of Graveyard Earth and Bleached Bone.

The shirt was given a basecoat of Dark Flesh, followed by a layer of Vermin Brown and highlighted with Vermin Brown mixed with Blazing Orange.

KNIGHTS OF MINAS TIRITH

A good force to aim for is one versatile enough to cater for different situations. So far the Warriors of Minas Tirith have a good selection of 'core' troops and some missile weapon troops; the missing element is speed, which is especially important when facing creatures such as Wargs. This can be ably provided by the Knights of Minas Tirith.

PAINTING THE KNIGHTS

The armour of the Knights was painted in a similar way to the Warriors. The differences were in the horses and weapons.

ADDITIONAL COLOURS

Dark Flesh	●	Chestnut Ink
Vomit Brown		

The horses' socks were painted brown, with small bits of white around the legs to distinguish them from each other.

Normally, spears, bows and other wooden weapons are made from the lighter heartwood of a tree. The Men of Gondor's weapons will have seen a lot of battle so were given an older appearance by being painted with a basecoat of Dark Flesh. A grain effect was achieved by painting strokes of Vomit Brown on before the basecoat completely dried.

BASING THE KNIGHTS

One trick that can be played to make cavalry bases stand out is to apply more detail to them than you can with the base of a foot soldier. Here we have used a plastic Warrior of Gondor model to make the body of a dead comrade on a Knight's base. Chestnut Ink can be used to represent dried blood stains.

CAPTAIN OF MINAS TIRITH

To create the Captain, we first swapped the body of one of the normal Knights with one from a swordsmen. Then the sword was replaced with a more impressive one from the Aragorn model in the Heroes of the West box.

Tip: When adding detail to a base you can add as little or as much as you like. This is particularly impressive on characters, as it can really make the model stand out, as with the pieces of ruined building on the base of the Knight Captain.

ADDING ALLIES

In The Return of The King movie, the warriors of Minas Tirith are joined by the forces of Rohan in their battle against Sauron. These character models from the Rohan range make use of all the techniques given so far.

A foot model and a mounted version of each individual has been painted, so they can be allied to any part of the Minas Tirith force as the battle dictates (and, more importantly, so they can be represented in games if their steed is slain).

COLOUR CHART

Black Ink	⬤	Bleached Bone
Terracotta	⬤	Golden Yellow
Blazing Orange	⬤	Chestnut Ink ⬤
Catachan Green	⬤	Skull White ⬤
Graveyard Earth	⬤	

THÉODEN

To make the body armour stand out more on this model and to also tone down the colour of the chainmail, a wash of Black Ink was applied to darken the colour down.

ÉOMER

When painting a model which is wearing a combination of different armour types, it is best that the two work together rather than one outdoing the other, Here the leather armour has been painted in muted tones with a base layer of Terracotta, that was then highlighted with Blazing Orange, so that it doesn't stand out too much compared to the chainmail and helmet.

MERRY

The cloak Merry wears is painted in the same style as the Rangers of Gondor. We began with a basecoat of Catachan Green. Then the next layer was a mix of this colour and Graveyard Earth. Muted highlights were added with a mixture of Graveyard Earth and Bleached Bone.

ÉOWYN

To create the striking effect of Éowyn's blond hair, we first used a basecoat of Bleached Bone mixed with Golden Yellow. This was then covered in a wash of Chestnut Ink and highlighted with a mix of Golden Yellow and Skull White.

CHOOSING BASES

Although basing the Rohan allies in the same way as the Minas Tirith models would have been a good solution, having them on grey bases just didn't seem to fit. Instead, we added a piece of ruin to each base and then covered the rest of the base in static grass and modelling sand to look like a mixture of earth and debris, the kind that might be found on the edges of Osgiliath or Minas Tirith. This tied them to their allies but still gave them their own identity.

Rider of Rohan base

Knight of Gondor base

WARRIORS OF ROHAN

The mounted Riders of Rohan and the warriors on foot were painted in the same colour schemes as the characters. To further tie the models together as a coherent force, their shields were all painted in a similar style.

THE FORCES OF MORDOR

Intent on destroying the White City, the Orcs of Mordor are bloodthirsty, foul creatures who live for death and destruction above all else. Whereas the Warriors of Minas Tirith have a noble appearance, taking pride in their armour and equipment, Mordor Orcs are the complete opposite. Their clothing is rough and poorly made, their armour barely fit for its purpose and their weapons of the lowest quality.

The techniques that follow show how to quickly paint a force that contains a large number of similar models. By keeping to the same basic colour palette, a lot of models can be tackled in a short amount of time, leaving you time to introduce some individuality amongst the horde by painting small areas on some models a different colour or adding a variety of weapons and equipment.

COLOUR CHART

Scorched Brown	●	Chainmail	●
Bestial Brown	●	Brown Ink	●
Codex Grey	●	Dark Flesh	●
Bleached Bone	●		

CLOTH AND FUR

Mordor Orcs care little for their appearance. Their clothes and furs are covered in dust and dirt, little more than tattered rags crudely stitched together. Unlike the bold bright armour of the Warriors of Minas Tirith, the colour palette for the Orcs comprises earthy colours such as browns and greys.

> *Tip: When trying to achieve a more natural appearance on your models, try to use colours that are similar in tone, and then use a lighter mix of the colour for the highlights.*

First we painted a layer of Scorched Brown over a Chaos Black undercoat. This provides a base colour for the cloth, fur and skin.

Bestial Brown was then applied to the undershirt, gloves, boots and shield.

The fur areas were overbrushed with Codex Grey so that some of the Scorched Brown showed through, giving the effect of dirt-encrusted fur.

Finally, the fur was lightly drybrushed Bleached Bone.

THE ARMOUR

Mordor Orcs wear a combination of chainmail, plate or scale armour, most likely scavenged off the bodies of the slain after a battle. The following method is a good way to tackle all of these armour types in one go.

Paint all the armour in Chainmail.

Then apply a wash of Brown Ink all over.

Once the wash of Brown Ink has been applied, the Chainmail colour will still keep some of its brightness on the raised areas but on flatter or recessed areas such as the plate armour, it will look tarnished.

THE SKIN

In the films, Orc skin ranges in colour from grey through green to dark brown and black. To keep the skin on the models suitably muted, we used Codex Grey or Bleached Bone on the models rather than Skull White when mixing highlights. With the armour and majority of skin painted, more effort was taken over the details of the face.

The skin of the face was highlighted with Codex Grey mixed with Dark Flesh.

Then more Codex Grey was added to the mix to lighten it.

Codex Grey was then applied to the features, such as the cheekbones, brow, lips and nose.

Finally, the teeth were painted with Bleached Bone. Rather than adding a bright colour to the model, the tongue was painted with a coat of Codex Grey – much more fitting for an Orc!

MORDOR URUK-HAI

Mordor Orcs are a terrifying foe to face, but there are those amongst their own kind who surpass even them. Stronger, smarter and better equipped than their lesser cousins, the Uruk-hai are devastating in their attacks – an almost unstoppable force bred for the sole purpose of massacring Sauron's enemies.

The addition of the Uruk-hai complements the basic troops we have chosen for this force. Whereas the Orcs rely on their vast numbers to bolster their courage and lack of individual strength, a single Uruk-hai is many many times stronger and faster. This makes them a devastating close combat troop.

Like the Orcs, the appearance of one Uruk-hai is slightly different from another but together the horde has the same basic colour scheme. A different way to achieve this look is to paint the models in groups, one colour at a time but on different parts of each model. The group still has uniformity but each model looks like an individual, as shown on the three Uruk-hai on the right. On these, Scorched Brown was painted on the tunic of one model, the cloak of the next, the hood on another, and so on.

Only a handful of colours have been used to paint these models, but they have been applied in different combinations.

This Uruk-hai force is commanded by a Captain and Standard Bearer. As there aren't any specific models for these characters, we picked one of the normal Uruk-hai to be the Captain and gave him a larger more ornate base, using some of the ruined wall scenery cut into pieces to represent piles of brickwork.

The Standard Bearer was created by first drilling a hole into the hand of an Uruk-hai and inserting a piece of wire to create the banner pole. Then a piece of torn paper was painted with the symbol of Sauron and glued to the pole as the flag.

MORDOR TROLLS

As deadly as they are ugly, Mordor Trolls add sheer brute force to a battle. These monsters are in no way subtle but there can be no doubt of their effectiveness. The Mordor Orc force consists of a vast number of basic troops, each painted in a similar manner. Although this can look quite impressive when arrayed on the tabletop, painting dozens of troops like this can become a bit monotonous. With large creatures such as the Mordor Troll, you can take a break from painting standard troops and really do something special.

COLOUR CHART

Dark Flesh	●	Chainmail	●
Chaos Black	●	Brown Ink	●
Terracotta	●	Kommando Khaki	●
Dwarf Flesh	●	Bestial Brown	●
Elf Flesh			

CONSTRUCTION

Large models normally come in multiple parts, such as a head, body, limbs and weapons. This Mordor Troll also came with separate armour plates to add to the helmet. For more information on assembling multi-part models see page 164.

COLOUR SCHEME

The skin of the Troll was painted with a layer of Dark Flesh, followed by a wash of Chaos Black. This helped to create shadow to the scaly texture.

The highlights on the scales were first built up with a drybrushed layer of Dark Flesh, then Terracotta, Dwarf Flesh and finally Elf Flesh.

The metal areas of the model were first painted with Chainmail, then with a Brown Ink wash. The edges of the metal were then given their own highlight, making them stand out against the dullness of the rest of the armour.

The claws were painted Kommando Khaki and the lines of the nails with Brown Ink.

Then the straps and cloths were painted Bestial Brown and washed with Chaos Black. To finish off, the buckles were picked out in Chainmail and the Troll's teeth were painted Kommando Khaki.

THE BASE

To add something special to the model, it was set further back on the base than normal. In the space at the front was added an Orc wielding a two-handed axe.

The models needed to complement each other, so the Orc was painted in a similar colour scheme to the Troll.

The remainder of the base was then finished in the same way as the rest of the force but with some larger gravel added to represent rocks and rubble.

CAPTAINS OF MORDOR

All forces need leaders to guide them in battle. This is especially true of the Mordor Orcs and Uruk-hai who, although brave in large numbers and when the fight is in their favour, tend to be rather cowardly when the odds are stacked against them. All leaders need to rise above the common trooper and stand out as a shining example to their warriors!

It's worth bearing this in mind with models too. So instead of just using the normal Mordor Orc and Uruk-hai Captain models, we chose to use conversions of the Shagrat and Gorbag models. Gorbag's armour is much more ornate than the common Orc's. Shagrat too stands apart from his Uruk-hai warriors, having no cloak and helmet but more armour on display.

CONVERTING THE MODELS

To make them unique, both models were converted by adding shields and weapons taken from Mordor Orc Captains.

These three models were the components used to create the two Captains.

Orc Captain

Mordor Uruk-hai Captain

Tip: *Whenever removing parts from models, it's worth taking a little care not to cause too much damage – you may find some use for the remaining model at a later date.*

Using a fine jeweller's saw, the shield was first removed from an Orc Captain and glued to Gorbag's arm.

Then Frodo's mithril shirt was cut carefully away from Shagrat's hand.

After the hand was cleaned up with a file, a pick from an Orc Captain was attached.

PAINTING THE CAPTAINS

The Captains were given the same dark colour scheme as their troops.

The Orc Captain's armour was painted Tin Bitz and the raised areas were picked out with Chainmail, making the armour quite bright compared to the dark base colour. Then the leather straps used to hold the armour together were painted Bestial Brown and highlighted with Vomit Brown. This made the leather stand out from the bright armour.

COLOUR CHART

Tin Bitz	●	Graveyard Earth	●
Chainmail	●	Dark Flesh	●
Bestial Brown	●	Dwarf Flesh	●
Vomit Brown	●		

The Mordor Uruk-hai Captain was painted exactly in the same palette as his troops apart from the introduction of Graveyard Earth on his clothing. The raised detail on his face was painted in Dwarf Flesh over Dark Flesh, a stark contrast that made his brutal features clearer.

THE MÛMAK

Nothing can inspire fear like the Mûmak. Not only can this colossus wreak havoc as it towers above the battlefield, but so too can the contingent of Haradrim warriors on its back, all picking off enemies with their deadly accurate shots.

The Mûmak is the centrepiece of any Evil force so it is well worth taking your time putting this model together. Consider not just how you are going to assemble the model but also how it will be painted.

The Mûmak shown was created in three separate parts: the beast itself, the howdah and its tower. Keeping them separate for painting meant all areas were easier to paint. Otherwise it would have been awkward to paint some of the supports, etc, on the final assembled model. The base has loads of details so that is worth painting separately before attaching. The front prongs and flags can also be painted before being glued to the model.

FIRST STEPS

THE MÛMAK'S HEAD

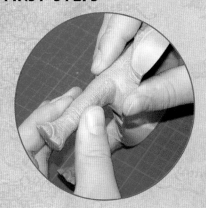

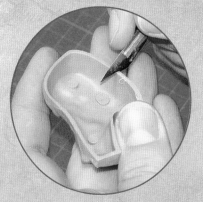

*The legs were assembled
and left to dry,*

*Next, the legs and two halves of the
Mûmak were joined together.*

*To improve the fit of the two halves of the
head, some of the plastic was scraped off.*

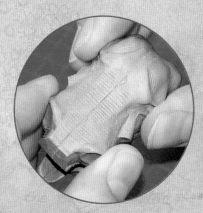

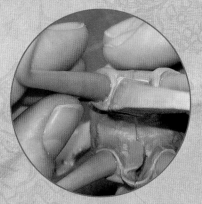

*The pieces were then
glued together.*

*The trunk was test-fitted and its base filed
down slightly so it matched up better.*

*Each tusk was then attached. Check the
attachment of the tusks from all angles to
ensure that they fit symmetrically.*

THE HOWDAH

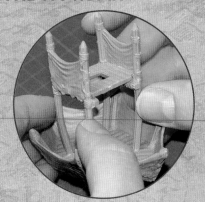

The tower was assembled
and left to dry,

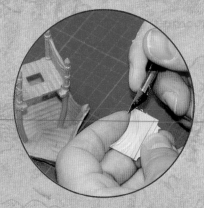

The cloth was first trimmed slightly
to fit better against the tower.

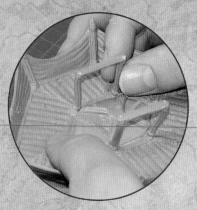

Then the supports were built up
on the base of the howdah.

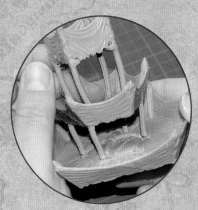

Resting the tower on top whilst the
supports were drying helped to keep
them in the right place.

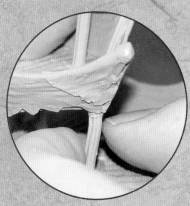

The tower was used again as a guide
when the single supports were positioned.
The supports come with pegs on each end.

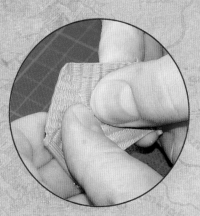

The platform was bent slightly
so its shape fitted that of the supports.

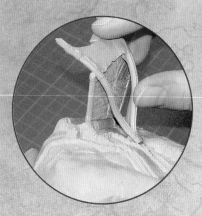

It was then glued to the Mûmak
with the supports underneath.

FINISHING TOUCHES

With the howdah in position, the
supports were attached to the
Mûmak's body. Once the head and
tail were attached, any gaps were
filled with Green Stuff and left to dry
before being filed smooth.

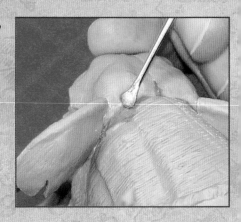

DRYBRUSHING & OVERBRUSHING

The best techniques to use on the Mûmuk are drybrushing and overbrushing, This suits the texture of the model. Drybrushing is explained in detail earlier in this section.

Overbrushing is a similar method to drybrushing where less painted is removed from the brushing prior to applying the finish.

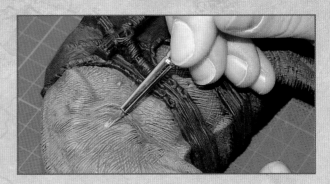

THE BODY AND HOWDAH

1) *The skin was overbrushed with an equal parts basecoat of Dark Flesh and Codex Grey. To achieve a more natural effect, some of the Chaos Black undercoat was left showing in the recesses. The howdah, including the canopy, ropes, wood and wickerwork fighting platforms were all painted with a basecoat of Scorched Brown.*

2) *Next, the skin was overbrushed with Codex Grey, and then the contours of the body were drybrushed with the remainder of the colour left on the brush. The howdah was heavily drybrushed with Bestial Brown.*

3) *Making more use of the hide's contours as a guide, the skin was finished with a drybrush of Bleached Bone. The strongest highlights were concentrated around the creature's eyes. The ropes, wood and wickerwork were drybrushed with Snakebite Leather, and the flat cloth of the saddle blanket was painted with a couple of coats of the same colour.*

4) *To finish off the howdah, it was drybrushed with Bleached Bone. Particular attention was paid to the ropes, slightly more colour was added to them to make them stand out.*

RED CLOTH

The red cloth was first undercoated with Chaos Black and then given a basecoat of Liche Purple.

Then a couple of layers of Scab Red were added to build up a solid colour.

Once dry. the cloth was drybrushed with an equal parts mix of Scab Red and Bleached Bone.

Finally, Bleached Bone was brushed along the folds of the cloth.

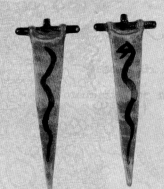

THE FLAGS

The flags were painted the same way as the cloth. Then the black Harad snake symbol was added. This was done by making a simple wavy line for the body, then painting in the head and leaving a gap for the eye.

THE TUSKS

Beginning with a basecoat of Scorched Brown, rough stripes of Bestial Brown were painted near the base of the tusk to give a ridged effect. This was then repeated with additional stripes of Snakebite Leather, Bubonic Brown, and finally Bleached Bone.

THE BASE

To contrast the colour of the Mûmuk's hide, the base was first drybrushed with Bestial Brown and then with Bleached Bone.

The colour schemes of the fallen troops are based on the palettes of the Rohan Riders and Mordor Orc troops detailed earlier in this section. Once painted, all the warriors were drybrushed with Bleached Bone, which not only highlighted them but also added a dusty effect.

To finish off, the whole Mûmakil was superglued together, the crew were painted and arranged in place.

COLOUR CHART

Dark Flesh	●	Bleached Bone	○
Codex Grey	●	Snakebite Leather	●
Chaos Black	●	Liche Purple	●
Bestial Brown	●	Scab Red	●
Scorched Brown	●	Bubonic Brown	●

SCENARIO – GRAND SIEGE

PARTICIPANTS

DEFENDERS

The defending force has up to 375 points of Warriors and Heroes.

It may neither include cavalry models nor equip more than 33% of its models with bows.

ATTACKERS

The attacking force has up to 500 points of Warriors and Heroes.

It may neither include cavalry models nor equip more than 33% of its models with bows.

The attacking force may also include up to 8 Siege Ladders, 2 Siege Towers and 1 Battering Ram.

LAYOUT

The scenario is played on a board 48"/112cm by 48"/112cm. The outer wall of the castle is made of stone and stretches across the board 12"/28cm in from the southern table edge.

The inner edge of the wall faces onto the streets beyond. The outer edge of the wall faces onto a morass of trenches and siege works (featureless to allow a clear field of fire).

DEPLOYMENT

The defending player deploys his entire force on or behind the walls of the castle. When the defending player has finished deploying, the attacking player may deploy his entire force up to 18"/42cm from the northern table edge.

OBJECTIVES

The game lasts for 12 turns. The attacking player wins if he has 12 or more models on or behind the wall, or has achieved two out of the following three objectives at the end of any turn:

• All defending Heroes slain.

• The defending force has been reduced to 25% or less of its starting numbers.

• The attacking player has six or more models on or behind the wall.

If the attacking player does not achieve his victory conditions before the game ends, the defending player wins.

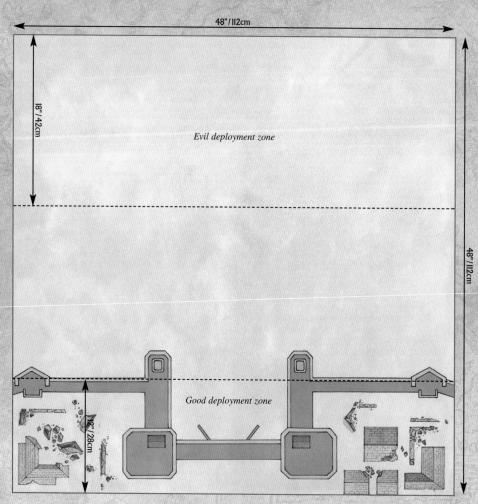

48"/112cm

18"/42cm

Evil deployment zone

48"/112cm

Good deployment zone

12"/28cm

BUILDING A FORTRESS

If you're planning on fighting a siege, you'll need to think about the terrain and buildings you plan on fighting over. You could use the Minas Tirith fortress set or, if you're feeling adventurous, you could build your own castle walls and towers. The next few pages contain easy-to-follow instructions and diagrams of how we made ours, which you can easily use as the starting point for your own projects. The castle is made from separate walls and towers that fit together,

with doors and walkways for your warriors to move to where the action is. When you come to make a castle for your games, you can start small by building just a tower. A lone tower can be used straight away, and you can then add more towers, and join them with sections of wall to form a complete fortress. A nice final addition is a gatehouse complete with opening gate.

MATERIALS

10mm foamboard, thin card, balsa sheet and grey textured paint.
Paints: Codex Grey, Fortress Grey, Bleached Bone and Bestial Brown.

TOOLS

Modelling knife, metal ruler, PVA glue, pencil and brushes.

THE TOWER

Below are the dimensions of the tower. Draw the different wall sections onto your foamboard and cut them out, including the battlements.

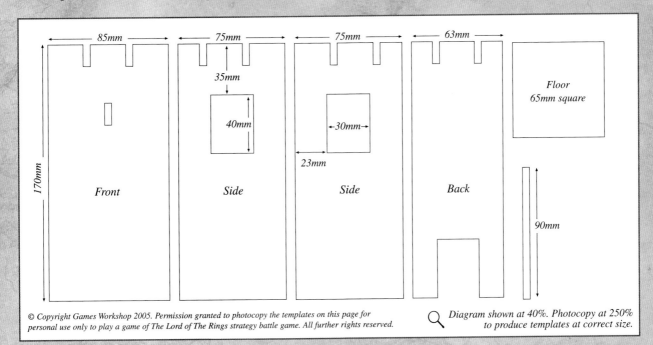

Diagram shown at 40%. Photocopy at 250% to produce templates at correct size.

Building a Fortress

Assembly

Begin assembling the tower by gluing the two side walls to the front wall, with the top and middle floors in place above and below the doorways. The two floors strengthen the assembled walls.

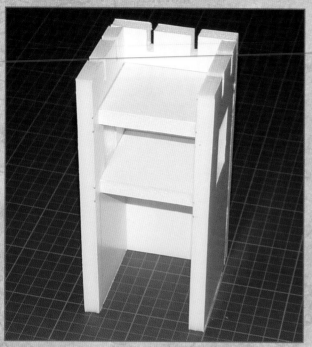

The tower features a removable back wall, so that you can place miniatures inside on the top and middle floors. To hold the back wall in place, glue supports in place flush with the bottom floor. This gives a 10mm gap into which the back wall can fit.

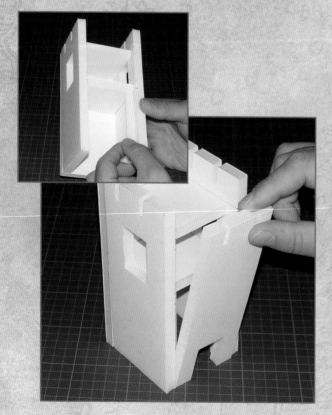

Trapdoors

To finish off the tower you can add trapdoors to the tower floors. Simply cut a 30mm square piece of card with a 25mm square piece of thin balsa sheet glued on top. This is then glued onto the centre of the tower floor.

Paint the card Codex Grey and the balsa wood Bestial Brown. To finish off both the wood and the card, lightly drybrush over the top with Bleached Bone.

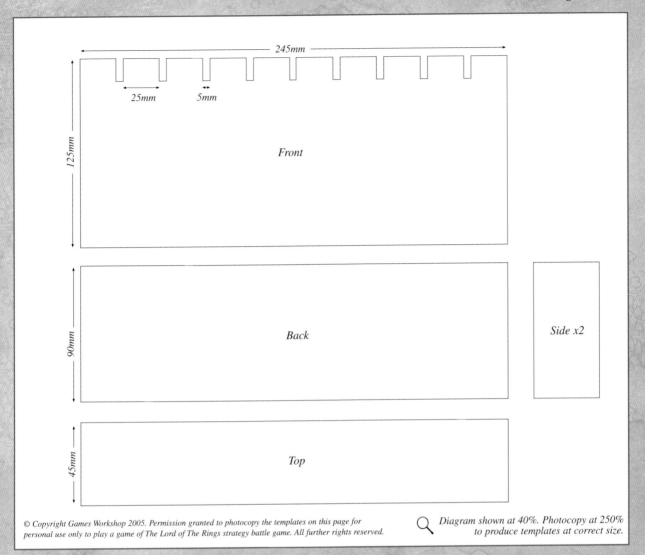

245mm

25mm 5mm

125mm

Front

90mm

Back

Side x2

45mm

Top

Diagram shown at 40%. Photocopy at 250% to produce templates at correct size.

THE WALL

Cut the walls to size based on these dimensions, including the battlements, in the same way as the tower. Glue the side walls to the front wall, with the walkway on top and then the back wall.

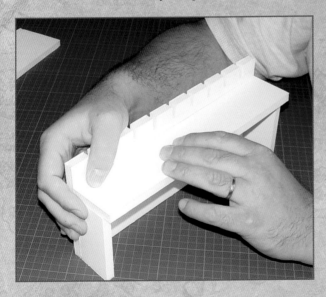

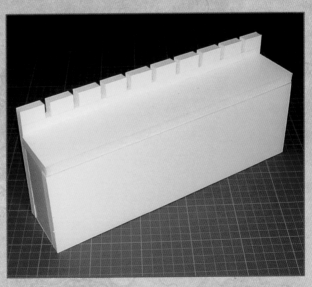

Cutting Foamboard

When cutting foamboard, you'll find it easier if you don't try to cut through the board in one go. Begin by cutting through the card layer first. You'll then be able to gradually cut through the foam underneath with a couple of light strokes of your modelling knife. Once you've cut through the foam layer you can finally cut through the card on the other side. Also try to keep your knife upright to get a square cut.

Cutting the Battlements

The castle features identically sized battlements. The arrow slit is 15mm deep and 5mm wide, the battlement itself is 25mm wide. You can use the tower template as a guide. When it comes to making battlements, there is a trick to cutting them so they look square.

Draw the battlements on both sides of the foamboard. Be careful to make them match each other.

Carefully cut through the card layer, first on one side, then on the other.

Put your foamboard on its edge and, using the cut card groove as a guide, slice through the foam from the top down.

Push your knife through the bottom of each arrow slit on both sides.

Then to finish off simply ease your modelling knife back, popping out the cut section of foamboard. You can use this approach to cut all the battlements on the castle.

The Gatehouse

We decided to add a gatehouse that is based on the castle wall with a gateway cut into both the front and back walls.

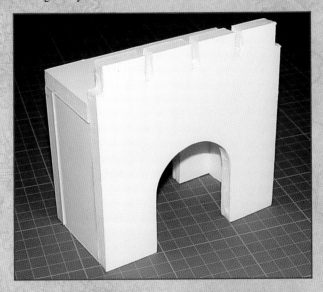

First of all, we constructed a gatehouse section in the same way as a wall. This piece is 125mm long, and has an inner and outer gate cut out, based on the gate dimensions below. This diagram also includes dimensions for the tabs used to attach the gates.

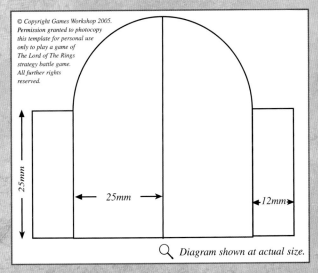

© Copyright Games Workshop 2005. Permission granted to photocopy this template for personal use only to play a game of The Lord of The Rings strategy battle game. All further rights reserved.

25mm

25mm

12mm

🔍 *Diagram shown at actual size.*

The Gate

Trace the dimensions onto thin card, then cut out the complete gate. The gate comes in two halves with tabs attached to glue onto the walls of the gate. Glue thin balsa wood to both the gate sections before cutting them in two. Once the balsa wood is dry, cut the gate in two and score where the tab and the gate meet.

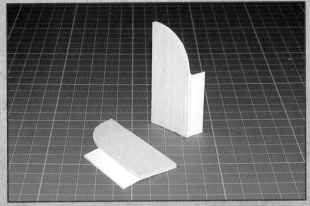

You may prefer to paint and texture the gatehouse before gluing the painted gate in place. Paint the gate Bestial Brown and lightly drybrush with Bleached Bone.

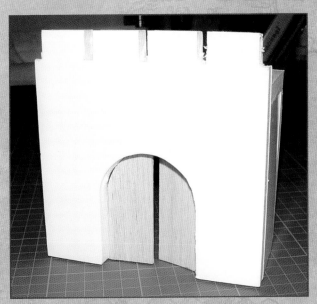

TEXTURING THE CASTLE

To paint the castle, apply a coat of grey textured paint. If you don't have textured paint to hand, mix Codex Grey paint, sand and PVA glue together.

To add the brick effect, use a knife to score horizontal lines across the foamboard 10mm apart. Then to give the effect of bricks, score alternating vertical lines 25mm apart.

Lightly drybrush over the surface with Fortress Grey.

Finish off painting the brick work by lightly drybrushing on Bleached Bone.

To help define the stone work, run a pencil along the grooves you've scored.

RIVER ASSAULTS

The rules given below enable you to recreate all many of exciting skirmishes that involve rivers or boats - what if Aragorn and The Fellowship were attacked as they travelled down the Anduin? The following rules are normally only used on deep water - for example a river or a lake. If a scenario describes a water terrain feature as being impassable (rather than as difficult terrain) then these rules are suitable, though players should agree their use when the game begins.

On a fast river, the boat drifts D6"/2D6cm in the direction of the current.

Drift

At the start of the game, players determine the rate and direction of Drift in the river or sea. Players are free to decide upon the amount and direction of Drift – either D3"/D6cm (standard current) or D6"/2D6cm (strong current). In the Priority phase, each model in the water (including boats) moves in the direction and speed of the Drift. The player with Priority may choose the order they move.

Moving Boats

Boats are always deemed under the control of the player with the greatest number of models touching either the sails or the oars of the boat (calculate before any models move) although if your boat model does not have a visible method of propulsion, simply count all the models on board. Models that are lying down or incapacitated for any reason (as the result of a Paralyse spell, for example) do not count for the purpose of determining control. Models with a Strength of 6 or greater count as three models. If both players have an equal number of models touching either the sails or the oars of the boat, neither player has control so neither can move the boat that turn.

Boats move in their controlling player's Move phase. Boats may be turned to face any direction at the start of their move – they may not turn later in their move. Roll on the Handling chart opposite to determine how far the boat can move.

Handling Chart

D6	Result
1	**Out of control.** The boat goes out of control. The warriors spend the rest of their Move phase trying to regain control – the boat may not move this turn but will drift with the current as normal.
2-5	**All ahead.** The boat must move up to D6"/2D6cm. It may move an additional 1"/2cm for each additional model beyond the fourth that is propelling the boat (a boat propelled by 6 models could move for example D6+2"/2D6+4cm).
6	**Excellent seamanship.** The boat may move up to 6"/14cm plus 1"/2cm for each additional model beyond the fourth that is propelling the boat.

The boat can move at full speed if there are four or more models propelling the boat; if there are less than four models then the speed of the boat is halved. Note the boats are unaffected by Heroic Moves.

If a boat collides with a model with a Strength of 5 or less, the model is pushed 1"/2cm back from the boat – the boat completes its move as normal. If a boat collides with a model with a Strength of 6 or greater, or another boat, it immediately comes to a halt. In both cases if the boat has travelled 4"/10cm or more, both it and whatever it collides with take a Strength 8 hit for each 1"/2cm of unused movement.

The good player has rolled a 6 on the Handling Chart so the boat moves 6"/14cm.

Docking

With careful guidance, a vessel can be directed to dock at a certain place, or with another boat, without suffering damage. To do this, the controlling player must nominate where the boat is going to dock before any dice are rolled on the handling chart. If the boat reaches the chosen vessel or coastline during that move it is guided in and neither suffers nor inflicts damage.

Embarking and Disembarking

Any model may make a Jump roll to embark or disembark using the normal Jump rules. If a 1 is rolled on the Jump roll then the model falls into the water. If a model attempts to jump onto a defended obstacle (the side of a boat, or a bank defended by the enemy), treat it as an attacker charging a defended obstacle.

Warriors in Boats

Whilst in a boat Warriors and Heroes may move, fight and shoot as normal – they count as being stationary for the purposes of shooting, even if the boat has moved.

Models in the Water

Warriors and Heroes may attempt to swim through deep water – indeed if they have been tipped into a river as a result of a boat sinking, they'll have no other choice. Refer to the rules for swimming on page 73.

Dropping Anchor

After a boat has moved, the controlling player may declare that it is dropping anchor. Mark the boat with a suitable counter or token to show that this has taken place. Whilst anchored, a boat will not move nor drift – the anchor must be raised for it to do so. The controlling player may raise the anchor at the end of any subsequent Move phase (after both players have moved) – the boat will then move normally from the next turn onwards following the normal Moving Boat rules as outlined earlier.

Attacking Boats

Boats may be attacked like any other model and have the following profile.

	Strength	Defence	Batter Points
Boat	–	8	4

Boats that are reduced to 0 Batter Points sink instantly – any models inside are tipped into the water. Cavalry models that are cast into the water are treated as if they had just rolled a 1 on the Thrown Rider chart. Models that have been tipped into the water may not move further that turn.

BUILDING A RIVER & BOATS

The Lord of The Rings contains a number of significant events that happen near water features. The Fellowship of The Ring movie in particular has two: first when the hobbits are fleeing the Ringwraiths as they race to cross at Bruinen Ford and secondly when the Fellowship are making passage of the Anduin.

Adding water features to your modular terrain boards is as easy as creating hills and uses a lot of the same techniques. As with adding anything to a board, it's best to make a few sketches first to decide how the feature is going to fit in. For the following river section, it was decided that the feature would go over two boards. To make sure the boards could still be used in any combination, the river sections started and ended at the same points on each board.

SCULPTING THE RIVER

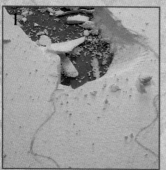

1 First, cut out the path of the river.

2 Then, even out the banks so they are at the same level and angle across the two boards.

3 Once this is done, texture and paint the boards to match the rest of your scenery.

PAINTING THE WATER

1 To create the water effect, first paint the board with Dark Angels Green. Then drybrush the area near the bank with Catachan Green, followed by a highlight of Graveyard Earth at the edges.

2 Once this is completely dry, apply gloss varnish to finish off the surface.

Tip: Avoid using paint effects that show the direction of the water. This way, the boards can still be fitted together in any combination or direction you like.

Below are a couple of examples of the combinations that can be made with the boards we have made.

Example 1

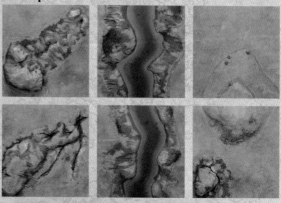

Example 2

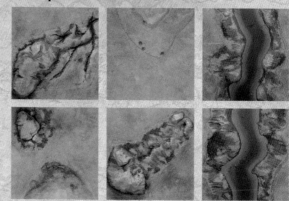

BOATS

When building boats to use in your The Lord of The Rings battles, it's important to decide first of all the maximum number of models you will want to fit in them. The boat below was designed to hold nine normal sized models.

Most forces will require more than one boat, so when you are happy with the design make a template so it can be easily replicated. We've reproduced the template we used to make our boats below.

To make this boat, its base was cut from 3.5mm foamboard and its sides from thin card. The side with the prow and tiller was glued first, then the other side was fitted together.

The boat was then undercoated with Chaos Black. Once this was dry, the deck and outside of the boat were given a coat of Codex Grey, followed first by a drybrush of Fortress Grey and then a final drybrushed highlight of Bleached Bone.

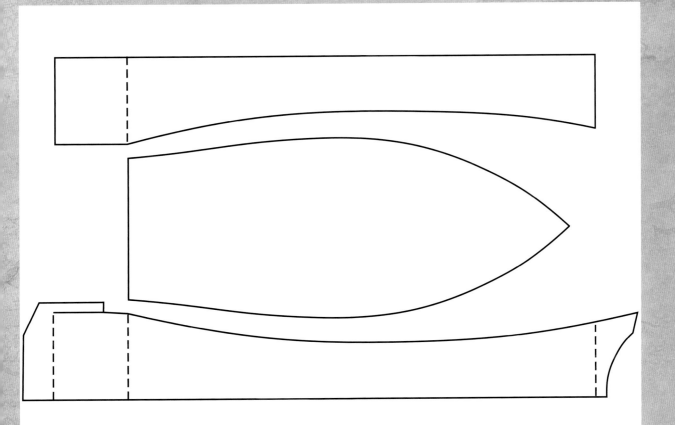

Q *Shown at 80% of actual size. Photocopy at 125% to produce templates at correct size.*

COASTAL RAIDS

Some of the most memorable moments in The Lord of The Rings centre around rivers and boats. Aragorn's arrival at Pelennor Fields, Gothmog's assault on Osgiliath and the passage of the Anduin are but a few examples – the story is full of many more. The fantastic thing about playing scenarios in this game is the depth to which you can take them. Once you've decided what, where, why and who (no small task in itself), then there's always the how. This is the bit that we're going to take a look at – by the time we're done you'll be fearlessly crafting your own scenarios and events within the world of Middle-earth.into the water may not move further that turn.

CHOOSING YOUR FORCES

Almost any protagonists will do for playing a coastal raid so spare a thought to the story that runs through your scenario. Will you recreate the folk of Anfalas defending their shores against Corsairs, for example? Are the Men of Númenor landing in Harad to end Sauron's control here once and for all? Only your imagination can limit the setting and scale of your game. Whatever your backdrop, both players should agree on a points value for the game – both the attacker and the defender should have with equally-sized forces.

Board Layout

Coastal raids are best played on a board 48"/112cm by 48"/112cm, although of course they can be played on gaming tables of any width or length. The quayside stretches 24"/56cm out from the landward board edge and should be covered with suitable terrain. It's worth noting at this point that the term 'quayside' is used as a term for a generic shoreline – it does not have to be an urbanised harbour. There is no reason why a quayside could not be a heavily wooded shore with just a few jetties to land boats at – or even have no conventional landing points at all! As normal, it's always best if players agree terrain (and its effects) before the game begins, although it is worth noting that some objectives will require specific terrain types. The rest of the board is the sea (or river) itself, and should be mostly empty of terrain, although there is no reason why there cannot be piers or jetties stretching into the water, or rocks or debris projecting through the waves.

When the board has been set up, the defending player may place 2D6 barricades (lines of obstacles up to 1"/2cm high and 6"/14cm long) anywhere along the quayside. In addition, he may place D3 boats of his own anywhere in the water, provided that they are touching the quayside itself, or a pier or jetty.

Deployment

Unless any of the special deployment conditions are being used, the defending player always deploys his forces first. In a basic game this is always on the quayside, within 12"/28cm of the landward board edge (see map). When he has done this, the attacker deploys his boats (and their forces within them) no more than 6"/14cm from the seaward table edge.

These rules are enough to play many coastal raids. That said, you can always vary the deployment a little to add more variation to your games by limiting where each side deploys, perhaps, or having them arrive late. To help add a little more variety to your games, we have created a series of tables for all manner of variations that you can add to your games – simply decide with your opponent which one you wish to use, or roll a D6. Over the next few pages are Deployment options, Game Length and Special Rules, and some Mission Objective variants to give your games extra variety.

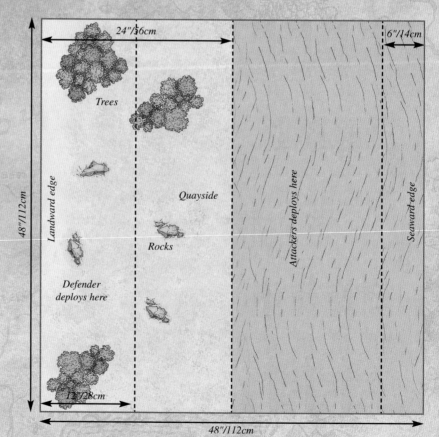

SPECIAL RULES

Of course, no scenario for The Lord of The Rings would be complete without a few special rules to keep both players on their toes, and coastal raids are no different. Any of the examples given below can be combined in any way, so you can have Gusting Winds and an Opening Bombardment, for example.

1. Gusting Winds

The winds along this particular stretch of coast are incredibly treacherous, making it very dangerous to walk along precipitous drops (or quaysides). If the Priority roll is ever drawn on the roll of 5 or 6, both players roll a D6 for each of their models that are within 2"/4cm of a sheer drop (a cliff, at the top of a wall etc…) or the edge of the quay. On the roll of a 4+, the model loses its balance and tumbles off the edge, taking falling damage or other effects as appropriate. If the model is within 2"/4cm of two or more hazards, the opposing player may nominate which way the model falls. Might may be used to modify this roll. All Shooting attacks must re-roll any successful hits.

2. Defensive Volley

The defenders have seen the incoming raid and have prepared a volley of fire to greet the attackers. By using such a trap they hope to strike an early blow. After both sides have deployed but before the first turn, the defending player may fire three volleys. Each volley has a total number of shots equal to the quantity of defenders with bows of any kind and follows the normal rules for Volley Fire, with the exception that the defenders do not need to be in base contact with one another.

3. Hearth and Home

The defenders have pledged to repel the attackers or die trying. Defenders do not have to take Courage tests in this scenario.

4. Opening Bombardment

As a prelude to a raid, vessels offshore can use their armament to harry the forces of the defender. Before the game begins, the attacking player may make D3 bombardments. For each of these, he rolls a D6. On the roll of a 4 or more, his catapults have found a target sending out a wave of crushing debris. The attacking player may nominate any defending model on the board. That model takes a Strength 10 hit and any other model, friendly or enemy, within 1"/2cm, takes a single Strength 6 hit as they are hit by rubble; any survivors with a Strength of 6 or less are knocked to the ground. If the attacking player rolls a 1, the same effect occurs, but the defending player may nominate the target. If a cavalry model is hit rider and steed take a Strength 6 hit, the rider is thrown, and both models are knocked to the ground.

5. Continuous Bombardment of the Enemy

If the battle is hard fought and desperate, leaders may risk firing siege engines into the thick of combat. This unusual tactic is used only by the most despairing commanders as a last gamble for victory. If using this special rule, the player who rolls the lowest dice when determining Priority may make a single bombardment (as described above) in the Shooting phase. If players tie in the dice roll then both players may make a bombardment in their respective Shooting phases.

6. Redoubled Efforts

The attackers, spurred on by their determination, have propelled their boats closer to the shore. At the start of the game, after both sides have deployed, the attacking player may move each of his boats D6"/2D6cm (roll separately for each). Drift and other factors have no effect on this move.

DEPLOYMENT VARIANTS

1-2 Prepared Defences

The attackers have taken some time to get organised, giving the defenders a breathing space to redeploy. After both sides have set up, the defending player may move all of his barricades and 2D6 of his defenders up to 6"/14cm.

3-4 Scattered Defenders

The defenders are thinly spread, holding several positions against the incoming assault. At the start of the game, the defending player splits his force into equal halves, dividing his Heroes equally between the two. He deploys one half normally, but keeps the other to one side. From the second turn onwards, the defending player rolls a D6 at the end of his Move phase for each model put aside in this way. If the roll is lower than the current turn number, the models may move onto the board from anywhere along the quayside. If the roll is failed then another attempt may be made next turn.

5-6 Flanking Manoeuvre

In an all out attempt to thwart the defences, the attackers have landed a portion of their warriors further along the shore. Before the game begins, the attacker may put up to a quarter of his force (including up to one Hero costing less than 60 points) on one side. He deploys his remaining forces as normal and nominates which board edge his other warriors will enter from. From the fourth turn onwards, the attacking player rolls a D6 at the end of his Move phase. If the roll is lower than the current turn number, the models put aside at the start of the game may move onto the board from any point along the edge he nominated earlier.

END CONDITIONS

Coastal raid games can last a few turns, representing a lightning fast raid, or several hours, re-enacting a desperate fight for supremacy. Players can agree on the game length before they begin, but note that the game should always end once one side has been eliminated. Alternatively, here are few suggestions:

1. Secure the Quay

The game lasts for at least six turns. If there are no attacking models upon the quayside at the end of any turn from turn seven onwards, the game ends.

2. Random Game Length

The game lasts for at least six turns. From the end of the seventh turn onwards, the player with Priority rolls a D6. If the result is a 6, the game ends.

3. Leaderless Attackers

The game continues until all of the Heroes on the attacking side are slain.

4. Leaderless Defenders

The game continues until all of the Heroes on the defending side are slain.

5. War of Attrition

The game continues until one side has been reduced to below 50% of its starting numbers.

6. No Quarter

The game continues until one side has been reduced to below 25% of its starting numbers.

ADVANCED MISSION OBJECTIVES

Hopefully by now you've had a chance to launch several of your own coastal raids, or at least to defend against those of your opponent. Let's face it though, piratical behaviour is as its best when you have a suitably piratical goal, like kidnapping, stealing or just razing things to the ground. the following rules allow all those sympathetic to the call for wanton destruction to do exactly that. As with the Deployment options, Game Length and Special Rules simply agree with your opponent on which of the options you want to use, or roll a D6 if you can't agree.

Every fight has a reason, even if it is just a case of two hosts meeting in battle to take land, and coastal raids are no exception. It's always worth trying to think up a good narrative for your conflict based on the forces you and your opponent are using. Perhaps Aragorn is trying to destroy the ships of the Corsairs, harboured in Umbar? Maybe Gothmog is trying to breach the defences of Osgiliath? Whatever your goal, you needn't worry too much about the game being balanced. Dice have a funny way of rebalancing these situations, and some of the most enjoyable games can be ones where you are struggling against the odds.

Included below are a few ideas to play your scenarios around, but feel free to come up with your own. Note that any objectives can be combined in any way, so if you want to play a scenario with Ransom and Plunder objectives, you can – the attacker has to achieve more objectives than he fails to achieve to win the game.

PILLAGE

The most common and straightforward of objectives, the attackers are attempting to steal whatever they can carry and burn the rest. There are several variations of the Pillage objective. Players can choose which one to use or, if they wish, roll a D6 to determine their mission objective.

1-2 Plunder

In this mission, the attackers are attempting to steal as much as possible. To play games with a Plunder objective, you will need five 'Loot' counters. These can be anything from small coins to modelled piles of weapons. At the start of the game, starting with the defending player, each player takes it in turns to place a Loot counter. Counters may only be placed on the quayside (you may not place them in the water, for example) and may not be placed closer than 6"/14cm to another counter, or 3"/8cm to a board edge. Attackers (or defenders) may drag Loot counters by moving into base contact with them. Once a model is alongside a Loot counter, it can complete its move normally, dragging the Loot alongside. If the model doing the dragging is engaged in close combat, it will drop the Loot. At the end of the game the attacker wins if he has successfully stolen three or more Loot counters. Loot counters are considered stolen if they have been taken aboard a boat that then leaves the board.

3-4 Burn the Village!

Houses and fortifications can be rebuilt, but it takes time and effort. Destroy your opponent's base of operations and you can win a significant advantage in the fight to come. There must be at least five buildings on the quayside to play this mission objective. To win the game, the attacking player must burn at least three of the five buildings. Attackers may attempt to set fire to a building during the Fight phase, providing that they are in base contact and have performed no action other than moving that turn. The attacking player may roll a D6 for each of his models that are trying to fire a building. On each roll of a 5 or 6, the fire catches hold – indicate this with a suitable marker. At the start of each turn, before Priority is rolled, add an additional marker to the building as the fire rages through its structure. If the winning roll for Priority is lower than the number of Fire counters on a building, it collapses, replace it with a pile of rubble. Any models inside the building suffer a single Strength 10 hit (as well as any falling damage) and are knocked to the ground). Defending models may attempt to douse the flames on a building in the Fight phase, providing that they are in base contact and have performed no action other than moving that turn. The defending player may roll a D6 for each of his models that are trying to douse the flames. For each roll of a 6, they have been partially successful – remove a marker.

5-6 Destroy the Fleet

This raid has come at a time when several enemy vessels have been moored up alongside the quayside, and the attackers take their chance to scupper these ships. The defending player must deploy five boats along the quayside to play this mission objective. To win the game, the attacking player must burn at least three of the five boats. Boats are set alight and put out exactly as described for buildings. Due to the flammable nature of boats, any vessel touching a boat that is on fire will itself be set alight at the start of the Priority phase if the defender rolls a 4 or more on a D6 – place a single Fire counter to show this. If a boat is destroyed due to the Fire counters on it, any models onboard take a single Strength 5 hit and are dumped ignominiously into the water.

KIDNAP

This raid has been initiated to kidnap one or more enemy warriors, to hold them for ransom or torture. If a Kidnap is part of the mission objectives, the attacking player can choose for his troops not to slay their enemies in close combat. To represent this, whenever a defending model loses its last wound in close combat, the attacker can choose for them to have been knocked unconscious, rather than killed. Attackers (or defenders) may drag unconscious models by moving into base contact with them. Once a model is in base contact with an unconscious model, it can complete its move normally, dragging the unconscious model alongside. If the model doing the dragging is engaged in close combat, it will release the model. In all Kidnap missions, the attacker must drag his victims to a boat, which must then leave the board.

There are several variations of the Kidnap objective. Players can choose which one to use or, if they wish, roll a D6 to determine their mission objective.

1-2 Ransom

A captured leader is always valuable to the opposition, whether in terms of concessions, or simple currency.

The attacker must kidnap one or more enemy Heroes (named or unnamed). If he does so, he wins the game.

3-4 Targets of opportunity

In this mission, the attackers are attempting to kidnap as many enemies as possible (to take away as slaves if the attackers are Evil, or for interrogation if the attackers are Good). At the end of the game, the attacker scores:

- 1 point for each Warrior kidnapped
- 5 points for each unnamed Hero kidnapped
- 10 points for each named Hero kidnapped (Aragorn, Gandalf, Gothmog etc.)

If the attacker scores 10 or more points, he wins the game.

5-6 Checkmate

Even more than the capture of enemy captains, the capture of an enemy king can often lead to great wealth or victory. The attacker must capture the most expensive Hero on the defending side. If two or more Heroes are of the same points cost, then the attacker must declare which at the start of the game.

RAID

There is nothing fancy about a Raid mission. The attacker simply wishes to cause as much damage as possible to his enemy, for as little loss in return. There are several variations on the Raid objectives though. Choose which one to use or roll a D6 to determine the mission.

1-2 Headhunt

In this mission, the attacker is trying to kill a specific enemy character, hoping that his loss will demoralise that foe. At the start of the game, before both sides have deployed, the attacker chooses one Hero in the enemy force to be his target.

At the end of the game the attacker scores:

- 5 points for each wound inflicted on the nominated Hero
- 10 points for killing the nominated Hero
- 1 point for each other casualty inflicted on the enemy

While the defender scores:

- 1 point for each enemy Warrior slain
- 5 points for each enemy unnamed Hero slain
- 10 points for each enemy named Hero slain

Note that models that leave the board due to failed Courage tests do not count as slain in this scenario, but models that are slain as a result of drowning (or other natural causes) do form part of the tally.

3-4 Let the Coasts Run Red

To achieve this objective, the attacker must slaughter as many of his enemies as possible whilst keeping his own casualties low. Each player scores:

- 1 point for each enemy Warrior slain
- 5 points for each enemy unnamed Hero slain
- 10 points for each enemy named Hero slain

Note that models that leave the board due to failed Courage tests do not count as slain in this scenario, but models that are slain as a result of drowning (or other natural causes) do form part of the tally. At the end of the game, the player with the most points, wins.

5-6 Destroy the Batteries

Siege engines defend some harbours and it is often necessary to eliminate these machineries to open the way for a greater assault. To play a game with this objective, the defender must include three siege engines of any kind (if there are no suitable siege engines to match the theme of the force, use either a Gondor or Mordor engine with different crew).

At the end of the game, the attacker scores:

- 1 point for each slain siege engine crewman
- 5 points for each slain Engineer Captain
- 10 points for each destroyed siege engine

If the attacker scores 10 or more points, he wins the game.

Example Coastal Raid:
THE ASSAULT ON LINHIR

In the middle years of the Third Age, the power of the Corsairs of Umbar was at its height. The great fleets of Umbar were bolstered by the smaller Haradrim vessels, forming a series of devastating raids and harassing pinpricks across the southern coasts of Gondor. These attacks came to a head during the late spring of 1711, when an enormous Corsair fleet came to Linhir, a town on the mouth of the river Gilrain. A full dozen Corsair vessels, and countless smaller Haradrim craft, set upon the town and its outnumbered defenders with appalling ferocity in search of plunder and spoils. Fortunately, as with all towns on the Belfalas coast, Linhir had been fortified against such an attack and, though the defenders were overmatched, the town held long enough for help to arrive.

Mission Objectives
Pillage: Plunder
Raid: Headhunt
Kidnap: Targets of Opportunity

Deployment Variants
Prepared Defences, Scattered Defenders

Special Rules
Defensive Volley

End Conditions
Secure the Quayside!

HISTORICAL PARTICIPANTS
Good
Captain of Gondor, heavy armour, shield, lance, horse
Captain of Gondor, heavy armour, bow
6 Knights of Minas Tirith
8 Warriors of Minas Tirith with bow
8 Warriors of Minas Tirith with shield
8 Warriors of Minas Tirith with spear and shield

Evil
Hâsharin
Haradrim Chieftain, bow, spear
Haradrim Chieftain, lance, bow, horse
Haradrim Warrior with Banner
24 Haradrim Warriors with spears
12 Haradrim Raiders with lances
6 Haradrim Warriors with bows

MISSION NARRATIVES

Don't be afraid to pick a narrative that you think will give you a good game. If you've an expensive Hero in your force, why not play a mission that centres around them – kidnapping Aragorn may be a greater challenge than abducting a Captain of Gondor, but will make for a much more entertaining game for both players. Similarly, don't be afraid to tweak the objectives and set-up to better fit the storyline you are enacting.

OBJECTIVES AND ALIGNMENT

Many of these objectives might look like they are told from one point of view and are not necessarily suitable for both sides (ie, would a Good army really try and assassinate an Evil Hero?). The answer is, of course, that absolutely they would. Players should feel free to come up with their own narratives to justify the actions of their forces. So, for example, while Orcs might pillage a village because they can, Elves would more likely raid an Orc military outpost. The same rules and objectives apply in each case, but the one paints a far nicer picture of the 'Good' models than the other.

CAMPAIGN NARRATIVES

A lot of these objectives combine well form campaign ideas. For example, if you play a 'Kidnap' game where the Orcs manage to spirit away an important Captain of Gondor, why not follow it up with a 'Raid' in reprisal? Or perhaps the Men of Gondor could attempt to rescue their lost captain, by playing a 'Kidnap' game against the Orcs – just change the victory conditions slightly, and have the Captain start the game unconscious in one of the Orc buildings. The sky really is the limit.

BUILDING COASTAL TERRAIN

Many other battles occur in The Lord of The Rings that don't appear in the films. In areas near the sea such as Gondor, coastal raids would have been a daily threat. When building a coastline you will need to make sure you have enough room for boats to be on the water and also for troops to form up along the shore. This type of board may not be as versatile as other scenery boards though. One way to solve this is to create a removable area of coast that you can use with your existing terrain.

PLANNING

Keep in mind the type of terrain you have already built when planning the design of the coastal terrain. For example, a large stone quayside will look out of place on a board that obviously represents untouched wilderness.

To maintain the theme of the grassland modular boards detailed on pages 182-185, a beach is probably the easiest and most versatile type of coastal terrain to build. The simplest thing to do is to make a flat board that can be placed on your current terrain. This has the slight drawback of making the sea level higher than the land, which can look strange, but the bank can be graduated around the edges to make the difference less obvious.

This method will use a row of dunes to serve as a raised bank, with the edge of the board cut into an irregular line to help make transition from board to table less obvious. If your terrain is more built-up, for example for fighting among the ruins of Osgiliath, you could replace the dunes with stone docks or moorings, and with steps leading up to them from the street level.

BUILDING THE BOARD

Tools and Materials

- 2' x 4' hardboard or MDF
- Static Grass
- Lichen
- Polystyrene
- Cork bark
- Ready-mixed filler
- Modelling sand and gravel
- PVA woodworking glue
- Sharp knife
- Saw
- Sandpaper

1 First mark out the MDF board with an irregular edge on one side.

2 Then cut away the edge with a saw. To blend it in better with the gaming table, round off the cut edges using a knife.

3 Next glue layers of polystyrene sheet to the board with PVA glue to build up the area of the dunes.

4 Once the glue has dried, carve the dunes out of the polystyrene, and then smooth down their edges with sandpaper.

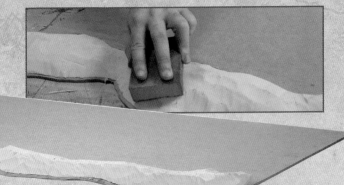

5 To add texture, glue pieces of cork bark, sand and gravel to the dunes to create rocky areas.

6 Finally, add ready-mixed filler to create waves and to fill in any gaps between the dunes and the rocks.

PAINTING SAND

1 Paint the dunes with a basecoat of Bestial Brown.

2 Then drybrush them with Snakebite Leather...

3 ...followed by a drybrush of Vomit Brown...

4 ...then drybrush on a layer of Bleached Bone to lighten up the colour a bit.

5 To break up the flat yellow colour, drybrush small areas with patches of Catachan Green.

6 Once this is dry, Static Grass and Lichen can be added to the dunes to blend them with the rest of the board.

PAINTING THE SEA

1 Give the sea a basecoat of Chaos Black, followed by a layer of Dark Angels Green.

2 Follow this with a layer of Scaly Green.

3 Painted Ultramarines Blue near the shoreline.

4 Next paint the tops of the waves with Skull White.

5 To give the surface of the water a wet effect, apply a few coats of Gloss Varnish.

THE GAMING HOBBY

The gaming hobby has grown enormously in recent years as has the variety and quality of games and models available. Where once gamers were few in number and scattered far and wide, now there are few who do not have the benefit of a local club or stockist. Furthermore, the development of the internet has brought the skills and talent of the most creative individuals into the homes of all.

Games Workshop is a specialised company that manufactures and sells fantasy tabletop games and gaming miniatures. The Lord of The Rings battle game is part of a whole range of tried and tested gaming products and is fully supported by Games Workshop's extensive club and tournament program. Every year we hold special events – some of these take place at our Warhammer World exhibition centre in Nottingham, England; whilst our biggest and most popular Games Days are held annually, usually in Birmingham in England and Baltimore in the USA. More recently we have started to hold Games Days in France, Spain, Australia and Canada.

GAMES CLUBS

Gaming is a sociable hobby and you will not be surprised to hear that there are many clubs that cater for gamers of all ages and tastes. If you live in a large city, you'll probably find there is a local games club where Games Workshop games are played. You don't need to be part of a club to enjoy gaming, but there are plenty of advantages, and it is always nice to meet people who share your own passion for gaming.

One of the great things about clubs is there's always someone willing to show you how to play a particular game or improve your painting or modelling skills. In particular, clubs always seem to harbour at least one expert scenery maker who will be only too happy to rope you in to whatever huge and ambitious project he happens to be working on. Many clubs also participate in bigger public events, putting on demonstration games or displays and helping to explain about the games and models.

EVENTS

These are the social occasions of the hobby – a chance to meet fellow hobbyists and swap ideas or just to hang out with old friends. As well as the major events of the gaming calendar, such as Games Day and the Grand Tournaments, there are many smaller local or specialist events held by independent groups or sponsored by Games Workshop. Many clubs hold their own events and, though these are usually small, intimate affairs, some of the larger club events attract hundreds of attendees.

Games Workshop's monthly hobby magazine White Dwarf is a great place to look if you want more information about The Lord of The Rings battle game or the wargaming hobby in general.

To coincide with the release of The Lord of The Rings – The Return of The King game, White Dwarf has loads of articles enabling you to get more out of your battles, including:

News on forthcoming releases.

A look at the background of both the movie and game.

How to play The Lord of The Rings battle game.

New scenarios.

Campaigns and battle reports.

Advice on painting and converting your models.

Scenery masterclasses.

Gamers' model collections.

Features with sculptors, artists and designers.

White Dwarf is also the place to look if you want to find out where your nearest Games Workshop store or local stockist is.

To make sure that you don't miss out on anything, you can buy White Dwarf from any of our stores or stockists, and most major newsagents. To be absolutely sure that you don't miss an issue, why not give Mail Order a call. They'll be more than happy to send your copy to you each month and if you take up a subscription you'll be able to take advantage of some of the brilliant deals available only to subscribers.

THE GAMES WORKSHOP THE LORD OF THE RINGS WEBSITE

Regularly updated as and when boxed sets and miniatures are released, Games Workshop's The Lord of The Rings website is an ideal place to go to buy your models.

As well as this, the website will link you to the main Games Workshop website where you can find lots of information about painting models, details of wargaming clubs and gaming events in your area and the location of Games Workshop stores and independent stockists.

A large part of the Games Workshop website is dedicated to the wargaming community. This is a major forum which links together thousands of people across the world who are totally devoted to wargaming. Here you will find an abundance of advice written by fellow wargamers on all aspects of the hobby and also links to some of the thousands of websites on the internet written by gamers.

Another great aspect of the site is that it enables players who live near each other to meet up and play a game. So even if you don't have a games store nearby you should be able to find a club near you or join up with someone wanting a battle.

To find out the latest releases and news on The Lord of The Rings releases visit the following website:

http://uk.games-workshop.com/thelordoftherings/

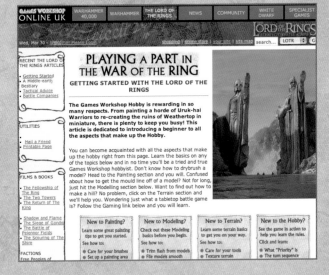

For more details on other Games Workshop releases, general wargaming and hobby information, and links to our wargaming community check out:

www.games-workshop.com

The products shown overleaf are just some of the releases we have planned to coincide with The Lord of The Rings film trilogy. New releases are being brought out each month so make sure you keep up to date by regularly checking out White Dwarf or the website.

MAIL ORDER

Should you find that you do not have a local store or stockist nearby you can give our Mail Order department a call. Staffed by experienced gamers and collectors, they can supply you with the products that you require, and also help with any questions you may have about The Lord of The Rings hobby. From army selection to rules queries, feel free to give them a call.

If you place an order with us, it will be delivered straight to your door. Call the relevant number below for your country for more details.

UK   0115 9140000

USA   1-800-394-GAME

Canada   1-888-GW-TROLL

Australia   (02) 9829 6111

The Netherlands   ++44115 9168255

Denmark   ++44115 9188506

Sweden   ++44115 9188507

HOW TO USE MAIL ORDER

Ordering by Mail Order is easy. If you have a credit card or debit card you can place your order over the phone.

- **TELL THE STAFF WHAT YOU WANT** – If you are not sure, just ask the telesales staff. They will be happy to help you out.

- **SIT BACK & RELAX** – After you have placed your order, just sit back, relax and wait for your parcel to arrive on your doorstep.

If you wish to pay by cheque (please include your cheque guarantee card number) or postal order, it is just as easy. All you need to do is:

- **FILL OUT AN ORDER FORM** – Printed in the Mail Order section of White Dwarf magazine, with what you would like.

- **COMPLETE PERSONAL DETAILS** – Fill out your name and address in the space provided at the bottom of the form.

- **THEN SIMPLY PLACE YOUR ORDER IN THE POST!**

GAMES WORKSHOP STORES

One of the best places to learn more about the game is at your local Games Workshop store. Not only can you find the entire Games Workshop The Lord of The Rings range there but our stores are staffed by experienced gamers who can advise you if you have any questions or wish to take part in an introductory game.

Our stores are also excellent places to meet other gamers. As most will have played other Games Workshop games they're a good starting point if you're new to gaming.

INDEPENDENT RETAILERS

You can also find our great The Lord of The Rings hobby products in a huge network of independent toy, hobby and game retailers across the world.

Many of these stores also offer modelling advice, in addition to stocking The Lord of The Rings range. They may also stock a wide selection of Games Workshop paints and modelling equipment.

If you would like to know where your nearest independent retailer is, you can find a contact number for your area on the opposite page. Alternatively, look in White Dwarf magazine or on the Games Workshop web site at **www.games-workshop.com**.

WHERE TO FIND US

If you would like any more information about The Lord of The Rings or other Games Workshop products, or if you would like to order something from our Mail Order service, please contact us by using one of the numbers below. Alternatively you can check out our website at www.games-workshop.com.

UK
GAMES WORKSHOP, WILLOW ROAD, LENTON, NOTTINGHAM NG7 2WS

TEL:
01159 140000
FAX:
01159 168002

USA
GAMES WORKSHOP, 6721 BAYMEADOW DRIVE, GLEN BURNIE, MD 21060-6401

TEL:
1-800-492-8820

CANADA
GAMES WORKSHOP, 2679 BRISTOL CIRCLE, UNIT 3 OAKVILLE, ONTARIO L6H 6Z8

TEL:
1-888-GW-TROLL

AUSTRALIA
PO BOX 576, INGLEBURN, NSW, 1890, AUSTRALIA

TEL:
(02) 9829 6111

NORTHERN EUROPE

GAMES WORKSHOP
WILLOW ROAD, LENTON
NOTTINGHAM
NG7 2WS

TEL: 00441159 168210 • FAX: 00441159 168470

COPENHAGEN: FREDERIKSBORGGADE 5.
TEL: 00 45 33 12 22 17

STOCKHOLM: REGERINGSGATAN 30,
TEL: 00 46 8 21 38 40

AMSTERDAM: ROKIN 36,
TEL: 00 31 20 622 3863

OSLO: MOLLERGATA 5/9,
TEL: 00 47 22 33 29 90

CHARTS

MOVE CHART

Type of Model	Maximum move
Man/Woman/Wizard	6"/14cm
Elf	6"/14cm
Eagle	12"/28cm
Ent	6"/14cm
Hobbit	4"/10cm
Dwarf	5"/12cm
Gollum	5"/12cm
Orc	6"/14cm
Moria Goblin	5"/12cm
Uruk-hai	6"14cm
Troll	6"/14cm
Spirit	6"/14cm
Giant Spider	10"/24cm
Fell Beast	12"/28cm
Warg	10"/24cm
Horse	10"/24cm

JUMP CHART

Dice	Result
1	Model halts at obstacle.
2-5	Model crosses obstacle and halts.
6	Model crosses and completes move.

CLIMB CHART

Dice	Result
1	The model falls to the ground. It takes damage (see page 21).
2-5	The model continues to climb up/down. If the top/bottom is reached, the model halts.
6	The model continues to climb up/down. If the top/bottom is reached, the model completes its remaining move.

THROWN RIDER CHART

Dice	Result
1	The rider falls and suffers a S3 hit. If he survives, rider is placed lying by mount and moves no further that turn. If engaged in combat, the model fights lying down.
2-5	The rider is placed standing by its mount and moves no further that turn. The model may not act further that turn, including shooting. If engaged in combat, it cannot strike blows.
6	The rider is placed standing by mount – there is no further penalty.

MISSILE CHART

Weapon	Range	Strength	Move Penalty
Short bow	18"/42cm	2	Half
Bow	24"/56cm	2	Half
Orc bow	18"/42cm	2	Half
Elf bow	24"/56cm	3	Half
Dwarf bow	18"/42cm	3	Half
Uruk-hai Crossbow	24"/56cm	4	All
Throwing weapon	6"/14cm	3	None

BATTERING CHART

Dice	Result
1	No effect.
2-5	Damaged. You score 1 Batter Point on it (strikes with a Strength of 10 cause 2 Batter Points of damage).
6	Broken in. The target suffers 2 Batter Points (strikes with a Strength of 10 cause 4 Batter Points of damage).

WOUND CHART

DEFENCE

		1	2	3	4	5	6	7	8	9	10
STRENGTH	**1**	4	5	5	6	6	6/4	6/5	6/6	–	–
	2	4	4	5	5	6	6	6/4	6/5	6/6	–
	3	3	4	4	5	5	6	6	6/4	6/5	6/6
	4	3	3	4	4	5	5	6	6	6/4	6/5
	5	3	3	3	4	4	5	5	6	6	6/4
	6	3	3	3	3	4	4	5	5	6	6
	7	3	3	3	3	3	4	4	5	5	6
	8	3	3	3	3	3	3	4	4	5	5
	9	3	3	3	3	3	3	3	4	4	5
	10+	3	3	3	3	3	3	3	3	4	4

Compare the Strength value of the attacker down the left-hand side of the chart with the target's Defence value across the top of the chart.

The result indicates the minimum dice roll required to inflict one wound on your enemy. A score of 6/4 or 6/5 or 6/6 means you must roll a single dice and score a 6, followed by a further dice that must score either 4+, 5+ or another 6. A '–' indicates the target is impossible to hurt – it is just too tough!

For example, a Man defeats an Orc in a fight. The Man has a Strength of 3, the Orc a Defence of 5, and both have 1 Attack. The Man therefore requires a dice roll of 5 or more to inflict one wound on the Orc.

DETONATION CHART

Dice Result
1 **Dud.** The charge has been damaged in some way and will not detonate; remove it from play.

2-5 **Instant Reaction.** The charge catches instantly, exploding in a roar of smoke and flame. See below for details.

6 **Titanic explosion.** The powder in the charge detonates with colossal fury as described opposite, but inflicts 2D6 Wounds rather than D6.

SCATTER CHART

Dice Result
1 Your opponent may nominate one of your Battlefield targets or a Siege target within 6"/14cm of the initial target as the new target. If no alternative target is within 6"/14cm, or if the player does not want to do this, the shot misses completely.

2-5 Your opponent may nominate one of his own Battlefield targets within 6"/14cm of the initial target as the new target, if he wishes. If there is no other suitable target within 6"/14cm, the shot misses completely.

6 The shot lands exactly on target.

SENTRY MOVEMENT CHART

Dice Result
1 The model may not move this turn.

2-5 The player with Priority may immediately move the Sentry the distance rolled in inches (or twice that rolled in centimetres) in a direction of their choice. Mounted sentries move double this distance.

6 The Sentry moves normally.

SWIMMING CHART

Dice Result
1 Remove the model as a casualty.

2-5 The model may move up to half its move through the water. If it reaches the bank it may make a Climb test to pull itself out of the water onto a bank.

6 The model may make its normal move through the water. If it reaches the bank it may make a Climb test to pull itself out of the water onto a bank.

Apply the following modifiers to the Swimming chart. These modifiers are cumulative:
• Model is wearing no armour/Mithril armour: +1
• Model is wearing heavy armour/Dwarf heavy armour: -1
• Model is carrying a shield: -1

RECORD SHEET

WARRIOR	Move	F	S	D	A	W	C	Might	Will	Fate

Please feel free to photocopy this page for your personal use.